Risk, Power and the State

Risk, Power and the State: After Foucault addresses how power is exercised in and by contemporary state organizations. Through a detailed analysis of programmatic attempts to shape behaviour linked to considerations of risk, this book pursues the argument that, whilst Foucault is useful for understanding power, the Foucauldian tradition – whether with its strands of discourse analysis, of governmentality studies, or of radical Deleuzian critique – suffers from a lack of clarification on key conceptual issues.

Oriented around four case studies, the architecture of the book devolves upon the distinction between productive power and repressive power. The first two studies focus on productive power: the management of long-term unemployment in the public employment service and cognitive-behavioural interventions in the prison service. Two further studies concern repressive interventions: the conditions of incarceration in the prison service and the activity of the customs service. These studies reveal that power, as conceptualized within the Foucauldian tradition, must be modified. A more complex notion of productive power is needed: one which covers interventions that appeal to desires, and which would govern both at a distance and at close range. Additionally, the simplistic paradigm of repressive power is called into question by the need to consider the organizing role of norms and techniques that circumvent agency. Finally, it is argued, Foucault's concept of *strategies* – which accounts for the thick web of administrative directives, organizational routines, and techniques that simultaneously shape the behaviour of targeted individuals and members of the organization – requires an organizational dimension that is often neglected in the Foucauldian tradition.

Magnus Hörnqvist is based in the Department of Criminology at Stockholm University.

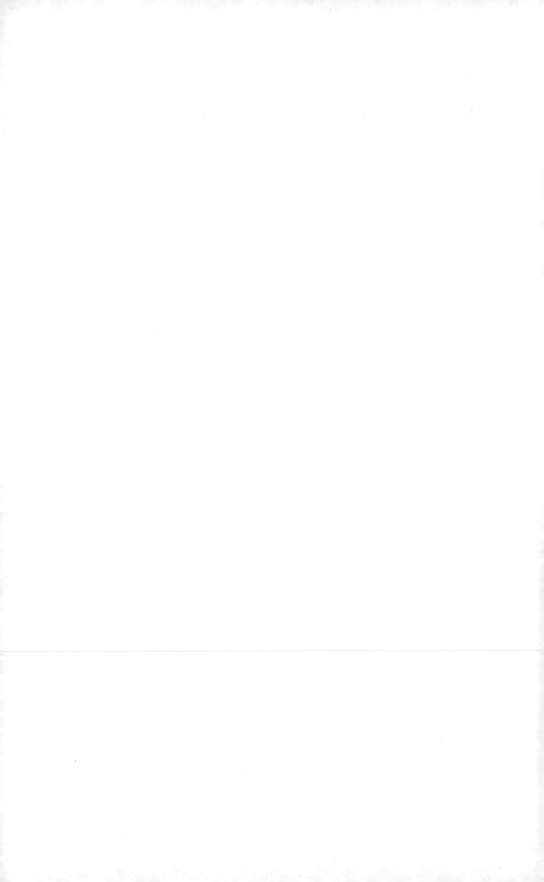

Risk, Power and the State

After Foucault

Magnus Hörnqvist

a GlassHouse book

First published 2010
by Routledge
2 Park Square, Milton Park, Abingdon, Oxon, OX14 4RN

Simultaneously published in the USA and Canada
by Routledge
270 Madison Avenue, New York, NY 10016

A GlassHouse book

Routledge is an imprint of the Taylor & Francis Group, an informa business

© 2010 Magnus Hörnqvist

Typeset in Garamond by
Taylor & Francis Books
Printed and bound in Great Britain by
CPI Antony Rowe, Chippenham, Wiltshire

British Library Cataloguing in Publication Data
A catalogue record for this book is available from the British Library

Library of Congress Cataloguing in Publication Data
Hörnqvist, Magnus.
    Risk, power, and the state after Foucault / Magnus Hörnqvist.
      p. cm.
    "A GlassHouse book."
    Includes bibliographical references.
    1. Power (Social sciences) 2. State, The. 3. Foucault, Michel, 1926-1984–
Influence. I. Title.
    JC330.H67 2010
    303.3–dc22
                    2009044983

ISBN10: 0-415-54768-7 (hbk)
ISBN13: 978-0-415-54768-0 (hbk)

ISBN10: 0-203-85705-4 (ebk)
ISBN13: 978-0-203-85705-2 (ebk)

Contents

List of Illustrations

Figures

Tables

Introduction

What follows is an empirical study of power in some contemporary organizations. By choosing *power* as the point of departure, I want to reawaken a number of insights elaborated by Michel Foucault in the course of a few brief but brilliant years in the 1970s. The ambition in this introductory chapter is to present an understanding of power which has for a long time been hidden beneath a thick layer of governmentality studies and discourse analysis. The presentation is structured around three distinctions. The distinctions provide the cornerstones for this study, as well as, arguably, any study of power. Although firmly rooted in Foucault's work, they have received far too little attention in the Foucauldian literature. The first distinction is that between power as a relation and power as an activity. The concept of power is ambiguous as it can refer to both. Foucault exclusively studied power as an activity, which was not always kept separate from the notion of power as a relation. The second focuses on the way in which power as an activity exists in two forms, productive power and repressive power. The distinction between productive and repressive power is primary in relation to all other concepts employed by Foucault to make sense of the business of regulating human behaviour. Discussions of 'sovereignty', 'governmentality', 'discipline', 'mechanisms of security', 'pastoral power', 'technologies of the self' and 'bio-power' presuppose – or would benefit greatly from – the distinction between productive and repressive power, which cuts across all historical manifestations of government. The third distinction is that between programmatic and non-programmatic acts of power. In this book, as in the Foucauldian tradition generally, it is the programmatic – rather than the singular and spontaneous – attempts to shape conduct that are of interest. Yet the distinction, in so far as it accounted for, tends to ignore the organized nature of power in favour of an exclusive focus on the element of thought and deliberation. By redrawing all three distinctions a new light can be cast on power and the process of social reproduction.

The ambiguity of power

Foucault's conceptual comments on power are shot through with a basic ambiguity. There is a tension between power as a relation and power as an activity. In *Discipline and Punish*, we are encouraged to view power as 'a network of relations, constantly in tension' (Foucault 1979a: 26). Power, in this sense, refers to *relations* between individuals. It is not confined to a specific domain. There is no such thing as a political domain, where power would be exercised, as distinct from other spheres of life that are economic, personal, and so forth. Every social relation is at the same time a power relation. For this reason, one must disentangle the relations of power that run 'between every point of the social body, between a man and a woman, between the members of a family, between a master and his pupil, between every one who knows and every one who does not' (Foucault 1980: 187).

This view is not uncontested however, even in Foucault's own writings. Alongside the relational conceptualization runs a rather different view of power. In one interview, Foucault says that 'power is nothing other than a certain modification, or the form, differing from time to time, of a series of clashes which constitute the social body, clashes of the political, economic type, etc.' (Foucault 1989: 188). On this view, power is an activity. If power is nothing else than a historically variable form of 'clashes of the political, economic type, etc.' it is essentially tied to a certain kind of activity – namely, the acts performed in these clashes. There is no longer room for power as a relation which in some sense underlies the clash. Power is *not* the balance of forces that predates the clash: it may change during the course of events, and in part it determines the outcome. Power is only what happens when two or more people clash; the concept does not capture the fact that a confrontation may take place under historically given and unequal conditions. At times, when the metaphysics of Friedrich Nietzsche make their presence felt, Foucault stresses the active nature of power to the extent that power *becomes* an activity and, as such, it is temporary and fluid. It is never stable and always exercised: 'Everywhere that power exists, it is being exercised' (Foucault 1977: 213). On this reading, there is no power (relation) behind the exercise of power. The concept is de-contextualized and reduced to particular cases of power in action.

After abandoning conflict and war as a matrix for understanding power (Lemke 1997: 144–45), Foucault would not so much conflate the two meanings of the term as downplay one of them. The notion of power as a relation disappears from the analysis. It has also been neglected in the secondary literature on Foucault. In the long dominant approach, inspired by the later work of Foucault from 1978, when the lecture series on governmentality was delivered, 'the conduct of conduct' is the preferred definition of power (Foucault 1982: 220–21; Gordon 1991: 2; Burchell 1996: 19; Dean 1999: 10–11; Rose 1999: 3). The expression refers to attempts at directing the conduct of others – or oneself. The formulation 'the conduct of conduct' is associated with straightforward attempts to delineate specific courses of action. Yet power could also be exercised by shaping the options at hand. To include this possibility, the late Foucault could define power in terms of structuring the field of possible action (Foucault 1982: 222). However, whether the emphasis is on direct procedures or indirect means, the underlying conception is that of power as an activity. Unless this conception is supplemented with a notion of power as a relation, the entire undertaking – the analysis of power – is bound to founder. More specifically, it will not be possible to separate power from what is not power. There are a tremendous number of actions that to some extent structure the field of possible actions. In a trivial sense, almost anything that people do at one moment may affect the options of others at the next moment. Similarly, a wide range of actions may immediately influence the conduct of others. Not least, Foucault has illustrated this in some detail. Quoting the French educational reformer Jean-Baptiste de La Salle, he enlarged the concept of punishment to include 'a certain coldness, a certain indifference, a question, a humiliation, a removal from office' (Foucault 1979a: 178). Inversely, a large number of acts could operate as rewards: a moment of confirmation, a nod, an extra benefit, or silent acceptance.

That somebody nods, however, or asks a question, does not necessarily mean that power is being exercised. If we want to restrict the courses of action that may be called power, how do we draw the line? There is no definitive answer. Conceptually, power as an activity presupposes power as a relation. Without inequality and relative positions of strength, there is no sense in talking about exercising power as opposed to exerting influence in more general terms. Consequently, since the late Foucault and the governmentality approach lack a notion of verticality – of the unequal nature of social relations – the term 'power' becomes superfluous. Peter Miller, one of the pioneers of the approach, saw these logical consequences and suggested that we should 'dispense with the term power' considering there to be 'quite simply practices' (Miller 1987: 17). We are left with a multitude of actors who are trying to influence one another in various directions. There is nothing qualitatively different about these attempts – they are 'quite simply practices'.

The problem concerns not only the notion of power as the conduct of conduct, but also other conceptualizations of power as an activity, including the one presented here. The distinction between power and non-power is admittedly vague. To exercise power is to influence the conduct of other individuals. On the other hand: which acts do *not* influence the behaviour of other people? To exercise power is to reproduce the existing order. On the other hand: which acts do *not* to some extent reproduce an existing order? Acts of power are not readily distinguishable from other acts; there are no shared inherent qualities. What separates power from non-power, I would suggest, is the context. If we want to retain the word 'power', as distinct from 'practices', it is necessary to look at the playing field of unequal social relations. Power is the activity that starts from *and* reproduces power relations. It comprises acts by a party superordinate in relation to another, to influence which acts are carried out by that second party, with the intention or the effect of reproducing the inequality between them. I am aware that the expression 'the intention or the effect of reproducing the inequality between them' is imprecise. The problem is that one cannot assume that those who exercise the power *always* share a specific intent; neither can one assume that *all* acts of power actually do reproduce such relations. Hence, to cover all acts of power, both the intention and the effect have to be included. In this way, the definition becomes wide enough – albeit at the risk of becoming somewhat too wide. Similar acts on the same playing field, performed by subordinate parties, may instead be called *resistance*. Resistance challenges the power relation. The difference is the relative position of strength.

To conclude: the term 'power' encompasses double meanings, which must be kept separate. This book deals primarily with power as an activity. For purposes of clarification, this will be called 'the exercise of power', or 'to exercise power'. At the same time, it is vital to *retain* the notion of power as a relation, since without it power as an activity cannot be identified. The conditions for, as well as the results of, power as an activity will be referred to as 'power relations'. Much of Foucault's work was devoted to 'the "how" of power' (Foucault 2003a: 24) – how power was exercised in specific settings. Little attention was given to the question of what constituted power relations. When the matter was brought up, Foucault emphasized the multiplicity of power relations – that they exist everywhere and are different from one another (Foucault 1980: 187–88). Yet relations of power do have something in common, something that distinguishes power from that which is not power. The notion of power as a relation is not foreign to Foucault. It is embedded in the original conception, and simply needs to be disentangled from the notion of power as an activity.

Power comprises 'unbalanced, heterogeneous, unstable, and tense force relations' (Foucault 1998: 93). Three basic characteristics stand out: the relations are unequal, contentious and unstable. First and foremost, power relations are unequal. One party can direct the conduct of the other party, whereas the other party has less influence over the course of action of the first party. For this reason, the former may be called superordinate and the latter subordinate. The imbalance may be rooted in material resources, access to information, experience, physical strength, social class, a formal command structure or indeed anything that influences the capacity to affect the conduct of others. There are no sources that per definition are more important than others. This conception of power makes no assumption about the relative weight of violence, science or capital.

Second, power relations are contentious. The struggle is not contingent but endemic (Foucault 1979b: 60, 1980: 90). Power relations are produced and reproduced through struggle. The inequality presupposes a history of conflict – over the allocation of material resources, knowledge, work efforts, and so on – which it perpetuates. In one sense, power is nothing but the momentary status in an ongoing struggle. At the same time, the struggle transcends the individual power relation. What is at stake need not be confined to positions of strength in the relation at issue. Every power relation exists in a society and is thereby surrounded by, and potentially affected by, a range of other power relations and conflicts. In all, there are 'innumerable points of confrontation, focuses of instability, each of which has its own risk of conflict' (Foucault 1979a: 27).

Third, power is unstable. The inequality may be only temporary. This characteristic is related to the element of struggle. The outcome depends on the actions and tactics deployed. Consequently, an 'at least temporary inversion of the power relations' is always possible (Foucault 1979a: 27). In addition, the uncertain outcome is related to the very nature of the original relation. Power is not fully on one side; the imbalance is never total. The subordinate part retains its freedom to a certain extent. There is always an option to act otherwise, or to actively resist. If pursued, this may change the power balance. Moreover, a power relation may be transformed even if none of the parties directly involved take action. Other processes can undermine or reinforce the power relation. A context consisting of multiple layers of contradictions and ongoing conflicts means that change can come from more than one direction. The freedom of the parties immediately involved, in combination with the uncertain outcome of related conflicts, results in a basic fragility. Foucault speaks of 'the moving substrate of force relations which, by virtue of their inequality, constantly engender states of power, but the latter are always local and unstable' (Foucault 1998: 93).

This concept of power is modelled on the particular situation where individuals are opposed to each other, face to face, without intervening institutions. It does not rule out the possibility of power relations at the macro level, the presence of organizations that stabilize power relations, or considerations that conflicts take place under historically given conditions. But the ambition is to *reduce* rather than to account for the complexity of power relationships. Complex power phenomena are broken down into their smallest components: individual relations that are unequal, contentious and unstable. A Foucauldian analysis is an immediate critique on the fetishism of power, that is, the tendency to turn power relations into objects, cut loose from a social context. The point of departure is that power is something which occurs exclusively between human beings. It is a relation between actors and not a property of one actor. By extension, to speak of 'the power of big corporations', for example, constitutes a major linguistic simplification.

The expression could and should be broken down into relations between human beings. Equally, the seemingly overwhelming power of the state falls apart into a multitude of relations, each of which is 'unbalanced, heterogeneous, unstable, and tense'. Ordinary notions of class and gender must also be analysed as being composed of unequal, contentious and unstable relations that occur between individuals.

At the same time, power transcends the level of individuals. Foucault's conceptualization includes phenomena at the macro level, which are referred to as 'wide-ranging effects of cleavage that run through the social body as a whole' or 'major dominations' (Foucault 1998: 94). Although local and unstable, 'the multiplicity of force relations' is also articulated 'in the state apparatus, in the formulation of the law, in the various social hegemonies' (ibid.: 92–93). These phenomena are of a different kind. Power relations at the macro level are in some respects the very opposite of power at the micro level: not unstable and constantly questioned, but 'permanent, repetitious, inert, and self-reproducing' (ibid.: 93). Foucault would also speak of 'states of domination' where the power relations 'remain blocked, frozen' (Foucault 1997: 283). In other words, a Foucauldian analysis would acknowledge that power is also collective rather than individual, stable rather than fragile, and structural rather than situation-dependent.

However, if power relations are – by definition – unstable and contentious, one needs to understand the reproduction of phenomena that are stable and inert. Foucault has little to say about the transition. He merely states that 'power comes from below', and describes higher order phenomena as 'simply the overall effect' of relations and activities at the micro level.

> 'Power', insofar as it is permanent, repetitious, inert, and self-reproducing, is simply the overall effect that emerges from all these mobilities, the concatenation that rests on each of them and seeks in turn to arrest their movement.
>
> (Foucault 1998: 93–94)

Yet the question remains: how is this 'simply the overall effect' brought about? What makes power structures stable when power relations are unstable? Through which mechanisms are the individual relations successively interconnected to form higher order phenomena such as 'the state apparatus', 'major dominations' and 'social hegemonies'? What can be said about the range of meso-level phenomena – organizations, discourses, strategies and technologies – that may account for this process? In what ways do they mediate between action and structure, between fragile individual relations and inert institutionalized relations?

This problematic is rarely acknowledged within the tradition. Instead, there is a tendency to reaffirm that 'power comes from below', combined with an ambition to show that the reproduction of relatively stable relations of power – or the element of permanency, repetition, inertia and self-reproduction – is not guaranteed. Hubert Dreyfus and Paul Rabinow formulate both points concisely: 'There is no inherent logic of stability. Rather, at the level of the practices, there is a directionality produced from petty calculations, clashes of wills, [and] meshing of minor interests' (Dreyfus and Rabinow 1982: 188). Yet what needs to be explained with this approach is the actual reproduction of institutionalized power relations, rather than why the reproduction is *not guaranteed*. Why is social order reproduced when its reproduction is not guaranteed, and when all that we know about the nature of power indicates that it will not be reproduced?

The assumption that the behaviour of all individuals would spontaneously reproduce social order is untenable, unless society is conceived of as being in a state of harmonious equilibrium. Given that the latter is not the case, the behaviour of all individuals must be *made* consistent with a given configuration of power relations. The 'multiple relations of power' that 'traverse, characterize, and constitute the social body' are not self-generating (Foucault 2003a: 24). Social order presupposes exercise of power. It was Thomas Hobbes who initially formulated the problem. In a society where some individuals attempt to acquire advantages over others unrestrained by normative considerations, there is a permanent tendency towards social disintegration. Stable social structures cannot be taken for granted in the face of 'a perpetual and restless desire of Power after power, that ceaseth only in Death' (Hobbes 1985: 47). Hobbes saw the precariousness of social order, and simultaneously identified a countervailing force. The existence of society depended on the presence of a sovereign, who was considered both necessary and sufficient to secure social stability. In *Leviathan*, the seventeenth-century absolutist state was the historical incarnation of the sovereign. Its activities consisted of legislation, law enforcement, taxation and the waging of wars against other nations (ibid.: 91–92). Talcott Parsons would later find this answer unsatisfactory. To Parsons, repressive power could not account for the stability of modern societies. Something else was also required. He found that this 'something else' lay in the normative dimension; society was held together through shared values (Parsons 1937: 89–94). As Axel Honneth has observed, Foucault's analysis could be seen as a different response to the Hobbesian question, as modified by Parsons: 'What means for the exercise of power do modern orders of power employ when they do in fact show a lesser degree of instability than would be achieved through the instruments of violence and ideology alone?' (Honneth 1991: 164).

The twin concepts of violence and ideology are not by themselves sufficient to explain the relative stability of current Western societies, so what *other* means are used to make individual behaviour consistent with the dominant configuration of power relations? Foucault did not agree with the answer given by Parsons, as normative, possibly stabilizing convictions were banished from the analysis. Relations of power are not kept in check by mutually shared values. But he accepted the question itself as a valid one. It is also the essential problematic for anyone who takes a Foucauldian concept of power as their point of departure. Conceptual tools other than the conventional must be employed to understand how it is possible that power relations, which are built up in local conflicts, extend into complex social institutions that display a high degree of stability. Foucault did not have an elaborate notion of social order itself; the references to institutionalized power relations never contain any characterizations (Hörnqvist 2007: 26–28). Yet the analysis of *what it is that does the reproducing* – that is, power as activity – is truly ground-breaking. The problem of social order was approached with an extended understanding of what it means to exercise power. Organizational discourses and technologies were brought to our attention as vehicles of power, which may account for the transition from fragile individual relations to inert institutionalized relations. The undertaking was built on the idea that power can be productive, as well as repressive.

Productive and repressive power

Foucault contributed to the analysis of power both conceptually and historically. A new framework was developed, on the one hand, and phenomena were studied that were previously unknown or known under other descriptions, on the other. Yet the two aspects have not always been distinguished; on the contrary, within the tradition the confusion between the historical and the conceptual is endemic. Along with the inability to separate power as a relation from power as an activity, the failure to distinguish historical transitions from conceptual advances has made it unnecessarily difficult to appreciate the latter. In the governmentality literature, as well as in the Deleuzian readings of Foucault, we find frequent references to the triangle 'sovereignty, discipline, and governmental management' (Foucault 2007: 107), suggesting new concepts to understand power, with the aim of demonstrating that the way in which power is being exercised has undergone fundamental changes through the years. The same point has been made in conjunction with the thesis of a transition from 'disciplinary societies' to a 'society of control', proposed by Gilles Deleuze and repeated by, for instance, Nikolas Rose as well as Michael Hardt and Antonio Negri (Deleuze 1990; Rose 1999: 233–34; Hardt and Negri 2000: 22–27). The later stage is associated with notions of 'bio-power', 'technologies of the self' and 'mechanisms of security', which are contrasted with outright coercion and fixed institutions. The argument is that power, historically, has become more productive, embracing and diffuse. Such a shift, whether it took place or not, must however be distinguished from the conceptual discussion. Foucault's primary contribution lies on the conceptual level, in the distinction between productive and repressive power. No doubt it was developed through genealogical studies, but once formulated it cuts across all transformations of government. The distinction between productive and repressive power is not, as opposed to the technologies of power themselves, subject to constant change. It does not depend on a gradual evolution from repressivity to productivity, or on a correlation between a specific type of society and the dominant mode of power. The distinction should be defined in categorical rather than historical terms, and I will explore that possibility in relation to Foucault's work.

The extended understanding of power as an activity can be seen as the antithesis of four basic assumptions that have traditionally been made in the social science literature. These assumptions delineate one specific conception of power. Foucault criticized it as the conception of power *tout court*. I will reconstruct its four basic assumptions, as they were formulated by Foucault.

R1
The fundamental operation of power is to dictate laws

'The pure form of power resides in the function of the legislator' (Foucault 1998: 83). On the most basic level, power is a speech-act. To enact a law is to say that 'thou shalt not!' (Foucault 1980: 140). This is the first act of power. It is the exercise of power that lays the platform for all further exercise of power. Enacting a law changes future conditions. It introduces a dichotomy, divides acts into two categories – those that are permitted and those that are prohibited. Individuals are confronted with 'a binary system' (Foucault 1998: 83); the sphere of possible action is circumscribed by a number of boundaries, each marking the difference between permitted and not permitted. The binary regime is not only made up of legal distinctions. The boundary may also be drawn between healthy and sick, between normal and abnormal, or between rational and irrational. Yet the principle is the same: to exercise power is to set enforceable boundaries.

R2
Power is mediated through conscious decisions

It is a conscious decision to enact the law – and it is a conscious decision to follow the law. The subjects are first told what to do, and then think how to respond. Power is played out in the arena of deliberation. Those who exercise power must make decisions that are linked to the existing rules in terms of application and justification. Every individual who is exposed to power is at the same time confronted with the opportunity as well as the necessity to choose. The basic question is: should I stay on the 'right' side of the established border? It follows that resistance is a conscious decision as well. Power relations can only be challenged by consciously transgressing the set boundaries.

R3
Power may be understood in strictly negative terms

There are basically two forms of power: repression and ideology. Repression punishes law violations, crushes resistance and excludes people. Ideology forbids texts, distorts reality and prevents insight. The former targets the body, the latter manipulates the mind. In both cases, power is essentially destructive. The setting of boundaries is the sole positive act. Repression is negative in relation to the individual, who is rejected, beaten, sanctioned or excluded. As power is mediated through conscious decisions, the impact of repression may also be indirect, to deter others from transgressing the set boundaries. Ideology is negative in relation to the truth, which is repressed, distorted or concealed. The impact of ideology is vital as it directly targets the ability to make decisions. While repression is associated with the state, ideology is seen to reside in the individual. 'When we turn to individuals,' Foucault remarked, power is found 'nowhere except in the mind (under the form of representation, acceptance, or interiorization)' (Foucault 1988: 119).

R4
The effect of power is either obedience or disobedience

Foucault comments ironically on the power of repressive power:

> it is a power that only has the force of the negative on its side, a power to say no; in no condition to produce, capable only of posting limits, it is basically anti-energy. This is the paradox of its effectiveness: it is incapable of doing anything, except to render what it dominates incapable of doing anything either, except for what this power allows it to do.
>
> (Foucault 1998: 85)

Passive obedience marks the successful use of power. The subordinate individuals perceive which rules are in force, and keep their behaviour within those boundaries. Power relations are conceived of as being reproduced through the lack of transgressions. A transgression, on the other hand, is an immediate threat. If power is deployed unsuccessfully, transgressions are provoked. This amounts to disobedience – acts that cross the line of the permitted. But if power is deployed successfully, it does not produce specific acts. Instead, it makes individuals *refrain* from specific acts, namely those that would challenge the power relation.

This conception is not inaccurate *per se*. Power is exercised in a way that corresponds to the four assumptions. But it does not *always* follow the same, repressive pattern. Power can also be productive.

The distinction between productive and repressive power is analytically just as central as the distinction between the relations of power and the exercise of power. In many ways, the two forms of power are each other's opposites. Productive power is organized around the norm, and not the law; the means are productive rather than negative; actions are created and not prevented; and the effects are achieved regardless of intentions and consent. There is, in Foucault's writings, an understanding of power which can be summarized in four assumptions. Taken together, these assumptions differentiate productive power from repressive power.

P1
Power is organized around the norm

Foucault describes the norm as 'the element on the basis of which a certain power is founded' (Foucault 2003b: 50). Productive power is organized around the norm, and that affects (a) the organization of the target group, as well as (b) which acts are targeted.

P1(a)   The norm does not divide acts into two categories, as opposed to the law around which repressive power is organized. Instead, all individuals are distributed along a continuum – 'a whole range of degrees of normality' (Foucault 1979a: 184). The norm is used as a yardstick. The behaviour of *all* individuals is monitored – not only those at risk of violating the law. While repressive power patrols the boundaries of accepted behaviour, productive power measures differences in relation to norms. The result will be used to construct power relations within the target group. Differences in individual performance are *activated* – transformed into privileges and positions in a hierarchical order. In the words of Foucault, the power relations are brought into play 'not above but inside the very texture of the multiplicity' (ibid.: 220). Individuals are not managed as a homogenous collective but as individuals occupying different positions. If they organize or act collectively for purposes considered illegitimate, the constructed power relations can be activated. The means are simple and unobtrusive – relying on the redistribution of ranks and privileges within the constructed order – as opposed to confronting the collective from an external position. Ideally, the ambitions of the recalcitrant behaviour will not be repressed but redirected and given new, exploitable expressions.

P1(b)   Repressive power targets potential or actual violations – and nothing else. This creates 'a measure of freedom' (Foucault 1998: 86), or a space which power cannot reach. Law-abiding citizens are left to themselves. There are vast areas of activity which are autonomous, in the sense that the courses of action are unrelated to, and even shielded from, repressive power. Productive power, on the other hand, may target any kind of behaviour. *All* behaviour is modifiable. There are no inherent limits. No activity is guarded from modifying efforts. What may appear as strictly private matters can nonetheless be subject to considerations of power. Foucault's analysis of discipline showed that a wide range of acts could be punished. 'The whole indefinite domain of the non-conforming is punishable: the soldier commits an "offence" whenever he does not reach the level required; a pupil's "offence" is not only a minor infraction, but also an inability to carry out his tasks' (Foucault 1979a: 178–79). Similarly, the case studies contained in this book will show how details of behaviour – attitudes, assertiveness, how to dress, body language, social skills, problem-solving techniques and the motivation to change – are targeted in relation to specific norms.

P2
The effects are achieved regardless of intentions and consent

The effects may be produced regardless of the intentions of those who exercise power or the consent of those over whom it is exercised. Unlike repressive power, there is no necessary element of deliberation and insight. Discipline is paradigmatic in that it subverts the level of conscious decision. 'The disciplinary systems favour punishments that are exercise – intensified, multiplied forms of training' (Foucault 1979a: 179) The exercises may be repeated until the behaviour no longer deviates from the established norm. The correct behaviour is produced automatically; it is an immediate effect of the punishment itself. Those who are punished need not regret or realize their mistakes. The intended behaviour will gradually become the default mode, through repeatedly practising the correct reactions. Although other modes of productive power, such as technologies of the self, to some extent rely on the choice of the individual, they also, typically, subvert the level of conscious decision. To influence behaviour it is not necessary to first access the consciousness. On the contrary; we must understand 'how power relations can materially penetrate the body in depth, without depending even on the mediation of the subject's own representations' (Foucault 1980: 186).

P3
Power must be understood in positive terms

Foucault speaks of a 'fundamentally positive power' (Foucault 2003b: 48). The positive feature of power is directly related to its perceived proximity. It is exercised *with* rather than over and against the disenfranchised individuals. Repressive power may be thought of as an external force that approaches the individuals from a radically different position. Productive power, on the other hand, lies much closer to the targeted individuals due to the nature of the norm, which is 'a mixture of legality and nature, prescription and constitution' (Foucault 1979a: 304). The norm is partly constructed from perceived regularities in the behaviour of the target group itself. This makes it appear natural. As a consequence, power 'conceals itself as power and gives itself out as society' (Foucault 1979b: 66). But it is not a form of ideology, which distorts and prevents insight. Productive power does not eradicate the space for deliberation. It is rather an endeavour that, in the words of Nikolas Rose, governs 'through the freedom and aspirations of subjects rather than in spite of them' (Rose 1998: 155; emphasis removed). Productive power is productive precisely because it addresses individuals as stakeholders in a common endeavour and appeals to their self-interests. Training is provided; positive incentives are preferred over negative incentives; and links are established between actions and existing needs and desires. In this way, individuals in subordinate positions are mobilized in collective projects with a shared vision. The target group is enrolled as active subjects in the maintenance of order; collective subjugation is linked to individual ambition.

P4
Power is productive

While repressive power prevents specific behaviours, productive power produces specific behaviours. The former reduces motivation and limits the ability to act; the latter enhances motivation and the ability to act. Power creates the competence to act in a certain way. This is the basic sense in which power is productive. Beyond this, the productivity of power has been elaborated in additional directions. For instance, Foucault might say that power produces 'knowledge', 'things', 'pleasure' and 'discourse' (Foucault 1980: 119). The creation of 'individuals' was another recurrent theme. The individual was described as 'one of power's first effects' (Foucault 2003a: 30). The governmentality literature would come to add new entities – above all citizens – to the list of phenomena produced in and through power (Bosworth 2007: 68).

Power is productive – and destructive. The problem with the conventional approach (R1–R4) lies in its one-sidedness. The Foucauldian account of power as an activity is potentially superior in that it covers power in both modes. Practices that otherwise might have gone unnoticed as power can be identified as such, as either repressive or productive power. It also provides a better platform to explore the question of social order. The conventional approach is inadequate because, as Foucault remarks, 'power would be a fragile thing if its only function were to repress' (Foucault 1980: 59). However, if repressive and productive modes of power are analysed together, a new dimension is added to account for the relative stability of social order.

Strategies: the organized form

There are a range of concepts in the social science literature – 'power', 'social control', 'governance', 'government' and 'regulation' – that perform the same analytical function. Across multiple meanings, they serve to account for that which reproduces social order. Some terms might be preferred over others.

e term 'power' as it is conceptually linked to social order and the lations that constitute it. In the work of the late Foucault, the preferred term is instead 'government'. Following the interest in 'the art of government', government replaced the notion of power (Foucault 2007). But there was continuity in one important sense. The attempts to shape the behaviour of others that reproduce social order were at the centre of interest. These attempts, whether productive or repressive, are programmatic. It follows that there is also a category of non-programmatic acts of power. This is the third fundamental distinction: that between non-programmatic acts of power and the programmatic attempts to shape conduct generally studied in the Foucauldian tradition as well as in this book.

The difference has been described in terms of intent and deliberation. Nikolas Rose, for instance, argues that 'the distinction hangs on the elements of thought, intention and calculation' (Rose 1999: 4). First of all, the activity must be carried out to achieve specific targets. Rose emphasizes this aspect when 'practices of government' are defined as 'deliberate attempts to shape conduct in certain ways in relation to certain objectives' (ibid.). In addition, the activity must be reflexive. Rose *et al.* speak of 'a way of doing things' that is not only 'oriented to specific objectives' but is also 'reflected upon itself in characteristic ways' (Rose *et al.* 2006: 84). This criterion is harder to specify. A target is or is not formulated, whereas the level of reflexivity to be expected is less clear-cut. Yet some amount of reflexivity should be required. The rational dimension – goals plus reflection – is doubtless one important aspect of the distinction. What makes Rose's distinction problematic is less what it contains than that which it omits. This conceptualization tends to neglect the organizational dimension. Programmatic attempts to shape conduct are thought through, yet, equally importantly, they are organized. The actions are organized in government agencies, political parties, families, voluntary associations or private companies. At one level, that is a trivial observation. But in theoretical terms, the organizational context has been neglected in favour of the cognitive, rational dimension. What does it mean that power is organized? The question is rarely posed within the Foucauldian tradition. It is the intention of this book to start filling the lacuna by asking that question. In particular, I will suggest an analytical framework that will account for the thick web of administrative directives, organizational routines, follow-up techniques and relations of accountability, which separate the organized from the less organized, the spontaneous from the calculated, and singular from recurring acts of power.

This entire book could be read as an elaboration of the proposition *that power is essentially exercised in an organized form*. I will describe this form as a *strategy*. In my usage, a strategy is a process made up of three stages, each of which is crucial in the exercise of power, in so far as it is programmatic: *setting the target, targeting, staying on target*. The concept captures the downward process, when policy decisions and research are translated into interventions at the level of individuals, and the upward process, when interventions at the level of individuals are followed up, both through and beyond the organization. In this sense, strategies are organized and calculated attempts to shape behaviour in relation to goals. It is a stipulative definition, which deviates from the usage of the word in ordinary language. This conception of strategies builds on the intuition that 'domination is organized in a more-or-less coherent and unitary strategic form' (Foucault 1980: 142), and that power can be seen as 'a machine in which everyone is caught, those who exercise the power just as much as those over whom it is exercised' (ibid.: 156). Although power is exercised by individuals and not by organizations, its exercise is to a large extent independent of individuals. Foucault also used the term *dispositif* to conceptualize this intuition, referring to a mix of tactics and technologies that transcended institutions (Foucault 2006: 14–15).

The organizational level is primary. Policy goals, behaviour-modifying techniques, prioritized risks and the choice of intervention should be analysed as properties of the organizational context rather than as phenomena that may be studied in isolation. I will draw on basic theorems of organization theory to understand the programmatic deployment of repressive or productive interventions and to elaborate the concept of strategies. According to Niklas Luhmann, the organization – every organization – distinguishes itself from society at large by deciding on membership criteria. The organization includes members in the organization on the conditions set, while it simultaneously excludes non-members (Luhmann 2006: 392–93). Members are incorporated in the organization as individuals. Each member assumes a formal position in a hierarchy of roles and responsibilities. While being part of a collective, they are monitored and mobilized as individuals. Depending on the member's position within the organization, some actions are mandatory, others are encouraged, and further others are prohibited. Non-members, on the other hand, are all those who are excluded from the rights and responsibilities reserved for members of the organization. A subgroup of non-members is immediately affected by the organization's activity from a position of dependence. I will call this the target group of the organization. The target group of the prison service, for instance, primarily comprises the individuals sentenced to prison.

Another basic feature of modern organizations is that they exist for a specific purpose. The organization acquires a goal in a trade-off with its environment. The goal is explicitly formulated and tends to be constantly talked about (Meyer *et al.* 2006: 44). In the customs service, described in Chapter 5, preventing illegal import is a main organizational goal. The primary target group is border-crossers. The goal implies that the behaviour of the target group is shaped in a particular direction: in this case, that border-crossers import commodities legally, or not at all. It further implies the exercise of power *within* the organization. Using power towards individuals in the target group in such a way that the organizations-specific target is attained presupposes mechanisms that shape and co-ordinate the behaviour of members of the organization. Put more briefly: for the organization to govern others it must itself be governed.

Organizations have emerged as a field in their own right for the exercise of power. Intra-organizational power was reflected upon in successive schools of management that introduced the techniques of target-setting, follow-up routines, quality measurement and team-building during the course of the twentieth century (Boltanski and Chiapello 2005). Yet this particular aspect of the exercise of power has not been theorized as such. Foucault (1979a) touched on the theme of intra-organizational power when describing the spread of discipline in the modern army to make it more governable and efficient. Within the Foucauldian tradition, management techniques have been analysed as technologies of power (McKinlay and Starkey 1998). But the sole focus was placed on the interventions themselves, and whether they were applied towards members or non-members has not been seen as significant. Failing to make the distinction between the use of power *within* an organization and the use of power *by* an organization, the crucial importance of the former as a prerequisite for the latter has been overseen. The notion of strategies will have to account for the double sense in which power is organized. On the one hand, power is exercised by members of the organization towards dependent non-members. On the other hand, power is exercised within organizations, towards members. The behaviour of members is shaped by features of the organizational context so that the first-order targeting – the application of targets and techniques in relation to non-members – becomes possible. Strategies perform both functions, shaping the behaviour of individuals in the target group as well as the behaviour of members in the organization.

The concept of strategies will be successively elaborated in the case studies. But I should make some preliminary remarks to clarify the peculiarities of the concept in my usage. Strategies are grounded on immediate interventions directed at a particular target group. What makes properties of the organizational context into elements of strategies is *the existence of a link* to interventions at the level of individuals. These interventions are acts of power, since they attempt to change the behaviour of individuals in the target group, either productively or repressively. If for some reason no such link exists, the presumed component does not constitute part of the strategy. To take an example from one of the case studies: the up-grading of the threat of pirate copies in the customs service had an immediate impact on ground-level measures. However, if the altered threat assessment had been unrelated to measures on the ground, as a result of non-existent routines or failure of communication, it could not have been considered part of the strategy. Further, strategies are *identified* through the links – consisting of information flows, organizational routines and oversight structures – which emanate from the immediate interventions. All parts of a strategy are perfectly visible. There are no hidden, latent or underlying components. Everything is on the surface: the policy goals are publicly stated; the statutory powers are regulated in legal documents; the interventions are observable social practices also described in manuals; the organizational routines are scrutinized in audits or accessible via interviews; evaluations are published in reports; and common visions are articulated in government bills and in educational material directed at employees. Finally, it will be assumed that strategies are the outcome of contestations and compromises. As such, strategies are not conceived in advance. Although a fair amount of conscious planning goes on, no one designs strategies. The links are established by various actors in the course of their daily work at different levels of the organization, or by groups outside the organization. The actors have different and sometimes conflicting goals. The contradiction between economy and security, for instance, is a common theme in the case studies. Business interests necessitate a balance between the will to control and the risk of controlling too much. Once in place, however, the strategy will possess an administrative inertia. The composition of strategies is contentious but relatively durable, as they are embedded in organizational routines.

Strategies are where action meets structure. The build-up of strategies, as an extended process of calculated attempts to shape behaviour in relation to goals within and beyond an organization, goes some way to account for how power relations that are inherently unstable and unequal can extend into complex social institutions which display a high degree of stability. As opposed to 'the moving substrate of force relations' which, to speak with Foucault, engenders 'states of power' that are 'always local and unstable', strategies may emerge as 'permanent, repetitious, inert, and self-reproducing' (Foucault 1998: 93–94). The power exercised is structural and collective rather than individual and situation-dependent. At the same time, strategies are also markedly different from structure. Power structures, conceptualized as cleavages that 'run through the social body as a whole' between collectives of individuals, or more specifically as capitalism – defined as a system of social relations characterized by private ownership of the means of production, commodity exchange and wage labour – are not organized, nor necessarily reflected. Structures are the effects of organized and reflected attempts to shape behaviour – that is, of strategies – but are not organized and reflected as such. In this way, strategies can be used to capture the mediations – scattered in techniques and organizations, policies and discourses – between action and structure.

Risk: the reflected nature

This notion of strategy was designed to capture the organized as well as the reflected nature of power. I have stressed the organizational element, but it is inseparable from the element of thought and calculation. Reflection is at the heart of strategies. Calculation is integral to the exercise of power at each stage: when assessing the risks, determining the performance targets or distinguishing the target group (*setting the target*); when designing treatment programmes, deciding control tactics or setting up administrative routines (*targeting*); and, finally, when evaluating interventions, monitoring performance targets or changing administrative routines (*staying on target*).

The element of reflection can be captured by notions of risk. Risk is used to communicate and think about the organized attempts to shape behaviour – within as well as beyond organizations. It has been constructed as the medium through which the past activity is communicated, contested, evaluated and reflected on, to produce decisions, demands, requirements and guidelines that will structure the future activity in general and the use of power in particular. First of all, risk plays a crucial role, as will be shown in this book, in directing power towards non-members who are part of the target group. Various tools for risk assessment and risk communication guide the deployment of interventions at the level of individuals, determining when and what types of interventions are activated in practice. Risk is moreover vital for guiding the intra-organizational exercise of power. Since the 1990s, risk has become 'implicated in new visions of the way in which organizations should be governed' (Power 2007: 3). Previously, considerations of risk were made use of mainly for control purposes: to secure the organization from things going wrong. Risk management meant assessing threats facing the organization, detecting dysfunctional routines and monitoring deviant behaviour within the organization. Yet increasingly, risk directs not only control practices but organizational performance in general. Tom Baker and Jonathan Simon have suggested an approach to the organized nature of power in terms of 'governing through risk'. The approach builds on the notion that the communication of risks is central to organizational performance or, in their words, 'the core idea of governing through risk is the use of formal considerations of risk to direct organizational strategy and resources' (Baker and Simon 2002: 11).

One might be hesitant to use the concept of 'governing through risk', since doing so runs the risk of isolating the element of risk from its organizational context. The calculation of risk takes place within a context of organizational exigencies, which constrain and structure it. Legal restrictions, organizational routines, available information, political expediencies, fiscal limitations, personal convictions, a shortage of resources, and discretionary tactics also shape activities at all levels of the organization, along with 'formal considerations of risk'. At the same time it should be conceded that risk has a special status. In the public sector, risk tends to be a hegemonic performance indicator guiding the attempts to shape the behaviour of members of the organization. Michael Power has observed that 'risk is the new concept for challenging the quality of public services in the absence of real markets' (Power 2004: 19). There is a *prima facie* case to be made that considerations of risk are superordinate in all state organizations. For private companies that operate on the market, profit is the ultimate indicator. There is no equivalent reality-check, stemming from the context in which the organization operates, for state organizations. But as goal attainment has moved to the centre of attention for oversight bodies, risk has proved a useful concept to evaluate performance across specific organizational goals within the state. Risk management captures organizational reforms which promise to improve organizational performance in terms of both avoiding the worst and achieving the best. It signifies both better protection and better use of existing resources. The dual character of risk has accompanied the concept from its commercial origins, as entrepreneurs balanced making a profit against suffering a loss when deciding on future investments (Bernstein 1996). Calculating risk was essential both to make a profit and to avoid economic ruin. When state organizations are evaluated and directed in terms of risk, this duality has been transferred to the public sector, where risk management, traditionally seen as avoiding adverse effects (Renn 2008), is equally achieving something positive.

As opposed to profit, however, which relates to a strictly economic logic, risk is not reducible to a singular dimension. It has been described as a fluid assemblage of different technologies, discourses and logics (O'Malley 2004). Put slightly differently, risk is a common language in which institutional discourses and practices are negotiated and connected. The communication of risks connects diverse phenomena and makes them work as parts of a single strategy. Figuratively speaking, risk is the language spoken within a strategy – by means of which the institutional players make themselves understood. To be effective, requests and expectations are of necessity translated to fit the risk communication system operating within the strategy. Competing goals, diverging interests, available information, moral and political convictions are phrased – or rephrased – as considerations of risks. In this way, risk becomes the common language. Goals that are not primarily associated with risk management – and that appear to have been drawn from a regime of welfare, of sovereignty or of cost efficiency – may be attached to the communication system. In administrative practice, considerations of efficiency, security, rehabilitation, due process, free trade and business opportunities are all negotiated in terms of risk. The common language does not erase the contradictions but makes different priorities and goals negotiable.

The characteristics of current risk-management practices themselves facilitate agreement. Risk assessments are surrounded by an aura of scientific accuracy, appear technical and promise increased efficiency. They incorporate findings from academic research. In many cases, and certainly in the cases examined in this book, either the analysis itself or the instruments for conducting the analysis are supplied by academics. The rational hallmark is reinforced by the apparent technical nature of the approach. As Hazel Kemshall has observed, risk-assessment instruments appeal to managerial concerns such as avoiding 'contentious disputes over appreciative systems by obscuring value choices behind checklists and weighting systems' (Kemshall 1998: 142). Difficult and inherently normative decisions are transformed into technical know-how and administrative routine. In addition, risk-assessment instruments carry the promise of improving the ability to manage an uncertain future. 'Risks are assessments of possible events,' in the words of David Garland, 'made by people in the face of an uncertain world' (Garland 2003: 52). Yet the case could be made that risk assessments are more present-oriented than future-oriented. The assessments are framed in terms of possibilities of future events but are present-oriented in terms of function. Risk is a way of addressing what to do with the present, based on past information, rather than thinking about the future. Present behaviour becomes actionable when past information is processed through the guiding notions of risk within a given strategy.

Risks are strategy-specific. There are no risks in general but only relative to a strategy. To borrow an expression from Richard Ericson and Kevin Haggerty, 'risks exist only in institutional knowledge about them' (Ericson and Haggerty 1997: 100). The risks are closely linked to the organizational goal. It follows that while members of an organization are able to communicate, the same risks are not necessarily understood elsewhere. Yet players outside an organization can learn to communicate. A strategy may extend beyond the boundaries of a single organization. Although the strategy is rooted in the interventions performed within the confines of one organization, it can be linked to a number of other institutional actors through target-setting or follow-up routines focusing on the management of the specific risks. The public employment service, described in Chapter 2, is enmeshed in an organizational network consisting of four further state organizations, which have successfully translated their concerns into the language of risk that directs ground-level interventions in the public employment service. In this way, all five organizations are part of the same strategy and can effectively communicate.

Finally, risk facilitates the reproduction of the organization in competition and negotiation with other institutional players. It mediates between singular actions of members and overall organizational performance. It is crucial in all three stages of a strategy. It is used, first, to set the target for interventions, then to target individuals and, finally, to ensure that the organization stays on target. In this way, the language provides a medium which links ground-level activity and policy-level planning. The strategy-specific risks are communicated upwards as well as downwards within the organization. Policy-level threat assessments are – via administrative guidelines, routines and forms – successively broken down into ground-level interventions. Conversely, the application of risk-based interventions is – via statistics, monitoring routines and audits – successively followed up throughout the organization. The communication of risk simultaneously individualizes and generalizes the pressure to perform and conform. It reaches every single member, regardless of whether they are involved in close encounter with the target group or making strategic decisions at the head office, and makes their performance visible and measurable in relation to the organizational goal.

The state: the blind spot

Strategies need not be situated in the state. Yet the strategies that will be studied in this book are integrated into a wider network of state organizations. But calling them *state* strategies does not necessarily mean anything. From a strictly Foucauldian perspective, two distinctions are crucial: between repressive and productive, and between programmatic and non-programmatic, acts of power. The distinction between state power and non-state power, on the other hand, is not significant. Governmental programmes of all kinds can be implemented by state agents as well as non-state agents. The state is theoretically redundant; whether a strategy is part of the state, and not part of the corporate world or of civil society, is a contingent historical fact, which has nothing to do with the state or the strategy itself. Although Foucault's own research on the asylum, the medical clinic and the prison are case studies of the state, there is no notion of the state. He made no attempt to gloss over this irony (Foucault 2008: 76–77). Within the tradition, the state is usually mentioned simply to make the point that power is *not only* exercised by the state. The call to seek power beyond the state was first issued by Foucault (Foucault 1979b: 59–60), and then became an axiom in governmentality studies (Rose and Miller 1992: 176–77; Miller and Rose 2008: 20). At the same time, few would deny that there is a state and that it exercises power. So what about when power *is* exercised by the state?

At some point, the question of the state and the possible specificity of its power must be confronted. In my case, there is little choice. All three of the organizations that are scrutinized in this book are parts of the state. The exercise of power by the public employment service, the prison service and the customs service constitutes a state activity. Are there reasons to assume that this particular circumstance affects the power that is being exercised? Drawing from other theoretical traditions, such as Marxist state theory, the answer would be yes. Following Joachim Hirsch, the state is characterized by its ability to exercise or authorize repressive power (Hirsch 2005: 18). This is the classic Weberian criterion: an organization that has monopolized the legitimate use of force within a given territory (Weber 1972: 822). It presupposes a concentration of the means to exercise force as well as a certain level of administrative capacity. Max Weber analysed the state as a specifically modern political structure. Marxist state theory adds that the state is a specifically *capitalist* political structure. It elaborates the links between the power exercised by the state and the capitalist relations of production. The state is distinct as compared to previous state-like structures precisely in this regard: the control over the use of physical force is separate from the extraction of economic value. Given the capitalist relations of production, value is not acquired by means of direct force, as was the case during feudalism and other historical epochs. Instead, those who own the means of production acquire value through the exchange of commodities, including labour power. This exchange is formally equivalent and voluntary. No one forces the economic actors to sell their commodities, and no one dictates the price. Although physical force went into the creation of market conditions, it is absent from the market itself. The use of force is monopolized in the form of the state, which is organizationally separate from those who own the means of production, as well as from all individuals and social classes (Hirsch 2005).

The state's monopoly on violence is by itself inadequate to the task of reproducing social order in general and capitalist relations of production in particular. For this reason, much attention in Marxist state theory, just as in a Foucauldian approach, is directed at *additional* mechanisms that make the accumulation of capital possible. These additional mechanisms are, however, conceptualized slightly differently in Marxist analysis, and include above all state interventions with an immediate economic relevance, such as the institution of money, commercial law, investment policies, central banks or industrial courts (Jessop 2001). These are institutional forms that regulate competitive economic transactions carried out by private actors. In this sense, the process of capital accumulation is embedded in the state, although the violence monopolized by the state takes no active part. It follows that the power exercised by the state is simultaneously internal and external in relation to the dynamics through which the capitalist relations of production are reproduced (Hirsch 2005: 25). Repression unfolds separately from the accumulation of capital, whereas other forms of state regulation are inseparable from the same process. The central tenet of Marxist state theory can also be expressed using the Foucauldian distinction between repressive and productive power. The characteristic feature of the capitalist state becomes, when cast in Foucauldian terms, that its repressive power is separated from the dynamics through which the capitalist relations of production are reproduced, whereas its productive power is part of the dynamics. *All* its repressive use of power is separate from the process of capital accumulation, whereas *some* of its productive use of power is integral to this process.

One achievement of Marxist state theory consists in accounting for the state's connection to economic structure. Institutional forms that are organizationally separate from all social classes and immediate business interests are analysed in their capacity to manage structural contradictions and secure the long-term as opposed to short-term profitability of individual companies. The mediations in one direction are well accounted for: the links running from state organizations to the conditions for capital accumulation. The concept of regulation, typically defined as 'the totality of institutional forms, networks, and explicit or implicit norms' (Lipietz 1988: 24), could capture the interconnectedness between capital and state. But the analysis is never followed through in the other direction, down to the level of action. How do 'institutional forms' or 'implicit norms' shape the behaviour of individuals? This question is never posed. The approach stops at organizational structures. What actually takes place within the state organizations that are meticulously positioned in relation to social forces and the process of capital accumulation is never analysed. The *power* exercised by the state is referred to in general terms – norms, institutions, modes of regulation, the monopoly of violence, historical blocs, and so on – but is not made into an object of study. To the extent that productive strategies of power, which are integral to the accumulation of capital, enter into Marxist analysis of the state, the focus is on the formation of institutions rather than on the shaping of behaviour.

The problem of social order comes down to shaping the behaviour of individuals – even given a materialist reading of social structure, whereby the behaviour of social classes which do not own the means of production has to be made consistent with, and must actively reproduce, capitalist relations of production. Among the actions that reproduce structure, performing wage labour is one crucial set of actions that must be produced with the additional support of the state. Wage labour presupposes the formation of skills and the motivation necessary to carry out paid work in accordance with the prevailing conditions on the labour market. This is not a spontaneous process. Historically, the creation of wage labour was necessary for the development of capitalism. In the first volume of *Capital,* Karl Marx analysed the original accumulation as a historical process. Through 'an accumulation [that was] not the result of the capitalist mode of production, but its starting point' (Marx 1954: 667), the direct producers were freed in a double sense – separated from their means of production and liberated from feudal constraints on the disposal of their labour power. Large numbers of individuals lost the ownership of their means of production but gained the full ownership of their own labour power. Marx described a unique historical transition. But the constitution of wage labour remains an issue. Wage labour that is accessible on the conditions set by a labour market, and that is equipped with skills and motivation that correspond to the current needs of production, is not a by-product of the original accumulation. The constitution of wage labour cannot be accounted for simply by reference to what Marx labelled 'the dull compulsion of economic relations' (Marx 1954: 689). This compulsion – the circumstance that all individuals have to make a living under conditions which are beyond their scope of influence – is no doubt significant, however it is not sufficient. For the great majority of individuals, the economic relations do exert a numbing and constant pressure towards performing wage labour. But that pressure cannot educate, and is by itself not enough to overcome their unwillingness or indifference to labour market participation, 'especially when the commitment demanded of them assumes active engagement, initiative and voluntary sacrifices' (Boltanski and Chiapello 2005: 8). The necessary qualifications, expectations and routines must also be actively created by other means.

The state is a key actor in the production of wage labour. The owners of the means of production presuppose a constant supply of skilled and motivated wage-labourers on the labour market, which they cannot produce themselves. They cannot compel people to work, since the use of force is monopolized by the state and separated from the extraction of economic value; nor can they, under circumstances of competition, take on the cost of educating and disciplining potential workers. The routines and skills for wage labour must be created elsewhere: in the family, in the associations of civil society and in the state. The economically relevant behaviour is shaped within as well as beyond the state. Yet the state undertakes the role of last resort, should the power exercised in the family, in the associations of civil society and in the regular education system fail. The state has taken on responsibility for all those who are – or are presumed to be – unskilled or unmotivated to carry out regular paid work. The productive interventions studied in this book are directed at those who are registered as long-term unemployed and those who are convicted to prison. The corresponding strategies shape the behaviour of front-line members of state organizations in such a way that they deploy technologies of productive power to develop the skills and the motivation to work within the target group. If successful, the actions of the targeted individuals will actively reproduce capitalist relations of production by selling their labour on the conditions dictated by the market. If not, the same individuals may be exposed to a combination of repressive and productive state interventions until they do so.

This study

The following chapters present four empirical case studies of interventions based on considerations of risk. Like all case studies, they were theory-laden from the outset. The very concept of a case implies that it is 'a case *of something*' (Gomm *et al.* 2000: 102; emphasis in original). The 'something' in my case was strategies of repressive and productive power. The concept of power came into play in choosing the *type* of intervention. The selection of cases reflects the basic distinction between *productive* and repressive power. Chapters 2 and 3 focus on *productive* interventions and Chapters 4 and 5 on *repressive* interventions. The *basis* for intervening was the other decisive feature guiding the selection of cases. I was looking for interventions that in one sense or another were triggered by risk. The choice was derived from a large body of literature on contemporary trends of government which suggests that risk was increasingly used to guide and to evaluate the exercise of power (Rose 1999; Baker and Simon 2002; Kemshall 2003; Hörnqvist 2004; Power 2004).

I gathered most of the data in 2004 and concentrated on recent documents. With a few exceptions, all the data come from the period 1994–2004. This reflects a basic methodological choice: to study strategies *as if* they had no history. The ambition is strictly to describe the composition of strategies, including the use of interventions and follow-up mechanisms, at a given time, which roughly corresponds to the period covered by my data collection. I have no ambition to diagnose a shift from one type of power to another. Plenty of other studies have been conducted with the aim of uncovering historical discontinuity in a constant quest for new, as opposed to older, forms of governance. This book does not claim to have found something radically new. I do think that many of the techniques described were developed recently, in particular during the late 1990s, but the element of change is not relevant to my concerns. I will focus strictly on how power is exercised at a given time, consciously bracketing out questions such as 'What is new?', 'Where do the components come from?', 'Who were the chief engineers?', 'Why did they do it?', 'What kind of resistance did they meet?' This may generate the false impression that strategies *are* a closed micro-system of power without a history. For this reason, the present study must be complemented with other studies to find the multiple layers of conflict and compromise beneath the surface of contemporaneity.

The three organizations examined are part of the state and perform core state functions, such as punishment, border control and market regulation. They interact with private actors that provide information and in some cases carry out the interventions. The private companies are acting on behalf of the front-line state organization, which in turn is monitored by an array of auditing bodies which are also part of the state. Hence, while involving non-state actors, the strategies were exclusively state strategies in terms of command and control. The same consideration applies to the choice of location. The case studies turned out to be case studies of the state in the old-fashioned sense. The domain is national, confined to Sweden. An international perspective is useful to understand *the spread* of the studied interventions. But their deployment, once imported, appears to be a national affair. The line of command and monitoring structures, as opposed to ideological influences and the diffusion of techniques, is a strictly national business. This need not be transferred into an argument against the ongoing internationalization of the state and the evolution of new forms of governance (Jessop 2008). It simply means that in the studied cases of punishment, border control, taxation and labour market regulation, the state did the steering and most of the rowing in relation to a target group that was defined on a national level.

All case studies were carried out with an identical design. The point of departure was one particular intervention to manage risk, and the research process consisted in pursuing all of the links extending from – and possibly guiding – the intervention that had been chosen as the starting point. These links comprised organizational routines and information flows, and they were pursued both towards the field of immediate application and upwards through the layers of the organization. Many links had already been documented – in manuals, audits, enquiries, instructions, evaluations, legal rules, forms, and so on. Consequently, I have retrieved all sorts of documents that were linked to the deployment of the four interventions. My ambition was to be as exhaustive as possible. Two routes were pursued. The first route went through libraries to find official documents – such as public inquiries, government directives, efficiency audits, activity reports and policy-relevant research – with an existing connection to the interventions. By 'existing connection' I mean that the documents guided, or were intended to guide, the deployment of interventions. This was the criterion I used for the inclusion of documents in the data set. The second route went through the head offices of the public employment service, the prison service and the customs service. I was granted access to extensive non-public documents, including internal policy papers, strategic assessments, training manuals, administrative guidelines and reporting forms. I was also able to retrieve data on the use of interventions at the level of individuals: action plans for 200 individuals enrolled in the public employment service and sentence plans for 188 prison inmates. In the customs service, equivalent data were non-existent.

The resulting data set was heterogeneous. A wide variety of documents were included: scientific work and administrative instructions, brief forms and comprehensive investigations, general overviews and assessments of individuals. The material was analysed in line with the concept of strategies. I started from the assumption that a strategy can be identified through the risks that it operates to prevent. Considerations of risk were identified in each document, and the traces were pursued across documents and organizational levels. The quotations presented throughout this text, which are drawn from threat assessments, training manuals, guidelines, audits, mission statements and individual case files, represent transmutations of the strategy-specific risks. In this sense, all quotations are representative. My results rely on what can be taken from the collected documents. The ambition has been to reconstruct the exercise of power on its own terms. This design made it impossible to tell whether – or in what ways – day-to-day practice deviated from what was stipulated or described in the documents. For instance, the account of exercises in the Cognitive Skills programme relies exclusively on the course descriptions in the manual. I have not observed the classroom implementation. It may well be that teachers in the local prisons have modified the classes, or that the education at times founders on prisoners' resistance. Or, to use another example, administrative guidelines may depict the routines for sanctioning in the public employment service, but have nothing to say about rule compliance, and in which cases employees abstain from sanctioning. The present study shares this limitation with other studies more firmly tied to the governmentality school. As a response to criticism, one could say that the documents portray 'empirically real plans and diagrams' that are part of the process of exercising power in practice (Rose *et al.* 2006: 99). One might also respond that the analysis concerns the organized nature of power in a slightly extended sense. It is not the exercise of power *per se* that is being uncovered but rather 'the architecture of power' (Ericson 2007b). The study captures how power is organized independently of individuals – regardless of both the preferences of those who exercise the power and the responses of those over whom it is exercised.

The concept of strategies dictated not only the research strategy but also the mode of presentation. All chapters have an identical structure. Each chapter proceeds from a single type of intervention. The presentation then follows the processes of:

Setting the target
Targeting
Staying on target

I will focus on each stage separately. Part (A) concerns the setting of the target; part (B) deals with the process of targeting; and part (C) accounts for the efforts to stay on target. Parts A–C represent the bulk of each chapter. They are followed by a section discussing the conceptual conclusions. The topic of these discussions is different in each chapter. The first chapter considers the mix of productive and repressive power, and captures the intra-organizational power in terms of layers of control. The second chapter specifies what productive power produces and proposes an outline of a generic concept. The third chapter questions the legal paradigm of repressive power and suggests that risk provides the element of calculated direction. The fourth chapter elaborates the claim that repressive power is mediated not through conscious decisions but through a common language of risk that negotiates contradictory expectations. In the final chapter of the book, the two main issues at stake will be reconsidered. Given the previous discussion, the first question could be formulated in the following way: do the interventions match the defining features of productive power (P1–P4) and of repressive power (R1–R4)? And if not, in what way do we have to modify the original distinction? The other question touches on the organized nature of power common to both productive and repressive interventions. Can the programmatic exercise of power be understood as a strategy – that is, as a process of setting the target, targeting and staying on target, in a way that makes sense of a wide range of phenomena related to the reproduction of social order?

Chapter I

Activation guaranteed

Individualizing the pressure to perform

During the 1990s, the obligation to work was extended into the duty to become employable. In Sweden, as in most other Western countries, governments would impose a strict regime of work-related requirements. The dual approach to simultaneously coerce and train individuals into wage labour came to be known as 'activation' (Gilbert and van Voorhis 2001; Lødemel and Trickey 2001; Goul Andersen and Jensen 2002; Hemerijck 2002). In Sweden, the assumption that everyone could and should be made employable was spelled out most explicitly in the 'activity guarantee' launched in 2000. Everyone who is, or is at risk of becoming, a long-term enrollee in the public employment service may be referred to individually designed labour market policy activities corresponding to full time activity. Participation is mandatory. For the duration of this open-ended intervention, the enrolled individual will circulate through a variety of training programmes and activation measures, which have a common focus on basic employability, including presentational skills.

The activity guarantee and similar schemes are usually contrasted against passive labour market policies, which entitle those who are unemployed to income provision without requiring any activity in return (van Berkel and Hornemann Møller 2002a). The overtly coercive nature is also stressed in the literature (Lødemel and Trickey 2001; Giertz 2004). In that sense, however, the activity guarantee was nothing fundamentally new. In a Swedish context, 'activation' had been official government policy since the 1920s (Junestav 2004). The emphasis on work-related activities, in order to be entitled to unemployment benefits or social assistance, was prominent from the very beginning (L. Eriksson 2004). By comparison with other countries, Sweden distinguished herself through the combination of a strict obligation to work and high levels of unemployment benefits. In a study from the late 1990s, Sweden was found to have both the highest level of compensation and the toughest legal requirements among a sample of 15 Western countries (ARM 1999: 154–55). The strict requirements to accept employment were not always enforced. During the period of the classical welfare state, 'these demands have been generously interpreted and the unemployed have usually had the possibility of rejecting the offered position or programme' (Johansson 2001: 66). In addition to a lenient interpretation of the require-ment to accept work, some groups were exempted from these requirements altogether. For instance, 'the ambition to make use of the residual work capacity of people on social insurance benefits was extremely low' (Lindqvist and Marklund 1995: 231). This was to change in the 1990s, when work requirements came to be enforced with more vigour and few groups were exempted. Individuals who had traditionally been exempted from the obli-gations of labour market availability were subjected to demands similar to those on other people out of work. Work requirements were extended to new groups such as those on long-term sick leave and social assistance clients. In addition, attempts were made to activate people with disabilities and han-dicaps (Bergeskog 2001). In principle, there was to be no exception. Under the assumptions of the activation policy, no one is exempted from the duty to become employable.

Each agency dealt with a segment of the target population in accordance with its own specific categories and routines. *In the social insurance system,* the notion of 'labour market oriented rehabilitation' was introduced in 1992 (SOU 2000a). It was made obligatory for persons on sick leave to participate in 'rehabilitative' measures that would enable a return to the workplace. If the individual was too sick to return to his or her present employment, any kind of work should be considered. The residual work capacity was to be tested in relation to the entire national labour market (Proposition 1996/97). Insurance benefits could be made conditional on compliance, and this con-stituted the incentive to participate in rehabilitation or to accept any posi-tion corresponding to the individual's residual work capacity. *In the social services,* the legislation was changed in 1998 so that social assistance could be made conditional on carrying out assigned work or training programmes. Those who were considered to be immediately job-ready would compete on the regular labour market, whereas social assistance recipients found to be 'in need of skill-enhancing measures' were referred to activities organized or contracted out by the social services (SFS 2001: section 4). These legal changes were significant. Although the new requirements were far from always enforced (Hetzler 2004; Salonen and Ulmestig 2004), the centuries-old distinction between the sick – who don't work because they cannot work – and the able-bodied – who don't work because they don't want to – was being blurred (Castel 2003). The conception of those who can, or can be made to, work was widened.

The extension of work requirements to new groups was implemented in close co-operation with the public employment service. Substantial minorities of social assistance recipients were managed in a joint venture undertaken by the public employment service and the social services, while interventions for those on long-term sick leave were co-ordinated by the public employment service and the social insurance agency (Lindqvist 2000; Giertz 2004). A total of 1.1 million individuals were enrolled at the public employment service at some point in the course of 2004 (AMS 2005a: 2). The sum total of enrollees during one year thus represents a substantial segment of the entire workforce, or one quarter of the population in the ages 16 to 64 years. Since its inception at the beginning of the twentieth century, the public employment service has confronted everyone formally registered as unemployed by means of a dual role of service provision and control – with a varying emphasis and level of vigour (Delander *et al.* 1991). While controlling that the unemployed actively seek work, the agency also provides a range of services to facilitate employment. Nowhere was activation turned into a more coherent strategy as in this agency, positioned at the centre of the state campaign to reconstitute labour.

The activity guarantee did involve a displacement towards more state-designed labour market intervention and more coercion. But it cannot be understood simply by contrasting passive and active labour market policies, or by using the distinction between coercion and consent as the sole point of departure. Instead of accounting for change using the dichotomies between passive and active, or between voluntary and involuntary interventions, activation will in this chapter be analysed as a strategy comprising a mix of repressive power and productive power towards the target group, built on a layered control structure within the organization. The analysis focuses on the momentary composition of the activation strategy, dealing with each of the three stages separately. At the target-setting stage, I will follow the way in which the risk of long-term unemployment was linked to a broader risk of social disintegration and came to be operationalized in terms of job-search activity and employability. The targeting, consequently aimed at increasing job-search activity and employability, involved the two main inventions of the decade – individual action plans and the activity guarantee – that revolutionized the business of laying down activity requirements. This will be followed by an account of the multiple layers of control within the public employment service that enabled and directed the first-order targeting. A disciplinary surveillance regime, assessing the individual members of the organization and shaping the organizational control performance, ensured that the power exercised towards the target group was on target.

A
Setting the target

The state is a key actor in the production of wage labour under capitalism. Activation may be seen as the historically specific form, directed at those who are unwilling or unable to work, involving a thoroughgoing individualization of state power. The goal has been described as 'personalized trajectories of integration' into the world of work (Procacci 1998: 74). It involves a tacit, but very specific, conception of the state's role in regulating the labour market. The state must design a solution for each and every individual, and the different responses must reflect the differences that exist between individuals in terms of employability and the motivation to work. This notion of social inclusion excludes the 'demand side' from policy considerations – neither the number of available jobs nor labour market conditions constitute an object for intervention. The performance of the private organizations operating on the labour market is similarly exempted. Jamie Peck and Nikolas Theodore have remarked that this is an example of 'supply-side fundamentalism', since the intent of the state is to 'work aggressively on the supply side to "flexibilise" and "motivate" the unemployed' (Peck and Theodore 2000: 729). More or less everything except the excluded themselves is excluded from policy considerations. The sole focus is on the unemployed as individuals who must be integrated into the workforce via state-designed 'personalized trajectories'.

The elusive long-term unemployed

In the mid-1990s, the government registered a new and growing problem through the lens of applications for unemployment benefits, social assistance and sickness benefits. Rather suddenly, after decades of almost full employment, individuals who were out of work for long periods of time became a prime policy concern. Different agencies defined the problem in different ways. In the public employment service it was defined as *long-term enrolment*. The group emerged during the 1990s and referred to those who had been out of work for more than two years. At the end of the decade, the government concluded that 'the number of long-term enrollees has increased dramatically during the 1990s, from having been virtually non-existent at the beginning of the decade' (Proposition 1999/2000a: 22). In the social services, the problem came to be known as *welfare dependency*. A government inquiry observed that the problem was growing at a dramatic pace: long-term dependency on social assistance increased fivefold between 1990 and 1996 (SOU 1999). Although most households receive social assistance for other reasons, those for whom unemployment constituted the primary reason were conspicuous. An OECD report noted that the 'long-term unemployed' had 'been the group showing the highest rate of increase among social assistance clients in most countries' (OECD 1998a: 68). Within the social insurance agency, the target population was perceived as *persons on long-term sick leave*. Long-term sick leave is not a medical but an administrative concept which is used to refer to individuals who lack the capacity to work for a considerable period of time because of illness. This group also grew rapidly, but its expansion started later, at the end of the decade. Between 1997 and 2002, the number of persons on long-term sick leave more than doubled. In addition, the number of persons in receipt of disability pensions grew steadily (Hetzler 2004: 81–88). Together these groups comprised a substantial proportion of the total workforce. At the beginning of the new millennium, up to 25 per cent of the total workforce was not supported by wage labour. And the majority of the members of this group were not actively competing in the labour market.

For the government, the trend represented both a threat and an opportunity. The economic cost to the state was a recurrent concern in the government bills (Proposition 1996/97, 1999/2000a, 2002/03). All those who were not performing wage labour had to be supported by other means, either through the state budget or, in the case of social assistance recipients, the municipal budgets. It was also assumed, however, that the threat that needed to be averted was far greater than both the economic ramifications and the personal costs of long-term unemployment. Long-term unemployment became a policy concern not least through its intimate connection with a perceived threat to social cohesion. Given the sudden proliferation of the concept of social inclusion in policy discussions, and the establishment across Europe of 'the new Durkheimian hegemony' (Levitas 2005: ix), societal integration became a prime consideration in its own right. This concern for social breakdown was not of a neo-conservative nature, framed in terms of a corrupted and culturally different underclass, but rather a social democrat one, articulated within what Ruth Levitas calls a 'social integrationist discourse' (Levitas 2005: 7). It was embedded in a normative analysis of the social order, yet its moral fragmentation was seen to be rooted in economic circumstances, something which distinguishes the approach from neo-conservatism. The central problem was not viewed as being the consequences of welfare dependency *per se*, but social exclusion 'understood as the breakdown of the structural, cultural and moral ties which bind the individual to society' (ibid.: 21). Exclusion in this sense was regarded as endangering society's capacity to maintain its own cohesion.

The threat became identified with – and visualized in terms of – the groups who were at risk of being excluded from the moral and economic order of society. It was labelled 'the new social question' in an influential book of the same name written by Pierre Rosanvallon. Similarly, Robert Castel points to a 'threat of breakdown', that is 'borne by groups whose very existence shakes the cohesion of the whole collectivity' (Castel 2003: 3). The groups are characterized as:

> vague silhouettes, at the margins of labor and at the frontiers of socially consecrated forms of exchange – the long-time unemployed, inhabitants of abandoned suburbs, recipients of national minimum income, victims of industrial downsizing, young people in search of employment who carry themselves from place to place, from menial jobs to temporary work.
>
> (ibid.: xv)

Together, they form a significant and growing segment of the total population. Yet these disaffiliated individuals have little in common with each other. As Rosanvallon notes, 'the excluded form a "non-class"' (Rosanvallon 2000: 98). The only thing that unites them is a common position in relation to the labour market – they are either out of work or in temporary work in the lower tiers of the labour market. This disaffiliated 'non-class' is loosely attached to the economic order and as a consequence their moral ties to mainstream society also become weaker. Employment is not seen as a strictly economic relation; 'it is through the attachments of the workplace that identity and social integration are effected' (Levitas 2005: 182). Consequently, being out of work involves a combined moral and economic estrangement, which endangers social cohesion.

The flip side of this threat was found in the constitution of wage labour. The growth of groups with a marginal attachment to the world of work was simultaneously seen as a potential waiting to be realized. According to an analysis conducted by the head office of the public employment service, there were 'substantial unexploited resources on the labour market' (AMS 2003: 3). The threat to social cohesion also constituted an unexploited resource. The government envisioned 'a mobilization of the large reservoir of labour power that exists today in this country among young as well as older people, immigrants and individuals with disabilities' (Proposition 2002/03: 36). Tapping into this 'large reservoir of labour power' was viewed as crucial.

The endeavours were framed in terms of social inclusion. Social inclusion was a cornerstone in the overall strategy to make Europe the most dynamic and competitive economy in the world (CEC 2001). In one of its submissions to the European Union, the Swedish government described its labour market policies as 'an expression of an ambition to make everyone part of society and prevent social exclusion' (Regeringen 2003a: 24). Social exclusion was prevented primarily by raising the level of participation in the labour market. According to the dominant conception, social inclusion means above all else being employed. As Rik van Berkel and Iver Hornemann Møller have noted, this assumption was shared by most European governments at the turn of the millennium, when regular paid work was 'considered both the most desirable form of inclusion, and the most important instrument for inclusion in a wider sense' (van Berkel and Hornemann Møller 2002b: 3). One cannot be socially included unless one is performing wage labour. The employment moreover serves as the stepping stone to inclusion in other areas of society. Thus, through its conceptualization as both a precondition and gateway, the focus on paid work is made consonant with the prevalent emphasis found within the 'social integrationist discourse' on a thorough embeddedness in society, in which the concept of social inclusion *also* refers to the individual's integration in the local community, housing conditions, levels of education, citizenship, health and political participation (Levitas 2005: 23).

To achieve social inclusion, everyone who is unemployed could be forced to participate in work-related activities based on their risk of remaining unemployed. This risk is framed in terms of their personal shortcomings in relation to a labour market that was excluded from policy considerations from the outset. It is the unemployed individuals who have to be changed. Yet to know *what* about them has to be changed presupposes a notion of their problems. One route towards this has been via empirical investigations asking the question 'What increases the risk of becoming long-term unemployed?' This line of enquiry is tied to a traditional risk-management approach, which has the goal of first identifying common characteristics among the long-term unemployed, and then intervening to target these characteristics, thereby reducing the risk of long-term unemployment. This has been attempted, but with only limited success.

One reason for the limited success is that the question 'Who are the long-term unemployed?' has proved very difficult to answer. One government inquiry attempted to pin down the long-term unemployed by pointing to 'people who have been struck by the restructuring of rural areas' and 'unemployed social assistance clients in the larger cities' (Proposition 1999/2000a: 1). This implicitly refers to two groups that occasionally appear in policy documents: older men in rural areas formerly employed in traditional industries, and immigrants living in poor suburbs on the outskirts of large cities. Attempts of this kind to constitute target groups discursively are never followed through in administrative practice, however. Moreover, even at the policy-level, the strategy operates without a precise conception of the target group. The same government inquiry was forced to conclude that 'simply put, you could say that long-term enrollees have more or less the same background as the unemployed in general' (ibid.: 23). They were found to be somewhat older, somewhat less well-educated, and more often born outside the country, but other than that, they did not stand out in any way. In terms of the usual socio-demographic categories, the long-term unemployed represented a rather mixed group, which managed to elude the statisticians. The long-term unemployed did not share any common identifiable characteristics.

The lack of knowledge is not merely the result of statistical limitations but is equally a matter of outlook. Rosanvallon's claim that 'there is no "typical" long-term unemployed person' (Rosanvallon 2000: 99) must also be attributed to the perspective within which the policy is framed. Individuals who are out of work are not *conceptualized* as being a different kind of people. In the official documents, no assumption is made that the long-term unemployed are fundamentally different from the population at large. The approach differs markedly from the neo-conservative discourse which describes the socially excluded as being qualitatively different from the rest of the population both morally and culturally (Levitas 2005). It also differs from the approach chosen by the prison service, to be discussed in the next chapter, in which a certain group of individuals is viewed as being different from the population at large as a result of a basic lack of cognitive and social skills. While the long-term unemployed are indeed considered deficient in the social integrationist discourse, their shortcomings cannot be described solely by reference to personal characteristics, and nor are they explicable in terms of culture or cognition. Their deficiencies exist in relation to the labour market – and only in relation to the labour market.

Several research projects have proceeded on the basis of a belief that it is possible to isolate the labour market related shortcomings of unemployed individuals. If successful, such research could be used to predict which unemployed individuals are more likely to remain unemployed for an extended period of time, and to guide the deployment of interventions. The promise proffered by a traditional risk-management approach is threefold. First, by predicting who will become long-term unemployed, interventions can start early. Second, long-term unemployment can be prevented by interventions targeting the identified risk factors. Third, scarce resources can be used more efficiently by channelling interventions towards those most at risk, and excluding low-risk categories from interventions. All three arguments have been made in the policy debate on profiling (OECD 1998b). Profiling involves a traditional risk-management approach to long-term unemployment which has been adopted by a number of countries, including Australia, the Netherlands and the USA. The newly registered unemployed are screened using assessment instruments to determine the risk level of the individual, who is then referred to a category that implies a specific intervention. One of the most highly developed profiling systems is the Job Seeker Classification Instrument in Australia. A set of characteristics relating to the unemployed individual – age, vocational qualifications, length of period of unemployment, family status, geographical location, disability, country of birth, offender status, and so forth – are considered to be risk factors and assigned a numerical value according to a pre-determined scoring system. Depending on the total score, the individual is assigned a risk level and then referred to an administrative category. A low risk of long-term unemployment equals job-matching services; medium risk equals job-search training; and high risk equals intensive assistance. The assessment tool thus translates a higher level of risk into more intense control and services (McDonald *et al.* 2003; Henman 2004).

But this risk-management approach suffers from serious limitations. First of all, it appears that long-term unemployment cannot be predicted at an early stage. Despite comprehensive attempts to assess the newly registered unemployed in terms of their risk of becoming long-term unemployed, conducted in several countries since the 1980s for the purposes of early intervention, no special risk factors have yet been identified which allow such predictions to be made. A team of Danish researchers working on the development of profiling tools noted, for example, that 'the predictive power of the various models' was 'to a large extent discouraging' (Rosholm *et al.* 2004: 3). Helmut Rudolph came to the same conclusion in Germany – 'there is no unique set of variables to predict LTU [long-term unemployment] correctly' (Rudolph 2001: 35). Moreover, many of the characteristics of the unemployed individual which *are* used in the process of risk detection – such as age, vocational qualifications, length of unemployment, family status, geographical location, country of birth, disability and offender status – are of limited value for risk *management*. The profiling tools may be effective in sorting out older members of the unemployed, the disabled, ex-prisoners, people living in rural areas, the unskilled and ethnic minorities, but characteristics such as being close to retirement age, work disabilities, immigrant background and rural residence can be targeted only to a very limited extent, or not at all. The risk factors used for prediction are for the most part static rather than open to change. In addition, they say little about the kind of intervention that is to be preferred. In the OECD report on profiling, it was pointed out that 'the indicators which might relate to the risk of long-term unemployment' may not in fact 'bear any relationship to the type of ALMP [active labour market policy] that is necessary' (OECD 1998b: 21). For all these reasons, the existing risk-assessment instruments are ill-suited to the task of setting the target for interventions. The empirical search for common characteristics that could be used for prediction and management found itself in a blind alley.

Job-seeking activity and employability

Instead, interventions would start from *the stipulation* that the individual remains unemployed because of a lack of the necessary skills or motivation to acquire and retain one of the jobs available. The absence of necessary skills and motivation are assumed to characterize all individuals who are long-term unemployed. Thus, even if the public employment service does not know *who* the long-term unemployed are, and does not try to find out who is at risk of becoming long-term unemployed at the individual level, it nonetheless has a general conception of *why* they are long-term unemployed. People who have been out of work for some time are assumed to lack basic prerequisites for paid labour. This amounts to explicating their predicament in terms of an explanation that borders on a truism. But during the 1990s, this assumption was further elaborated by researchers at the Institute for Labour Market Policy Evaluation, by policy-makers at a number of major international organizations and in the guidelines to local service providers. As a consequence, the target was formulated in terms of increasing job-search activity and employability.

Increasing job-search activity

In the mid-1990s, a general lack of motivation to apply for available positions was detected among the unemployed using self-reported job-seeking activity as an indicator. Almost half of those who were registered as unemployed estimated that they spent less than two hours a week looking for work. In an international perspective, this level was described as 'remarkably low' by comparison with findings from similar studies conducted in the USA and in the UK (Ackum Agell 1996: 13). Among those who were taking part in labour market interventions, job-search activity was even lower. Two-thirds of those who were enrolled in labour market interventions did not look for work *at all*, despite the fact that they were unemployed. In addition, there was a considerable unwillingness to accept available work opportunities. Of those who had been unemployed for more than 18 months, only one in six stated they would be prepared to accept any kind of job (ibid.: 14–17). Despite a long period of unemployment, the vast majority still viewed applying for a job in terms of a choice, at least to some extent.

According to the government, this had to be changed (ARM 1999) – and according to research it could be changed. Research reports published by the Institute for Labour Market Policy Evaluation showed that the motivation to apply for available positions was affected by the activities of the public employment service. In particular, motivation could be increased by altering the administrative framework: rules, sanctions and monitoring. Summarizing the state of the research, Peter Fredriksson and Bertil Holmlund assert 'that monitoring matters for search behavior and that more stringent search requirements are likely to speed up transitions to employment' (Fredriksson and Holmlund 2003: 25). Other researchers, such as Gerard van den Berg and Bas van der Klaauw, note that monitoring and search requirements need to be backed by an effective sanctioning practice – not for all unemployed but 'for individuals whose chances to find a job are lower'. As regards low-skilled and long-term unemployed workers, 'monitoring (in combination with the threat of punishment for non-compliance) has a positive effect on re-employment rates' (van den Berg and van der Klaauw 2005: 7).

As a consequence, job-search activity was made a target. The reforms of the 1990s and later proceeded from the conviction that the level of job-seeking activity was too low as a result of insufficient control. The existing control routines were scrutinized by government inquiries in the latter half of the 1990s and were found to be encouraging passivity. The restraint inherent in the traditional work requirement – that sanctions await those individuals who turn down an offer of 'suitable employment' – was now viewed as inadequate. It could only ensure a very rudimentary level of activity. The public employment service had – and still has – a limited capacity to assign individuals to specific job opportunities. And as applying for assigned job opportunities was sufficient, job-seekers were not compelled to take any initiatives on their own. The old notion of 'being at the disposal of the labour market' did not require independent job-seeking activity. In this way, the legislation was seen to encourage passivity (ARM 1999: 169). The call for increased control was also echoed in audits and evaluation studies. Insufficient enforcement of the existing legislation, non-existent follow-up routines and ambiguous rules constituted a common concern in several reports from the National Audit Office and the Institute for Labour Market Policy Evaluation (RRV 1996, 1999a; Lundin 2000; Persson and Johansson 2000).

Based on an analysis which concluded that control in general is efficient, and faced with criticisms that the existing control structure was insufficient, the government and the head office of the public employment service introduced changes to rules, monitoring routines and sanctioning practices. First of all, the legislation was rewritten. To avoid encouraging passivity, the responsibility was more firmly placed on the individual to *seek* job opportunities. This was made explicit in the legislation; the formulation 'being at the disposal of the labour market' was amended with the obligation to 'actively seek suitable employment' (SFS 2000a: section 9). To seek *and* accept available jobs became a basic condition for unemployment benefits.

Yet as they were stated in the law, both requirements – 'actively seeking' work and accepting 'suitable employment' – were abstract. There were still a number of links missing in the chain, which involved specifying the way in which general rules were to be applied in individual cases. Effective monitoring and sanctions required the formulation of unambiguous demands. To this end, administrative guidelines were issued describing in detail what the legal requirements meant in practice. Active job-seeking was operationalized as time spent engaged in activities to acquire a job. The norm was specified as 'the equivalent of full time activity' (AMS 2003: 10). The notion of suitable employment was also closely specified. A job is primarily deemed 'suitable' in relation to the current state of the labour market – that is, the jobs that are open to that particular individual on the Swedish labour market as a whole. The individual may have to move or accept a lower wage, although under certain circumstances he or she can refuse jobs on the grounds that they are not suitable – with respect to the individual's education, geographical location, family obligations, previous income and commuting options. The geographical distance to the potential workplace has been subject to particularly detailed operationalization. An individual may refuse to seek work elsewhere during the first 100 days of unemployment if commuting would involve the individual being away from the home more than 12 hours per day (IAFFS 2004). In order to specify what this means at the local level, every branch of the public employment service has a predetermined search area, defined in terms of the surrounding cities that are within the relevant distance. In this way, the notions of suitable employment and active job-seeking were transformed into useful tools for monitoring and sanctioning.

Improving employability

Since the 1960s, human capital theory has maintained that a highly qualified and trained workforce has a significant impact on economic growth and productivity. To meet the demands of a 'high skills economy', investing in education and skill enhancement has consequently been seen as a crucial task for governments (Brown 2001). The Swedish government is no exception. The level of education within the population has increased over the last thirty years, resulting in the paradox that the qualifications of the workforce have improved significantly while there is nothing to indicate that the work itself demands more highly qualified workers (Bäckman 2006). In the mid-1990s, this policy became further entrenched, being accompanied by a discourse on lifelong learning, and with the belief in high skill levels reaching a status that was 'almost religious' (Svensson 2004: 89). The preoccupation with skill improvement also applied to the *entire* workforce. The long-term unemployed were confronted with this preoccupation in the form of an emphasis on basic employability rather than high skills.

The notion of employability that guides the interventions of the public employment service emerged in strategy papers published by the European Commission and the OECD in the mid-1990s. Employability was discussed in terms of its capacity to tackle unemployment, and specifically long-term unemployment (Jacobsson 2004; McQuaid and Lindsay 2005). From the outset, the concept was defined narrowly, in terms of characteristics of the individual job-seeker. But the range of individual characteristics that went into the definition of employability was broad: social skills, personal appearance, formal education, job-specific qualifications, employment history, access to transport, household circumstances (children at home), health and wellbeing, demographic characteristics (age, gender), language skills, geographical mobility and wage flexibility (McQuaid and Lindsay 2005: 209–10). This may suggest – misleadingly – that employability is an intrinsic property of individuals. In fact it is relative to the current demands of the labour market. As has been noted by Phillip Brown *et al.*, 'employability is primarily determined by the labour market rather than the capabilities of individuals' (Brown *et al.* 2003: 110). In the same vein, Fredrik Hertzberg has stressed that employability is 'an aggregate of individual employers' preferences and desires' (Hertzberg 2003: 51). Hence, individuals are more or less employable depending on the match between, on the one hand, the competence and the characteristics of the job-seeker and, on the other, the characteristics and competence that are in demand. By implication, an individual's employability may improve. The skills of the individual can be made to better correspond to labour market demands. This aspect – the dynamic aspect – makes the issue interesting from the point of view of interventions.

There is also a bottom line, namely the state in which one is considered not to be employable *at all*, as opposed to not being employable in relation to a specific job. In such a case, the immediate aim becomes creating – or restoring – basic employability. It was in this form that employability became a target in relation to the long-term unemployed. A general lack of basic employability was assumed, and deemed possible to correct. Both assumptions were spelled out in the guidelines issued by the Stockholm County Labour Board to the private companies competing for contracts to provide 'activating and motivating interventions' for the long-term unemployed.

> Many job-seekers have experienced long periods of passivity. Therefore, they may be in need of activating and motivating interventions, which aim at increasing their capacity to work, creating and restoring the habit to work, and providing certain basic skills for subsequent work or education.
>
> (LAN 2004: 5)

Although many of the long-term unemployed were hardly employable at all, they could be made employable in relation to some forms of employment by means of interventions.

Studies of the temporary staffing business in Sweden have shown that flexibility constitutes a crucial aspect of employability. For the individual employee, this implies the ability to adapt to varying demands and working conditions with no apparent effort (Garsten 2004). This notion of employability is not confined to the service sector but is also gaining ground in manufacturing industries. In a study of a bus plant, Margareta Oudhuis traces a shift in the demands and expectations placed on workers. Passive obedience has given way to an ideal of active accommodation: 'today, being employable means being able to make one's own decisions, to be creative and independent or at least to act on one's own behalf without being told what to do' (Oudhuis 2004: 189). Alongside the importance of flexibility, there is a growing emphasis on 'soft employability skills' – personal presentation and social skills. Since many entry-level jobs are found in the service sector, social competence and appearance are vital for employability in the sense of retaining one's job. Soft employability skills are also important, however, in terms of acquiring a job, and, in this respect, in all interactions with potential employers. Ronald McQuaid and Colin Lindsay list the following items under the general heading 'individual factors of employability': basic social skills, honesty and integrity, basic personal presentation, reliability, willingness to work, understanding of actions and consequences, positive attitude to work, responsibility and self-discipline (McQuaid and Lindsay 2005: 209). This enumeration could be viewed as a definition of basic employability. Self-discipline, a positive attitude to work, responsibility and integrity are not job-specific skills but generic qualities required at more or less any workplace.

The process of target-setting involved several state organizations. The discovery of large groups of individuals not supported by wage labour spurred the threat of social disintegration, the ambition to reconstitute labour and the quest for the individualized risk of long-term unemployment. The risk was processed in government inquiries and research institutes, transformed into an approach that deflects any concerns that are not immediately associated with the unemployed as individuals, and was further specified in terms of job-seeking activity and employability in relation to the available jobs on the labour market. In this way, the competence and the motivation of the unemployed were transformed into the primary goal of interventions. This goal was to be achieved through an individualized combination of coercion and training, generally known as 'activation'.

B
Targeting

The activity guarantee and the individual action plan were the most important inventions. Designed to minimize the risk of long-term unemployment, they simultaneously increased the capacity and the motivation to perform wage labour. The long-term unemployed, or those at risk of long-term unemployment, constituted the sole focus of the activity guarantee, which was launched in 2000. The individual action plans, introduced in 1997, were also originally intended to manage long-term unemployment, although they were soon extended to cover everyone enrolled at the public employment service. The inventions significantly increased the administrative capacity, in line with the government instruction to 'prioritize those who have difficulties in finding work and those who have been out of work for a long time' (Regeringen 2003b: 3). In particular, the instruments revolutionalized the business of formulating activity requirements. For the first time, activity requirements could be individualized, extended and monitored. Demands were tailored around individuals, the obligations were made specific, and stringent follow-up routines enabled more efficient controls. The idea was that individualized activity requirements would increase both employability and job-seeking activity, thereby bringing the ultimate goal of social inclusion closer. Although any distinction between interventions to increase motivation and interventions to increase competence is eventually destined to founder, such a distinction may still be useful for presentational purposes. Therefore, interventions associated with the individual action plan will appear under the heading 'increasing job-search activity', whereas interventions associated with the activity guarantee will be presented under the heading 'improving employability'.

Increasing job-search activity

The target-setting involved a detailed account of what can be expected of the unemployed in terms of 'suitable employment' and 'active job-seeking'. The specification of the legal framework was part of the process of making activity requirements effective at the level of individuals. The crucial step, however, was the formulation of specific, unambiguous demands tailored around individuals. The innovation which made this possible was the individual action plan. It marks out the path that the individual has to follow to return to the world of work. Each plan is based on information supplied at the time the individual registers as unemployed, which is done using an online form covering areas such as reasons for unemployment, current job-search activity, search area, possible professions, employability needs, plans for the future, possible paths to employment, and assistance needed from the employment service. The individual is also asked to specify his or her expectations of the counterpart in the relation, that is, the public employment service. The completed form is then discussed in a personal meeting with a case worker, and is finalized into a quasi-contract which 'must clearly and unequivocally describe the division of responsibilities between the job-seeker and the public employment service' (AMSFS 2001: section 4).

The contract form means that requirements are binding. Every step is mandatory, from the initial formulation of the plan to carrying out the assigned activities. The unemployed individuals cannot refrain from conforming without endangering their unemployment benefits, which may also be their only source of income. The unemployment benefits have been made dependent on filling out an individual action plan in co-operation with the assigned case worker and performing the designated activities. The legal requirement is reproduced in the form itself as a personal reminder:

> as a recipient of unemployment benefits, you have to participate in the formulation of an individual action plan in co-operation with the public employment service. It is important that you conform to the agreement in the action plan and actively seek work. If you do not, this may affect your right to benefits.
>
> (AMV 2001: 3–4)

In 2004, four out of five unemployed individuals had an action plan (AMS 2005a). The plans structure almost all interaction between the individual and the agency. In internal policy documents, the individual action plan is described as 'the most important tool of the public employment service for concretizing the job-seeker's rights and responsibilities and planned activities' (AMS 2003: 14). It is appreciated by practitioners because of the control implication. Interviewed employees are in favour of the action plan since it 'enables follow-up and control of the activities that the case managers and the job-seeker have agreed upon' (Statskontoret 2004a: 33). Its ability to structure the interaction between the unemployed individual and the employment service, including the work of monitoring and control, is directly related to the level of detail with which the activity requirements are specified in the individual case. The activity requirements are articulated in terms of both job-search activity (how exactly is the individual going to find a job?) and employability needs (how exactly is the individual going to become employable?). More specifically, according to the internal directives for completing the form, the action plan should specify:

- suitable employment (type of vocations and mandatory search area),
- the set of employability needs (participation in job-specific education, training programmes, work experience, workplace adjustments, vocational guidance, self-employment projects),
- the job-search activities to be undertaken (which search tools to use, which kind of jobs to apply for, and minimum number of applications),
- interventions on the part of the public employment service (assignments, monitoring, and the provision of job-specific education, training programmes),

for every unemployed individual.

(AMV 2004)

Each item should be addressed by the case manager who completes the form. In practice, however, the compliance of case managers is not overwhelming in this respect. As several evaluation studies have noted, many action plans are incomplete. Out of a sample of 431 individual action plans, the Agency for Public Management found only one that was completed entirely in accordance with the regulations (Statskontoret 2004a). On the basis of another sample, the Unemployment Insurance Board noted that the vast majority of action plans contained no verifiable information on how the activities undertaken by the unemployed were going to be followed up by the public employment service (IAF 2005a). I have myself studied 200 randomly selected action plans for individuals enrolled in the activity guarantee in the Stockholm region. The sample differs from other studies, since it focuses specifically on the activity guarantee. For this reason, the requirements for the unemployed individuals might be expected to be specified in more detail. One might also expect the monitoring activities of the case manager to be better accounted for (Fröberg and Persson 2002; RiR 2005b). In my sample too, however, many of the plans are very rudimentary. For example, the only activity to be undertaken by AA is visiting the employment office '3 times a week to seek work', and the responsibility of the public employment service is simply described as 'assigning suitable employment'.

The information in this action plan can be used for the purpose of making assignments, and only for that purpose. 'Suitable employment', for AA, is specified as purchaser, order administrator, office worker or teacher's assistant. This information is then matched against all available work opportunities, which are reported by employers, and those that fit the profile are assigned to AA. The matching is taken care of by special software. The only auditable obligation on the unemployed individual is that of applying for the assigned work offers. AA agrees to seek work – but basically nothing else – and it is difficult to check whether she does so. AA can fulfil the requirement by being physically present at the employment office three times a week, without necessarily using the available computers and telephones to contact potential employers.

At the same time, there is a noticeable ambition to lay down the employability needs and the expected search activity in great detail. Several action plans contain detailed and auditable requirements. The following is one example. AB is willing to start working immediately. The goal is to work as a financial assistant, specialist salesperson, office worker or data collector. Her employability needs are twofold: she 'needs to seek work' and 'needs work experience'.

To be hired as a financial assistant or in some other capacity within the range of suitable employment options, AB is requested to carry out a detailed list of activities:

> hand in lists of jobs every week, containing five–ten jobs that have been applied for;
> get in touch with a previous organizer of practical vocational training;
> promote practical vocational training and reinforced hiring support, when contacting employers;
> participate in a special intervention for long-term unemployed on Wednesdays and Thursdays 8.30 a.m.–2 p.m.;
> be present at the premises of the intervention for long-term unemployed and seek work or practical vocational training, Tuesdays 9 a.m.–11 a.m., unless otherwise instructed;
> by the following week provide the name and telephone number of two employers that have not advertised any vacancies.

This action plan illustrates what could be called 'targeting by target-setting' in three respects. First of all, the action plan delimits the range of the professional and geographical mobility that can be required of the individual. AB is expected to apply for positions as a financial assistant, specialist salesperson, office worker and data collector. The case manager added a note that AB is 'aware that she also has to seek other jobs that are possible to acquire'. This implies that AB must apply for any job. But the search area is restricted. AB is only expected to apply for jobs in the Stockholm region, as opposed to the entire country, which would normally be the case after such a long period of unemployment. The legal concept of 'suitable employment' is thereby defined exhaustively in relation to AB.

Second, the detailed operationalization of the legal requirements facilitates monitoring. Taken as a whole, the list constitutes a definition of what active job-search means in the individual case. This is broken down into six activities, each of which is auditable on its own terms. AB is given a fixed number of jobs to apply for – at least five a week. She is required to contact previous employers, as well as other possible employers not known to be hiring, and to enquire about work opportunities. Every Tuesday morning, AB must be present at the premises of a local service provider and apply for work. Wednesdays and Thursdays her presence is required at the same place, to participate in education. The level of detail makes it easy to check whether the individual requirements have been met. In addition, the task of monitoring is in part transferred to the unemployed themselves. AB must produce verifiable evidence of her activity, such as contact information relating to employers. All pieces of evidence should be delivered in written form before a specified date. Actually confirming the individual's activity thereafter becomes easy should the case manager wish to do so.

Lastly, specifying the responsibilities of AB, in terms of search activity and reporting routines, simultaneously defines non-compliance, thereby enabling sanctioning on the basis of the requirements taken down in the action plan. This gives rise to the paradox of individualized rule violations. The requirements – and thus non-compliance – are operationalized differently from individual to individual and with a varying degree of detail. The central variable is the number and type of job-search activities, which is quantified differently across the sample. Other examples include:

[AC] is to apply for at least three jobs a week for which he is qualified, and three jobs for which he is over-qualified.

[AD] is to actively seek work by using the terminals at the public employment service as well as other media. This means applying for at least three jobs a day. Presented in written form to the case worker once a month, on the 10th.

[AE] is to go through 150 jobs posted in *Platsbanken* (jobs which do not require prior qualifications) and e-mail the case manager before the next appointment.

Not seeking the required number of jobs, not attending training programmes, seeking jobs within an overly restricted geographical area or form of employment, all amount to a rule violation as laid down in the individual action plan. Strictly speaking, there are no general rules. Every unemployed individual inhabits his or her own legal universe. What constitutes a rule violation for one individual might not be a violation for another. The legal concepts of 'active job-seeking' and 'suitable employment' are defined in the individual action plan. If the unemployed individual does 'not perform his or her part of the undertaking according to the action plan', this involves a rule violation (AMSFS 2001: section 5). Consequently, the individual requirements become unique instances of general rules. The individualized rule violations can, moreover, be punished. Neglecting to apply for a specified number of jobs may result in the removal of the right to unemployment benefits. Anyone who violates the individualized terms may either be suspended from unemployment benefits altogether or be deprived of a part of their benefits for a limited period of time, for instance losing 25 per cent of the total amount for eight weeks. Although such rule violations are far from always enforced (Statskontoret 2004a), the case manager *can* sanction every failure to fulfil the activities agreed in the action plan, such as producing a better résumé for the next appointment, or applying for a fixed number of jobs. By specifying the job-related activities for every unemployed individual, the action plan thus enables the public employment service to carry out the kind of close monitoring and strict sanctioning considered necessary to increase the willingness of the unemployed to accept available work opportunities.

Improving employability

The activation strategy involves a gradual increase of the level of control and of interventions as the period of unemployment grows longer. Instead of sorting out some unemployed individuals for more intensive interventions on the basis of a technical assessment procedure, as is the case in the profiling systems, everyone is seen to be at risk to the same extent upon registration. No attempt is made to predict which individuals are likely to remain unemployed. The model is based on self-selection. Yet it produces the same effect as traditional risk-management models, by sorting out a subgroup for special treatment. The difference is that the selection is delayed. Depending on the length of the period that has elapsed since their initial registration, the unemployed find themselves in one of three categories, which differ in terms of control and activity requirements. Those who have been unemployed for less than 20 weeks, which is the majority, are only loosely supervised, have been entrusted to search for employment on their own and are given greater freedom to choose which jobs to apply for (RiR 2004a). The rule is online self-service. After 20 weeks, the demands and the level of control will increase. The geographical and vocational search area is extended; the individual is expected to apply for jobs outside his or her geographical region and professional field. After 60 weeks, the level of interventions and monitoring increases further. This model bypasses the risk category and goes straight for the individual. Instead of trying to operationalize risk into various categories and then refer individuals to the categories, the public employment service designs auditable requirements tailored around every single individual. All attention is placed on individuals without mediation. The approach takes risk management a step further – shifting from groups to individuals. While monitoring every unemployed individual on their own terms, and without looking for special risk indicators, time is left to establish which individuals will require more intensive interventions. Taken together, they comprise the target group for activation.

After 60 weeks, when the first period of unemployment benefits expires, a significant number of individuals are referred to the activity guarantee (IAF 2005b). In 2004, on average 38,000 individuals, representing 15 per cent of the total number of unemployed, were enrolled. The term 'activity guarantee' does not refer to a specific programme, but rather to a series of interventions of indefinite duration. It stands at the extreme end of the control and service spectrum inherent to the organization's mission. According to the legislation, anyone 'who is, or is at risk of becoming, a long-term enrollee in the public employment service' may be referred to 'individually designed labour market policy activities' (SFS 2000b: section 21). This referral serves as a *guarantee* that the individual will perform labour market related *activities* – hence the name – until he or she acquires regular work or enters education. Participation is mandatory. Retaining unemployment benefits is conditional on participation in the assigned activities. Counselling, skill-enhancing measures, practical vocational training and temporary employment are among the activities which could be assigned, depending on the employability needs of the individual and the programmes available in a given area. Together, the activities should amount to 'full-time activity' (SFS 2000b: section 21). The decision is non-reversible. Once referred to the activity guarantee, there is no escape from the duty to become employable. For the duration of the intervention, that is, until the enrolled individual finds regular employment or education, or alternatively is expelled from the activity guarantee as a result of misconduct, he or she will circulate through a variety of training programmes and activation measures, with a common focus on employability.

The employability needs analysed in the sample of individual action plans, as well as the training programmes for participants in the activity guarantee, correspond to 'the rise of the "soft" employability skills increasingly demanded by employers' (McQuaid *et al.* 2005: 192). It is not infrequent in the completed action plans that employability needs are defined in terms of presentational skills. AF, for example, 'can start working immediately'. There are some health concerns, but basically AF is job ready, and primarily needs to improve the ability to seek work; specifically, 'writing applications' and 'presentation in job interview situations'. The emphasis on presentational skills is followed through in the specification of the activities to be undertaken. AF is requested to take part in lectures on personal marketing, to improve her curriculum vitae, and to work on a marketing letter. Personal marketing and the writing of a curriculum vitae constitute typical examples of presentational skills. At the same time, it should be said that a number of more traditional employability needs are taken down in the individual action plans. Presentational skills are far from being the only preoccupation in the activity guarantee. Work experience, job-specific education and workplace adjustments are noted equally commonly among the employability needs, and corresponding programmes and measures are available.

The importance of appearance and the ability to communicate is maintained in the training programmes. Although it cannot be claimed that any single activity is typical for activation, one type of activity – called 'interventions for activation and motivation' – is designed specially for participants enrolled in the activity guarantee. The interventions for activation and motivation are conceived of as targeting the most basic prerequisites for paid labour. The goal is that of making long-term unemployed individuals employable rather than employed (AMS 2005b: 97). Organizationally, the interventions are contracted out to private service providers. The County Labour Board made the purchase and specified the criteria that were to be met. The courses share three fundamental features: they are short – the maximum course length is 14 weeks; they combine lectures and practical exercises, in equal parts; and they teach basic social skills.

During the first half of the course, the activities are conducted in a physical space provided by the contracted company. Members of company staff are always present during the activities. Exercising control over the individual's time is one important element, as has been stressed in studies of municipal activation projects (Hjertner Thorén 2005; Ekström 2005). In a request written at the bottom of the schedule, found at one of the service providers at the time of my visit, the participant is reminded to be active at all times. 'When you are not booked for a class, you must seek employment, look for a practical vocational training place, or if possible, prepare yourself for a class.' If there are no organized activities, the responsibility rests with the unemployed individual to remain active. The service provider monitors attendance and the progress of the individual. In particular, it has undertaken to report to the public employment service if a participant is absent or 'unable to profit from the training in a satisfactory way' (LAN 2004: 4).

The classes represent a mixed bag in terms of content. To pick some of the subjects from the schedule reproduced in Table 1.1 in the class labelled 'Personal marketing', which is on Monday and Thursday mornings, the participants are to learn how to design a curriculum vitae and write an accompanying personal letter to a potential employer. How to eat correctly is dealt with under the subject 'Health – Diet'. The class 'Start your own business' conveys the rudimentary know-how to become self-employed, and also promotes self-employment as a way out of long-term unemployment. The class called 'I, the company' is based on a video aimed at building self-confidence and motivation. If there is one recurrent theme, however, it is the emphasis placed on soft employability skills. Basic social skills, such as conflict resolution and problem-solving, are taught in all courses. And the participants are instructed in the central importance of appropriate appearance, including how to dress, and of arriving on time. Appropriate appearance is likely to signal that all the other attributes of basic employability are present. The participant will come across as somebody who is honest, reliable, willing to work, positive, responsible and self-disciplined. The characteristics

Table 1.1 Weekly timetable

Time	Monday	Tuesday	Wednesday	Thursday	Friday
9–11am	Personal marketing Start your own business I, the company	I, the company	I, the company	Personal marketing I, the company	Weekly evaluation
11–12pm	Personal time – time with mentor	Personal time – time with mentor	Personal time – time with mentor	Personal time – time with mentor	
1–3pm	Advertisement analysis I, the company Health – Diet Start your own business	Mind Map I, the company Practical training group	Start your own business I, the company	I, the company Health – Diet Practical training group	
3–4pm	Personal time – time with mentor	Personal time – time with mentor	Personal time – time with mentor	Personal time – time with mentor	

themselves are at best only marginally affected. Although one of the service providers says, in its written tender, that the course will affect, among other things, 'commitments and values' and 'personality characteristics' (Lernia 2004: 14), in practice the ambitions are more modest.

The skills taught are centred on self-presentation – on the telephone, in an interview situation or in writing. The education often takes the form of role-play. The emphasis on role-play reflects the choice of a teaching approach, where 'understanding' involves the participant 'managing to solve realistic tasks as a preparation for a future working life' (ibid.: 5). In the scenarios, these 'realistic tasks' typically take the form of a job interview or a telephone call to a potential employer. The teacher designs a scenario which resembles such situations as much as possible. Two course participants play the job-seeker and the employer respectively in front of the group, with the teacher interrupting occasionally to ask questions such as 'Why did that happen?' or 'What did you feel?' Other members of the class are also encouraged to provide feedback. Special attention is paid to details of the presentation: attitudes, assertiveness, how to dress, body language, invisible codes, and so on. The service provider promises that focusing on these details will produce rewards, since it improves the participants' 'ability to communicate effectively' (ibid.: 9). The participants are also expected to practise on their own based on recommendations in the course literature. *The Jobseeker's Handbook* is one popular booklet with exercises for self-practice. Exercise number two, to take one example, encourages the job-seeker to 'write down a few of your patterns and qualities that you would like to improve'. The suggested problem is 'I am too shy at meetings'. The job-seeker should then think of a possible solution. The solution must be concrete: for instance, 'From now on, I will insist on speaking once every meeting and present something' (Åkesson 2004: 22). The element of practical exercise is crucial, just as the concept of employability is narrow.

Targeting motivation and skills simultaneously

Individual action plans could be said to primarily target the motivation of the unemployed, to increase their search activity, whereas the activity guarantee primarily targets the skills of the unemployed and aims to improve employability. Motivation and skills are, however, deeply intertwined in the current regime of long-term unemployment. Interventions to increase employability and interventions to increase search activity tend to coincide. The most frequently mentioned employability need in the sample of action plans is simply 'needs to seek work'. The motivation to seek work, on the other hand, is targeted through activity requirements, including participation in programmes aimed at producing basic employability. This fusion at the level of interventions is rooted in an uncertainty about where the problem lies.

The uncertainty is manifested in the analysis and the treatment of individuals. The present status of AG is described as 'can start work immediately'. But AG has not applied for any jobs, justifying this by saying that 'there are not any jobs around to apply for'. No specific employability need has been detected. Why is AG still unemployed? Is it lack of motivation, or is it lack of ability? If it is merely motivation – as indicated by AG's unusually blunt attitude – the problem might be solved by close monitoring. The referral to programmes like the 'interventions for activation and motivation' might constitute a way of testing the level of motivation. This procedure has been described as 'the threat of training' (Black *et al.* 1999). Training programmes might work primarily as a threat if the content is such that it reinforces the motivation to accept available jobs rather than the skills of the participants. On the other hand, if AG does not get a job despite the dual threat of training and sanctions, maybe the problem is one of ability. If so, forced participation in elementary training programmes will provide some basic skills, and if *this* does not help, the individual may be referred to one of several other state agencies that can provide more specialized rehabilitation, sheltered employment or medical assistance.

From this perspective, coercive interventions and close monitoring become a way of simultaneously probing and solving the problem, whatever it may be. In this particular case, AG was referred to a preparatory course similar to the ones described above. In addition, AG was referred to a special unit within the public employment service for a closer 'examination of the pre-requisites for work'. The objective of the former intervention was to make AG employable, and the objective of the latter was to find out more about why AG was not employed. However, the aspects of investigating, motivating and training are difficult to disentangle; AG is investigated, motivated and trained in the context of both interventions.

C
Staying on target

Activation is reserved for the long-term unemployed, persons on long-term sick leave, social assistance clients, and people with disabilities and handicaps. It is dispensed along parallel administrative tracks, with different mechanisms for detecting those in need of activation. In the public employment service, the target group is singled out by means of self-selection. Those who remain enrolled experience a gradual intensification of productive as well as repressive power, culminating in the activity guarantee. The productive power was structured around activity requirements, and the repressive power enforced individualized rule violations. But the strategy also involved a reorganization of power within the public employment service. The intensification of power towards the target group presupposed an intensification of power within the organization. Evaluations of the management of the risk of long-term unem-ployment produced by different state audit organizations showed that the strategy was incomplete. The exercise of productive power lacked direction and the repressive power was unreliable. Failure to fulfil the activity require-ments was too often not sanctioned in the form of withdrawn unemployment benefits. To make use of the repressive interventions and to direct the pro-ductive interventions, an elaborate control structure was constructed on top of the first-order interventions. As a result, three distinct layers of control were in operation. The first layer was the control of the unemployed individual – conducted by the case manager – to increase their motivation to carry out work-related activities. The second layer was the control of the individual case manager – conducted by other members of the organization – to increase their motivation to monitor and sanction. The third layer of control was the control of the public employment service – conducted by other state organizations – to improve the routines for control.

Targeting to the motivation to control

The use of the available control instruments was to a large extent discretionary – with the discretion lying in the hands of the case managers. All parts of the process leading up to the imposition of sanctions rely on active decisions made by the individual case manager. The precise procedure differs depending on the kind of rule violation. In the simplest and most institutionally entrenched cases, where sanctions are based on assignments, the process involves three stages. The case manager must first of all assign a programme or an available position (within the range of suitable employment) to an unemployed individual; then follow up the assignment and check whether the individual has actually applied for the job (or participated in the programme); and, finally, if the assigned activity is found not to have been carried out, the case officer must notify the Unemployment Benefit Fund. The final step – the issuing of sanctions – lies outside the scope of the public employment service. The Unemployment Benefit Fund is organizationally separate from the public employment service, but its decisions to sanction are totally dependent on the controls performed by the public employment service and, more specifically, by the individual case manager.

For a long time, the public employment service was to some extent designed as a service organization for the unemployed to help them find work or build a career (Delander *et al*. 1991). This is a legacy of the welfare era now considered to be an obstacle for consistent enforcement practices. The State Audit Institution reported that the case managers displayed 'a certain resistance towards questioning job-seekers' right to benefits' (RRV 1996: 106). The interviewed case managers thought that control would undermine confidence between themselves and the job-seekers. The same resistance is visible in the statistics. Although policy decisions require that all control instruments are to be used frequently, and in some cases always, the extent to which they are actually applied varies. This is evident in the information contained in official sources regarding the three stages of the assignment procedure. In 2003, a total of 970,000 assignments were made to available positions. This meant that on average 2.6 assignments were made per vacant position. Approximately half of these assignments were followed up by a case manager (AMS 2004a: 8–9). By implication, possible rule violations in the other half went undetected. In the same year, 5,100 notifications were sent to the Unemployment Benefit Fund. This constituted an estimated 20 per cent of the total number of *detected* rule violations (RiR 2005a: 9, 23). In other words, far from all rule violations are detected, and far from all detected rule violations are reported to the sanctioning body.

Auditing bodies, such as the National Audit Office and the Agency for Public Management, repeatedly revealed significant differences between offices in terms of the use of the control instruments – both quantitatively and qualitatively. Local and regional differences constituted a major theme

(Lundin 2000; RiR 2004a; Statskontoret 2004a). The studies followed the same pattern: several units within the public employment service in different parts of the country were compared in terms of their use of control instruments; significant differences were detected, followed by a call for more consistent enforcement practice. The National Audit Office, for example, found that the number of assignments per case manager and year varied greatly depending on the geographical location of the office. The average case manager at the highest performing offices was almost ten times as productive as the average case manager at the lowest performing offices (RiR 2004a: 30). Evidently, the control instruments *could* be used more extensively at some offices.

The intention to control more extensively had to be translated through all organizational layers to reach the front-line employees who monitor compliance and initiate the sanctioning process. The individual case managers became the focus of attention. Their disinclination to make use of the existing control instruments had to be overcome. Their behaviour was shaped to apply all instruments to the disposal of the public employment service, including removal of monetary support in response to passivity, in order to influence the behaviour of individuals in the target group towards increased search activity and employability. In terms of being an impetus for administrative redesign, the lack of motivation to control on the part of case managers was comparable with the lack of motivation to apply for available positions on the part of the unemployed. The detected lack of motivation triggered a variety of interventions, based on a view that the case managers themselves had to be monitored more closely in order to increase their propensity to conduct measures of control. In addition, the power itself resembled the first-order targeting of the unemployed. As in the case of the unemployed, the measures involved a mix of education, individualized monitoring and a specific incentive structure. The case managers were first of all given education in how to effectuate stricter enforcement. The traditional self-conception of many case managers as essentially being service providers was challenged by 'comprehensive education and information campaigns' within the organization 'to improve the control function' (RiR 2005a: 19). The education involved training in how the system works – when to issue assignments, how to interpret 'suitable unemployment', how to specify the requirements in the action plan and how to complete notifications to the unemployment benefit funds.

The case manager's control activity was moreover transformed into an object that could be *monitored at the level of individuals*. The ambition to increase control motivation was matched by the opportunities offered by custom-designed software. The director of every local office can monitor the management of individual cases as well as the total performance of individual case managers through an information system called the Director's Window (*Chefens fönster*). The name gives rise to associations that could be taken literally. To some extent, it is like having a manager peeping through a one-way window to see what is going on. The difference is that the Director's Window is limited to quantitative variables and cannot access qualitative data. It produces statistics on variables such as 'number of assignments made' or 'number of up-dated action plans'. The statistics relate to the performance of the entire unit – the local office, or all the local offices in a particular region. But it can easily be broken down to the level of the individual case manager with a few strokes on the keyboard. In this way, case managers are incorporated into a high-tech panopticon. They can be watched without being able to see the watcher. They can be controlled without knowing when they are being controlled. The suspicion of being controlled is constantly present, and this suspicion may in itself be an effective mechanism to ensure compliance. To borrow an expression from Foucault, an apparatus of 'circulating mistrust' is erected (Foucault 1980: 158).

Underperforming case managers, who refrain from controlling, can be singled out. They will not be formally sanctioned. Yet they might be confronted in a so-called result-dialogue, which constitutes the main follow-up routine. Result-dialogues are based on facts produced by, for instance, the Director's Window. Every second week the director of the office will discuss the measured performance of the employees as individuals or as a group. The Agency for Public Management describes the objectives of these result-dialogues as threefold. They provide the director with an opportunity to 'clarify existing expectations of the employees'; then, 'the employees' performance will be exposed', which may be followed by a discussion on 'the need for skill enhancement displayed by the employee' (Statskontoret 2004b: 60). Although case managers who fail to exercise sufficient levels of control cannot be formally sanctioned, the director may well 'clarify existing expectations' in order to avoid further misunderstandings and raise their 'needs for skill enhancement' through the mechanism of result-dialogues. In some offices control behaviour is moreover tied to positive incentives. Indicators of good monitoring, such as a high rate of follow-ups on assignments, may have a positive effect on the case managers' salaries (RiR 2004a: 31). The surveillance regime mobilizes the case managers by appealing to their own ambitions. Further, just as in the interventions they themselves authorized for the target group, motivation and skills are influenced simultaneously. The result-dialogues target both motivation and skills, without probing further into whether the case managers follow up few assignments because of a reluctance to do so, or because of a lack of knowledge in how to do so.

The result-dialogues and the Director's Window constituted a second layer of control directed at the case managers who were applying the rules. To ensure that the case managers exercised the relevant repressive power over the unemployed – by specifying individual rules and monitoring compliance – the case managers' motivation to control was itself controlled.

In this case, however, there was a limit to the amount of pressure that could be applied. The intra-organizational power was exclusively productive, trying to mobilize the case managers by appealing to their own ambitions. Repressive power could not be used towards under-controlling employees. The case managers were not inscribed in a legal space where inactivity was punishable. In addition, the streamlining towards consistent enforcement had to be balanced against the interests of the employers outside of the agency, who were looking for labour power. Exposing bogus job-seekers was not necessarily in their interest.

The control of organizational control

The problem was not reducible to the case managers' motivation. Shaping the behaviour of the target group by an efficient use of the disposable means of the public employment service also required that attention was being paid to wider matters of organizational policy, in particular the control routines throughout the organization. In the mid-1990s, the organization appeared to be off target. Auditing bodies detected serious incongruities within the public employment service: budgets were not kept, performance targets were not met, and existing rules were not enforced (Persson and Johansson 2000; RRV 2001a). The government was unusually explicit in its critique.

> Many County Labour Boards have not been able to perform satisfactorily, and the head office does not administer the required systems for governing, follow-up, and control to a sufficient extent.
>
> (Proposition 1999/2000a: 69)

The activation strategy was incomplete; the policy goals were not being matched by corresponding control routines. As a consequence, the government instructed the public employment service to use the available control powers more accurately and more extensively: 'The assignment instrument and the questioning of the right to unemployment benefits shall be used more efficiently and more frequently' (Regeringen 2003b: 14).

The use of the terms 'more efficiently' and 'more frequently' in one and the same sentence points to the dilemma of control in the public employment service. Increased control is considered necessary to ensure that the unemployed comply with the activity requirements. At the same time, increased control inflates the workload for employers who are looking for labour. As a rule, the detection of rule violations requires the time and the co-operation of employers, and enforcing the regulations too strictly floods the labour market with control functions that threaten its operation. The use of the assignments procedure illustrates this predicament. The assignment procedure is a computerized matching process initiated by the case manager.

A specific function in the public employment service's information system matches the job categories in the action plan with the positions that are currently available within the designated search area. The outcome consists of referrals to available positions which are forwarded to the unemployed individual, who must then act upon this information (that is, apply for the job) or face the withdrawal of benefits. Assignments constitute an operationalization of the legal requirements to be at the disposal of the labour market and accept suitable employment. The process is both a service instrument, to speed up the quasi-natural matching of the labour market, and a control instrument. As such, it is double-edged: on the one hand, it may provide employers with labour power, but it may also leave them with an unnecessary workload. Using assignments 'more efficiently and more frequently' is a contradictory expectation.

The head office of the public employment service describes assignments as 'an important instrument for the public employment service to detect whether an unemployed individual is not sufficiently active in seeking work'. It is 'particularly important' for those who tend to be unwilling, the 'less resourceful job-seekers who need a good deal of support to maintain an active search for work' (AMS 2004a: 7). It is practically impossible to increase volume and efficiency at the same time. Efficiency is measured as *the percentage* of all assignments that lead to employment (RiR 2005a: 22). In this sense, a larger number of assignments tends to decrease efficiency. Efficiency will decline, particularly if the assignments are made purely for control purposes, that is, to test the willingness to work rather than to offer a position that the individual might be interested in. Moreover, a larger number of assignments, and particularly of those that are issued for control purposes, may have a detrimental effect on the individual employer. Clearly, neither processing a large number of work applications nor responding to enquiries from the public employment service as to whether applications have really been filed correspond with the business interests of employers. Instead of getting the intended service from the public employment office, that is, filling a vacant position with new labour, they end up themselves serving as a supplementary institution of control to detect rule violations among the unemployed. This limits the extent to which the control instrument can be used. It was not seen as tolerable that 'employers perceive that assignments to vacancies are made on grounds other than the needs of the employer to fill the vacant position with suitable applicants' (AMS 2004a: 7).

For this reason, the first layer of control – the control of the unemployed – was reorganized in the tension between political demands to increase levels of enforcement and the interests of businesses in avoiding excessive levels of control. The head office designed an approach that would satisfy the potentially contradictory requirements of increasing levels of control without choking the labour market. The principal goals were 'uniformity, legal safeguards, and efficiency' (ibid.: 4). 'Uniformity' and 'legal safeguards' meant much the same thing and signalled increased enforcement. Launching a campaign of increased enforcement under the banner of the legal safeguards might seem odd. The justification, however, was that, if sanctions were more or less automatic, then this would eliminate any arbitrary elements of enforcement and sanctions would be foreseeable. Rule violations should result in sanctions, regardless of the preferences of the case manager or the location of the public employment office. The drive towards increased enforcement was balanced against efficiency, the third guiding notion, which required the very opposite: selectivity and accuracy.

One response was technical – inscribing enforcement in an automatic system. In some cases, manual monitoring can be avoided. A large part of the monitoring was already carried out by the unemployed themselves, since they were required to report back to the public employment service on the activities they had undertaken online. This information could trigger an automatic sanction. The inability to fulfil the formal requirements – such as not showing up for an appointment, not responding to assignments or not reporting on activities in the action plan – could result in a notification to the sanctioning body (AMS 2004b: 29). There is no need to interpret the rules, and sanctions are no longer dependent on anybody's decision to send a notification. In this way, the case managers, who often refrain from implementing controls, could be circumvented, and the employers would never be involved.

In other cases, however, which require an interpretation of the rules, the case manager cannot be bypassed. When an individual refuses to apply for an assigned work offer and gives reasons for not doing so, it is necessary to determine whether the assigned work constituted suitable employment. As Åsa Mäkitalo has shown, establishing a rule violation involves a bargaining situation between the case manager and the unemployed individual. The type of failures on the part of the unemployed person that in fact constitute a rule violation may be open to negotiation (Mäkitalo 2002). According to a survey conducted among case managers, the need to show that the assignment fell within the range of suitable employment was also often what kept them from reporting non-compliance to the Unemployment Benefit Fund (RiR 2005a: 9). The reporting form was subsequently redesigned to help the case managers overcome precisely this hesitancy. A decision to refrain from sending a notification now has to be justified by specifying the reasons for inaction. For instance, when an unemployed individual turns down an assignment, the case manager must justify the decision to report as well as the decision *not* to report the event (AMS 2004b: 27–28). A possible rule violation can no longer simply be ignored.

The control of organizational control performance – the third layer of control – was taken to a new level with the creation of the Unemployment Insurance Board. It was established in 2004 as an independent state agency with 50 employees. The objective was to monitor the internal control systems from a position outside the public employment service (Proposition 1999/2000b). What was scrutinized was not the control performance of the individual case manager but the control performance of the organization. In the very first activity report, the Unemployment Insurance Board described its field of operation as 'uncharted territory' (IAF 2005c: 12). Earlier, the head office of the public employment service was formally responsible for supervising enforcement, but in practice no one – that is, no administrative unit – performed this function. And none of the existing auditing bodies could focus *continuously* on the control routines of the public employment service. This would become the prerogative of the Unemployment Insurance Board. From this point on, the control exercised by the public employment service was itself subject to continuous control.

The Unemployment Insurance Board identifies routines which inhibit strict enforcement of the existing regulations. It has, for example, scrutinized the operationalization of the concept of suitable employment in the individual action plans. The routine was that the unemployed individual completed a draft online, which was later finalized in a personal meeting with the case manager. In terms of suitable employment, the individual listed what kind of jobs he or she intended to apply for and the geographical area within which positions could be accepted. The case manager was to correct this information and make it consonant with the legal requirements. But, as the study found, the case managers often simply accepted the information provided on the online form, which resulted in too much leeway being given to the unemployed individual's preferences. This was described as a conflict between the 'operative' and the 'legal' search area.

> IAF [the Unemployment Insurance Board] means that there is an obvious conflict between the operative search area, within which the assignment to available positions is probably taking place, and the legal search area, within which the job-seeker is obliged to apply for and accept work opportunities.
>
> (IAF 2005a: 25)

This conflict was to be resolved by enforcing the legal search area. The operative search area was too narrow, and the public employment service was recommended to change its routines to close the detected gap.

Another area of concern has been the quality of the notifications to the Unemployment Benefit Fund. The National Audit Office found that around one third of all notifications made between 1999 and 2003 did not result in sanctions (RiR 2005a: 23). The Unemployment Insurance Board took a closer look at the routines. It found that in most cases the reported individuals were not sanctioned because they did not receive unemployment benefits in the first place. These individuals could obviously not be punished by withdrawn benefits, but notifications were sent anyway. How could it be that the public employment service was in good faith sending notifications regarding individuals who were not in receipt of benefits? The study found that this was attributable to deficient information routines. In some cases, the case managers did not know precisely which individuals received benefits because they did not have access to the registers of the Unemployment Benefit Fund. In other cases, when the reported individual did receive unemployment benefits, the problem was instead one of neglect: the case managers did not submit all the necessary information with the notification. The Unemployment Benefit Fund was not provided with basic information concerning the refused assignment – such as the name of the employer, a rudimentary work schedule and the prior work experience of the job-seeker. As a consequence, it was sometimes not possible to establish whether the individual had turned down an offer of *suitable* employment, which is the legal prerequisite for sanctioning (IAF 2004). With the establishment of the Unemployment Insurance Board the control of organizational control performance was institutionalized. The routines surrounding notifications and search area are just two examples from the continuous stream of audit reports; more than forty reports were published during the first two years.

Conclusions

A mix of repressive and productive power

Activation comprises interventions that simultaneously create basic employability and the motivation to acquire available jobs, backed by the threat of tangible monetary sanctions. It is a complex mix of productive and repressive power. As exercised in relation to the target group, at one and the same time it shares all the characteristics of productive power and all the characteristics of repressive power. Activation has all characteristics of productive power (P1–P4). The power is organized around the norm (P1a), in this case the imperative of wage labour and the norms of employability. As a consequence, activation distributes individuals along a continuum constructed from the norms of employability. Long-term unemployed individuals are not managed as a homogenous non-employable collective, as distinct from the collectives who are already in work or who are immediately job-ready, but as individuals with a specific set of employability needs. Further, activation may target any kind of behaviour found to be deficient with regard to the norms (P1b), including a displayed lack of motivation to apply for work or lack of presentational skills. The corresponding interventions produce effects independent of the consent of those who are targeted (P2). The long-term unemployed learn how to behave at job interviews or how to contact potential employers through role-playing in the courses for activation and motivation. They learn to apply for work by satisfying the individually set job-search requirements. In this way, the interventions subvert the level of conscious decision. By complying, the competence to act in a certain way is created regardless of what the targeted individuals think of this competence.

Moreover, activation targets the motivation to perform the required acts by appealing to the aspirations of the unemployed (P3). Motivation is not only affected by an incentive structure based on the threat of sanctions. Power is also exercised with – rather than over and against – the long-term unemployed. They are mobilized as entrepreneurs of their own labour power who will embark on individualized trajectories of integration. At the same time, they are addressed as stakeholders in a common endeavour. The vision of social inclusion links the government's ambition to maintain social cohesion with the aspirations of those who are currently excluded from the world of work and other social arenas. Lastly, activation is productive (P4). The definition of activity requirements, along with the close monitoring of the progress of the individual, produces specific acts related to labour market participation, such as writing work applications and curriculum vitae, and learning basic social skills in training programmes. This constitutes the immediate effect. The mediated effect relates to participation on the labour market itself. By performing acts specified in the individual action plan, or by performing *other* acts to avoid having to do so, the long-term unemployed may eventually perform acts that amount to paid work over an extended period of time. That is, employment as well as employability is produced.

At the same time, the surrounding system of rules and sanctions incorporates all four characteristics of repressive power (R1–R4). First of all, the use of power proceeds from the law (R1). The legislation on unemployment insurance is operationalized in administrative guidelines and broken down into individual rules. *These* rules form the basis for all subsequent monitoring and sanctioning. Further, the exercise of power is mediated through conscious decisions (R2). The case manager determines the individual rules, based on an assessment of employability needs. The rules are communicated through the individual action plan to the unemployed, who are aware that not carrying out the listed requirements could result in tangible monetary sanctions. On the other hand, they also know how to avoid sanctions and be on safe ground. The use of power is actualized after – and only after – a foreseeable rule violation. If actualized, it may also be changed through conscious decisions. The resulting sanction can be appealed and possibly overturned in an administrative court of justice. Third, the power is strictly negative in the sense that it takes away resources from the targeted individual (R3). The sanctioning system is built on an elaborate mix of self-monitoring, automatic monitoring and manual monitoring by case managers. But the only means of intervention is the removal of unemployment benefits – on a fixed scale of punishments, depending on the severity and frequency of the violations. Finally, the effects of power are either obedience or disobedience (R4). Satisfying the individualized requirements in the action plan amounts to obedience, whereas the failure to do so amounts to disobedience. There are no other alternatives.

Hence, activation is a mix. Power is productive as long as the enrolled individual complies with the requirements. Participation in the assigned activities creates skills – whereas non-participation entails sanctions. There is no middle ground. Repression is the immediate flip side of the productive exercise of power. But the two forms of power follow different logics. The relation to acts, skills and motivation differs. Productive power produces a specific behaviour in relation to a target, defined as reducing the risk of long-term unemployment or, and which is the same, constituting wage labour. Repressive power, on the other hand, aims at rule compliance, conceived of as not breaking the terms stipulated in the individual action plan. The sanctions bear no relation to the activities themselves; they are based on the mere fact that the individual has failed to fulfil the requirements. Moreover, repressive power does not affect the skill set of the individual, or the ability to act in one way as opposed to other allowed options, whereas productive power enhances the capacity to work. Employability is at the centre of the exercise of productive power, but plays no part in repressive interventions. Lastly, both forms of power affect motivation, but in different ways. Repressive power is designed to increase the motivation to work negatively, through the fear of sanctions, whereas productive power is designed to increase the motivation to work positively, by stimulating self-interest. Yet, although the two forms of power follow different logics, they interfere at the level of interventions. Repressive power takes on features of productive power, and vice versa. Repressive power can produce specific acts and skills through the mechanism of individualized rules formulated in terms of activity requirements. And productive power can increase the motivation to work negatively through the threat of training – skill-enhancing interventions that are perceived as sanctions by the unemployed.

The triple layers of control

The mix of productive and repressive power towards the target group presupposes a no less sophisticated exercise of power within the organization. The first-order interventions are linked to a range of mechanisms within and beyond the public employment service to make sure that it is on target. A layered control structure is the backbone of the activation strategy. At the bottom, there is the control of the unemployed, conducted by case managers, which targets their motivation to satisfy individualized activity requirements. Above that level, there is the control of the case managers, conducted by other members of the organization, which targets their motivation to issue and enforce activity requirements. And beyond the organization, there is the control of the organization, conducted by other state organizations, which shapes policy priorities to adopt efficient control routines.

In terms of intra-organizational power, the strategy is structured around two poles: the individual member and the organization. As to the first pole, since the advent of corporate governance, no member escapes the impact of management techniques (Boltanski and Chiapello 2005). Within the public employment service, employees in all positions, including at managerial level, such as directors of individual offices, are affected by auditing routines. Yet the case managers are of particular interest as they are positioned in the intersection between the organization and the target group. They constitute part of the strategy in two ways: they exercise power over the unemployed, while power is also exercised over them. The performance of each case manager is made visible through completed action plans, issued assignments and notifications sent to other organizations. Documented and traceable to individuals, performance is assessed in terms of compliance and goal attainment through techniques such as the Director's Window, which incorporates the case managers into a high-tech panopticon. It is a disciplinary surveillance that measures the level of compliance and goal attainment of the case managers as individuals, intervening only if irregularities are detected, and shapes their behaviour in one particular direction: applying all available instruments of the organization to motivate the unemployed towards increased search activity and employability.

The second pole of the strategy is the organization itself. The public employment service was from the outset inscribed in a network of control that extends from other state organizations. The Unemployment Insurance Board, in particular, was entrusted with the task of monitoring the internal control systems from a position outside the public employment service. The agency scrutinizes routines surrounding the use of the assignment instrument, the completion of individual action plans and the questioning of unemployment benefits. What is monitored is the operation of control routines, as opposed to the control performance of individual members. But the evaluated aspects are the same. The routines are assessed in terms of rule compliance as well as performance. The two aspects are not always kept separate in contemporary audit practice. Along with the general expansion of auditing, demands of increased efficiency have been superimposed on the requirement of formal compliance. The control of performance tends to coincide with the control of compliance (Power 2007). In this particular case, the published audits interchangeably point to lax routines in relation to the legal framework and to inefficient routines in relation to the organizational goals. The monitoring shapes the policy priorities of the public employment service to adopt more efficient control mechanisms that are more frequently applied, balanced against the countervailing interest of not choking the labour market with control.

The multiple layers of control are the organizational prerequisite for the complex mix of productive and repressive power towards the target group.

The second-order control shapes — or makes it possible to shape — employee behaviour in such a way that power is exercised towards the long-term unemployed in accordance with the targets set within the strategy; and the third-order control makes it possible to reorganize the public employment service correspondingly, to improve control in such a way that activity requirements are issued, individualized and backed by sanctions.

Chapter 2

Subjected freedom

The productivity of power

Therapeutic techniques appear to be fully immersed in contemporary culture. Counselling and coaching are accessible everywhere, online, on the market or within institutions, and capture the endeavour to remake oneself, and others (Furedi 2004; Johansson 2006). Cognitive behavioural training, in particular, has spread like wildfire, both across countries and across different areas of policy (Kyvsgaard 2006). In the Swedish prison system, coaching and cognitive behavioural training programmes have been the preferred means of intervention since the mid-1990s. Inmates are encouraged, for instance, to participate in role-playing exercises where the objective is learning to respond to mixed messages. One scenario is:

> You have applied for a position, and you ask when you will hear from them. The supervisor responds ironically and scornfully (as you perceive it): 'We don't want to keep a promising person like you waiting. We'll put you at the top of the list.'
>
> (KVV 2000: 201–2)

Acting out different responses to mixed messages constitutes part of the overall task of the prison service, which is described in its mission statement as 'providing offenders with skills, knowledge and thought patterns that will leave them better equipped to meet society's demand for a life without crime when they leave prison' (KV 2005a). The cognitive behavioural programmes in prison, just like therapeutic interventions in other settings, build on the assumption that the individual needs remodelling to get by in the contemporary world. Learning to respond to mixed messages is part of a skill set considered necessary for social inclusion. From a different perspective, it is necessary for societal reproduction. The neo-liberal stage of capitalism relies on techniques that enable individuals to 'optimize choices, efficiency, and competitiveness under turbulent market conditions' (Ong 2006: 6).

The dispersion of therapeutic techniques into all parts of society appears to correspond to the shift diagnosed by Gilles Deleuze, from 'disciplinary societies', where power was exercised within institutions such as the prison and the school, to 'control societies', in which institutions have lost their grip on the exercise of power. In control societies, behaviour modification is unobtrusive and inscribed in everyday social practices. The mechanisms have escaped their institutional origins and are distributed throughout society (Deleuze 1990). But has the disciplinary society really been superseded? Although the techniques themselves are similar, it could be questioned how far the similarity goes when the prison-based coaching and cognitive behavioural programmes are compared to the therapeutic techniques provided on the Internet or on television shows, by contracted consultants at the workplace or by professional therapists paid for by the individual. In the latter cases, the techniques are chosen freely, or even purchased on a market. In the prison, however, the same or similar techniques are dispensed by the state. The element of coercion is also more pronounced in the prison, and programmes and objectives are determined by the prison service, not chosen by the individual, nor inscribed in everyday practices.

As a description of temporal change from one type of society to another, Deleuze's thesis may have to be refuted. Both 'societies' exist simultaneously. All the case studies in this book, with the exception of the control by the customs service, deal with the operation of power in the *other* society – in the disciplinary society. And the claims made relate to the inhabitants of the disciplinary society; this is how power is exercised in relation to those who are considered socially excluded. It was argued earlier that the socially excluded constitute a non-class in policy terms, united only by a common *position* in relation to the labour market (Rosanvallon 2000; Castel 2003). It could now be added that they share a common *experience*: the experience of being targeted by interventions in the name of social inclusion until they become part of the regular workforce. They are enrolled in one state institution or another. Those who are out of work and try to make a living within the *formal* sector must accept enrolment in the public employment service, the social services or the social insurance agency in return for financial assistance. Those who try to make a living within the *informal* sector, on the margins of the law, face the risk of forced enrolment in prisons, forensic psychiatric clinics, detention centres or institutional care. It follows that the mechanism of enrolment is generalized: *everyone* who does not carry out wage labour will be managed by some state organization. The generalized mechanism of enrolment secures the grip of institutions, since it delivers those who are out of work to whatever interventions have been prepared for them by the organization in which they are enrolled at the moment. If the interventions examined in this and the previous chapter are representative, this mechanism serves as a guarantee that those who are out of work will be exposed to productive and repressive interventions for the duration of their period as non-employed, regardless of the particular mission of the organization in which they are enrolled.

The enrolled individuals are routinely measured and managed in accordance with the risks and routines characteristic of the organization. At the same time, all state organizations share the governmental goal of social inclusion. But the outcome of the risk management in terms of social inclusion is secondary. Put more strongly: the question of whether the interventions are successful at the level of individuals is irrelevant. The rate of unemployment of former inmates is, for instance, of little relevance to the operation of the prison service or other parts of the criminal justice system since the internal system for ensuring quality does not consider employment or other indicators of legal income. Hence, the outcome of the programmes does not matter in organizational terms. But the sum total of organizations in the disciplinary society present a readiness to manage every outcome. If the interventions are successful, there is a multitude of private companies operating primarily at the lower end of the labour market that are ready to exploit the newly constituted wage-labourers. If they are unsuccessful, on the other hand, there is a range of state institutions operating in the welfare or criminal justice sectors that are prepared to take care of the failed wage-labourers.

The disciplinary society is constituted by the state. There are organizational routines within each state organization that respond to the progress of those who are enrolled, and there are *other* organizations that manage the outcome, whatever that outcome may be. Someone who is registered at the public employment service, for example, and remains unemployed will eventually end up in the activity guarantee. If an individual is still unemployed after a period in the activity guarantee, he or she might be sent to the employability institute for closer examination. At the same time, there are a number of exits from each institution. The system works in all directions – independently of whether the enrolled individuals comply with the ready-made organizational pathways. For example, an individual formerly involved in regular work but now enrolled in the activity guarantee may venture into illegal activities and end up in prison. And later on, once the prison term has been served, the same individual is enrolled in the public employment service and the social services. Without finding work but steering clear of the police, he or she may eventually end up in the activation interventions administered by the local municipality. Foucault described the disciplinary archipelago in the nineteenth century as 'a continuous gradation of the established, specialized and competent authorities' which 'moved gradually from the correction of irregularities to the punishment of crime' (Foucault 1979a: 299). Every individual organization of the state has changed since, but as a disciplinary archipelago it is remarkably unchanged. As Loïc Wacquant observes, 'the same population cycles through from one pole of this institutional continuum to the other in a near-closed orbit that entrenches their socioeconomic marginality' (Wacquant 2008: 29). At all stages the state will be there, exercising productive and repressive power. The only way to escape this predicament is through wage labour.

In this chapter, I will show how the targets for productive interventions in the prison service are set using the theory of criminogenic needs in combination with risk-assessment instruments, such as the sentence plan and the psychopathy checklist. This is followed by an analysis of two interventions, Cognitive Skills and Motivational Interviewing, in relation to the demands of the lower tiers of the labour market. A discussion of the techniques to ensure programme effectiveness and employee compliance, such as video surveillance of the teachers and questionnaires covering attitudinal changes among the inmates, completes the account of this strategy. The final section of the chapter addresses the question of what it means that power must be understood in positive terms (P3) and as productive (P4). I argue that the cognitive-behavioural interventions cannot be understood as either discipline or technologies of the self; instead, a generic concept of productive power will be suggested to account for the combination of contradictions, where elements of both empowerment and subjection are always present. In addition, a central theme in the Foucauldian literature, that productive power creates self-governing citizens, is criticized. What power produces must be conceptualized as actions rather than subjects.

A
Setting the target

'Of all the tasks which the prison is called upon to perform,' Gresham Sykes once wrote, 'none is more ambiguous than the task of changing criminals into non-criminals' (Sykes 1958: 17). The theory of criminogenic needs and the instruments of classification have to some extent dissolved this ambiguity. The theory constitutes the core of the cognitive-behavioural approach. All efforts rotate around criminogenic needs. The prison service is preoccupied with the identification, targeting and measurement of such needs. According to the theory, criminogenic needs are causally related to offending and can be changed. In their work *The Psychology of Criminal Conduct*, Don Andrews and James Bonta spell out the central assumptions underlying the current rehabilitation strategy, and define criminogenic needs as 'dynamic attributes of the offender that, when changed, are associated with changes in the probability of recidivism' (Andrews and Bonta 1998: 243). These attributes should be the target for all correctional intervention since, by definition ,'criminogenic needs' are those which can be changed and those which, if changed, will reduce recidivism. This is also known as the 'need principle' (KVS 1998a: 49). The use of the word 'need' – as in criminogenic needs or the need principle – may be misleading, since it indicates that the prison service is addressing something that the inmate would also perceive as a deficiency and would themselves strive to satisfy. Yet the perception of the inmate is irrelevant. Criminogenic needs are not needs in a straightforward sense, but rather 'dynamic attributes of the offender' which ought to be changed by the prison service, no matter what the individual inmate thinks. The connection to reoffending is all that is necessary, and this is established by means of science and statistics.

Need selection

The label 'need principle' might also misleadingly suggest that the prison service tries to change everything that is linked to recidivism. However, although a wide range of problems and shortcomings are formally acknowledged as criminogenic, only some are targeted. The criminogenic needs surveyed in the form for the individual sentence plan cover a total of 14 areas: financial situation, education, employment, accommodation, parenthood, family, friends, leisure activities, physical health, mental health, alcohol/drug abuse, compulsive gambling, criminal acquaintances and criminal values. All of these 14 'attributes of the offender' are considered criminogenic by the prison service, that is, as having an established relationship with reoffending that is supported by scientific evidence (KVVFS 2004a: 3). Moreover, a single inmate may have several criminogenic needs. As studies of the Swedish prison population have shown, this is a population that, as a group, is plagued by financial problems, low education, unemployment, homelessness, problematic social relations, health problems and drug use. In many cases, the problems are multiple (Nilsson 2002). However, the current rehabilitation strategy presupposes a specific selection of needs. It is based on the prioritization of a set of individual attributes, which is translated all the way down from policy-oriented research into administrative guidelines and finally into the instructions embedded in the form employed for sentence plans. In the end only two of the 14 listed criminogenic needs are prioritized: criminal acquaintances and criminal values.

The selection process can be reconstructed in three steps, each of which is corroborated using empirical evidence. First of all, criminal acquaintances and criminal values are what characterize prison inmates as a group. Psychologists have described the typical features of offenders, and these clinical observations have been supplemented by large quantitative studies. The research supports the claim that offenders often exhibit deficient social skills and anti-social cognition. The Cognitive Skills theory manual concludes that 'many criminals' are marked by 'a different and distinct "thought process"' (KVV 2002: 6). Second, criminal acquaintances and criminal values are features that are strongly correlated with offending. This claim is based on meta-analyses summarizing the findings from a whole range of studies. In one such meta-analysis, Paul Gendreau et al. found that the strongest predictors of recidivism were anti-social attitudes, identification with offenders and an anti-social personality (Gendreau et al. 1996). The same predictors are also stressed by Andrews and Bonta in their review of existing research (Andrews and Bonta 1998). Finally, those features which constitute the strongest predictors are also viewed as the most suitable targets for intervention. The selection of criminogenic needs is intimately connected with a set of preferred interventions – namely, uniformly delivered cognitive-behavioural programmes. The theory manual asserts that correctional interventions with a cognitive-behavioural focus are the most effective in reducing offending, based on studies conducted by, among others, Don Andrews, Robert Ross and Frank Porporino (KVV 2002: 93–99). Other types of interventions targeting other types of criminogenic needs are considered ineffective. In particular, providing inmates with vocational training and work opportunities is seen as futile, in and of itself, since many inmates are incapable of retaining employment. Instead, interventions must target the *underlying* inability – 'a different and distinct "thought process"' – that prevents inmates from benefiting from vocational training and work opportunities.

The policy-level selection of needs is operationalized in the individual sentence plan. The sentence plan is a key invention within the strategy, designed to draw information from many different sources: the judiciary (prior and present convictions), the police (the criminal investigation), the parole service (the pre-sentence report), forensic medicine (the forensic psychiatric examination), the inmate, as well as from sources within the prison service, such as the investigation conducted by the central intake unit (for example, a psychiatric diagnosis), data from the client administrative register (misconduct during previous terms in prison), information from other screening tools such as the ASI (Addiction Severity Index) and the placement form. In principle, all of the information that exists on the individual within the criminal justice system is collected and collated on up to ten sheets of A4 paper. The sentence plan belongs to an administrative series of tools, employed in many Western countries, which transforms 'offenders' backgrounds, behaviour and needs' into criminogenic needs (Maurutto and Hannah-Moffat 2006: 447). The prison officer on the ground assigned to the inmate is responsible for both completing and revising the form. The inmate is encouraged to take part in the planning process, and to sign a printed copy. Should the inmate refuse, however, the plan will be drawn up anyway. The form includes information on all criminogenic needs as well as on those that are prioritized in the individual case. Initially, all the criminogenic needs of the individual inmates are noted by prison officers. None of the 14 fields should be left blank. The prioritized criminogenic needs are then summarized under the heading 'factors which need to be managed to reduce the risk of reoffending'. This makes it possible to study the process of need selection at the level of individuals. In the last section of the form, a course of action is recommended, thus indicating whether the selected needs are acted upon.

To trace the target-setting at the level of individuals, I visited seven prisons in the Stockholm region, one female prison as well as six male prisons containing all security classifications, and, assisted by the staff, I retrieved 188 sentence plans on prisoners who were permanently settled in the area prior to their sentence. The impact of the theory of criminogenic needs was noticeable. For instance: according to the survey of criminogenic needs, BA has no income, a large amount of reparation to pay, no housing accommodation, expresses a wish to talk to a psychologist 'to sort things out', has many criminal acquaintances and wants to earn quick money regardless of whether this entails criminality. That is the sum total of the criminogenic needs of this individual. Some of the needs then recur as the selected criminogenic needs.

> [BA's] *liberal position on hash* [and] *the urge for quick money* can be counteracted by participation in programme activity and talking with a psychologist. [BA] is also in need of education in the Swedish language as he suffers from dyslexia. Needs also to *break with his current acquaintances*, as his closest friends are criminals, and to *establish new non-criminal relations*.

This is a paradigmatic example of the application of the cognitive-behvioural approach. Emphasis is added to highlight criminogenic needs prioritized within the framework. The 'liberal position on hash' and an 'urge for quick money' are criminal values which need to be changed, whereas the demand to break from old relationships and find new friends is related to the second criminogenic need, that of having criminal acquaintances. The need selection is followed through in the choice of interventions. The preferred intervention in this case is *One-to-One*, a cognitive-behavioural training programme geared towards social skills and self-control.

The cognitive-behavioural approach is almost never found in its pure form. In the example above, dyslexia is highlighted among the inmate's criminogenic needs, and BA was later offered a basic course in the Swedish language. Yet there are exceptions where only the policy-related attributes are identified and targeted. For instance: according to the survey of criminogenic needs, BB has debts to the Enforcement Administration, is poorly educated, homeless, depressed, has not had a job for ten years, has poor physical health, is addicted to drugs, and is quoted as saying that she will probably never stop stealing. Despite the multitude of problems that could be changed, her real problem is framed as a lack of motivation and coping skills. In particular, BB is said to have 'a problem in coping with setbacks' which makes her prone to reoffending. The only programme activity which was offered focused on strengthening her resolve to change her life. At the time when the sentence plan was completed, BB was about to start a series of individual talks with prison officers trained in Motivational Interviewing to address her lack of motivation for change. In this case, the prison staff adheres to a strict cognitive-behavioural focus in the face of a wide variety of needs.

A more welfare-oriented approach, emphasizing criminogenic needs such as unemployment, lack of accommodation and education, is also noticeable in the completed sentence plans. The pre-selected criminogenic needs are sometimes disregarded in favour of material needs. The guards who collect the information, along with the superior officers who make the decisions, disregard the written guidelines and instructions embedded in the forms, and instead display a commonsense understanding of risk and needs, emphasizing the importance of the social situation of the inmate. In these cases, the official frame is, using Keith Hawkins' formulation, 'overlaid by subsequent frames which reflect different values and sets of priorities' (Hawkins 2003: 197). For instance: according to the survey of criminogenic needs, BC is unemployed, lives with his mother, has previously been convicted, stays in touch with criminal acquaintances and openly states that he cannot see the problem with 'committing crimes, for example taking money from the state'. But criminal acquaintances or the persistence of criminal values are neither mentioned nor targeted in the ensuing selection of criminogenic needs. Instead, the focus lies on the fact that BC is *living in a chaotic social situation*. Moreover, *'unemployment'* is the only factor which needs to be managed, and *'establishing contact with an employment agent'* is the only proposed measure. The attention to aspects of the inmate's social situation is a vestige of the welfare era, when social inclusion was seen to be predicated upon meeting the inmate's needs in terms of drug treatment, accommodation, education and vocational training (Tham 1995; Duguid 2000; Garland 2001). Emphasis is added to highlight criminogenic needs prioritized within that framework. Another example is the sentence plan of BD, which documents the presence of criminal values as well as criminal acquaintances. But the high risk of reoffending is attributed to ongoing drug abuse and *'a chaotic situation with regard to employment and housing'*. Hence, BD will be supported by the prison staff in contacting the social services about drug treatment and possible accommodation, as well as in contacting the employment services about possible employment. However, a total disregard for criminal values and acquaintances is just as uncommon as a total disregard for the social situation. More typically, the cognitive-behavioural approach will be mixed with a commonsense emphasis on socio-economic factors.

To the extent that the activity of the prison service is shaped by the welfare-oriented approach, it is by remnants of an older strategy that exist in spaces not occupied by the current rehabilitation strategy: in the discretion exercised by prison officers, in parts of the legislation, and in the prison education system. Most prisons are still able to provide services directly geared towards employment needs, such as basic school education and vocational training. In terms of the daily activities of inmates, regular prison work and school education are much more common than cognitive behavioural programmes. Official statistics indicate that only 10–15 per cent of all inmates participate in some kind of cognitive-behavioural intervention during their prison stay (KVS 2004a; BRÅ 2005; KV 2006). However, unlike the components of the cognitive-behavioural approach, the elements of the welfare-oriented approach are not connected. There is no communication system in operation whereby risks and needs are successively broken down from policy-level analysis to administrative routine while the deployment of interventions is being monitored at every step. In short, the elements are not organized into a strategy.

The marginalization of the welfare-oriented approach does not necessarily involve a denial of the influence of the inmates' material circumstances. As Kathleen Kendall has noted, 'many proponents of correctional cognitive behaviouralism acknowledge the social context', but only in a form where the weight assigned to social factors is reduced to their impact on cognitive factors, 'such as the role social factors play in misshaping cognition' (Kendall 2004: 80). At the turn of the millennium, only 13 per cent of the entire Swedish prison population was employed with regular work before the prison term (Nilsson 2005: 152). The unemployed status of most prisoners before the punishment is reflected in the current cognitive-behavioural ideology. Although the vast majority of inmates are formally able – in medical terms – to perform some kind of work, they are no longer seen to be employable. Actual labour market participation presupposes skills and motivations which inmates lack according to the theory of criminogenic needs. In the Cognitive Skills manual, 'offenders' are described as being different from other members of society precisely in that they 'lack the values, attitudes, reasoning and social skills which are needed for social adjustment' (KVV 2000: 9). But the goal of steady employment is by no means out of sight. The rehabilitation strategy is part of the wider government agenda of managing social exclusion productively. Therefore, the inmate, like other individuals out of work, has to change and become employable by learning a pre-selected set of social skills and actively pursuing available social options.

The meaning of impulsivity and irresponsibility

The central criminogenic need is criminal values. As such, it covers a wide area that can be reconstructed with the assistance of *The Psychology of Criminal Conduct* and its operationalization in the prison service. Andrews and Bonta emphasize the 'Big Four' – four main risk factors for reoffending: 'antisocial cognitions, antisocial associates, a history of antisocial behaviour and a complex of indicators of antisocial personality' (Andrews and Bonta 1998: 143–44; emphasis removed). The same set of features is reiterated as the top priority in the directives regulating the deployment of interventions in the prison service. Although 21 possible individual features, or situations in which individuals could find themselves, are enumerated as constituting risk factors according to current research, ranging from age at first conviction to psychopathy-diagnosis and economic problems, some are deserving of closer attention than others.

These are 'previous criminality', 'antisocial personality in a wide sense', 'criminal acquaintances' and 'criminal attitudes and values' (KVVFS 2004a: 4–5), factors which could be seen as identical with the 'Big Four'. In the sentence plan itself, however, the four main risk factors are reduced to two, of which criminal values is the most prominent. In terms of the theory, this constitutes an understandable move. Of the original four features, only three can possibly be considered criminogenic needs. 'Previous criminality' is not a criminogenic need at all since it cannot be changed. Moreover, in the commentaries contained in the form, the term 'criminal values' is said to comprise both 'criminal attitudes and values' and 'antisocial personality in a wide sense'. That is, in this particular context, the term covers not one but two of the original features – the element of cognition as well as that of personality. The fourth feature – criminal acquaintances – is generally treated as a secondary target.

The reduction to criminal values is not only a matter of administrative simplification, but also the result of a basic terminological indeterminacy. In the writings of Andrews and Bonta, 'criminal attitudes and values' are at times referred to as 'antisocial attitudes' (KVS 1998a: 47), and at other times as 'antisocial cognition' (Andrews and Bonta 1998: 143). It is moreover hard to differentiate 'antisocial cognition' from 'antisocial personality', since the latter is defined in terms of the former. The enumerated indicators of antisocial personality are also essential characteristics of anti-social cognition: 'indicators of antisocial personality include restless energy, adventuresomeness, impulsiveness, poor problem-solving skills, hostility and a callous disregard for other people and responsibilities' (Andrews and Bonta 1998: 143). In other words, at the level of theory, the target area for interventions remains vague. The criminogenic needs seem to be dissolved into a single cluster by means of a frequent use of the adjective 'anti-social', positioned interchangeably in front of nouns such as 'attitudes', 'values', 'cognition' and 'personality'. The entire strategy operates on the basis of a series of pro-social–anti-social dichotomies, rather than on the distinction between legal and illegal. There is one attitude that is conceived of as pro-social and one that is anti-social; one set of values that is pro-social and another set that is anti-social, and so on. But the concept of anti-sociality is never defined as such.

The vague cluster of anti-social dichotomies is narrowed down in the risk-assessment tools and programme manuals adopted in daily practice. The norms that organize the exercise of productive power in the prison can be disclosed through a somewhat heterodox reading of HCR-20, PCL-R and DSM-IV – three risk-assessment instruments which are used to scrutinize inmates at the central intake unit. Administratively, these instruments are utilized for different purposes. The HCR-20 is an assessment schedule for predicting future violence. It measures 20 risk factors, divided into *h*istorical, *c*linical and *r*isk-management factors. PCL-R stands for *p*sychopathy *c*heck*l*ist – *r*evised and it is used to detect psychopaths. The DSM-IV is the fourth version of the *Diagnostic and Statistical Manual of Mental Disorders*, which contains a set of criteria for the diagnosis of, among other things, anti-social personality disorder.

I will argue that these assessment instruments, along with the manuals of the Cognitive Skills programme, delineate a common conception of what constitutes the proper target for correctional intervention. The various 'items', 'factors' and 'criteria' that are being stressed also point out what must be changed. At first sight, this might appear to be a far-fetched undertaking. Not only are the instruments used for different purposes, but the terminology employed differs across the different instruments. The HCR-20 focuses on *dynamic risk factors* for future violence; the PCL-R detects psychopathy, conceptualized as stable *personality traits*; the DSM-IV is used to diagnose personality disorder, defined as an '*enduring pattern of inner experience and behaviour*' (DSM-IV 2000; emphasis in original); while Cognitive Skills addresses *cognitive deficiencies* to reduce reoffending. The indicators are strikingly similar, however. The headings are different, but the observable indicators are the same. The indicators of future violence, of psychopathy, of anti-social personality disorder and of cognitive deficiencies refer to much the same kind of observable conduct. That which has to be changed is more or less identical, irrespective of whether it is referred to in terms of 'dynamic risk factors', 'personality traits', 'patterns of antisocial behaviour' or 'cognitive deficiencies'. This convergence can be traced back to the two pairs of opposites around which the entire strategy is organized: responsibility and irresponsibility, self-control and impulsivity.

The essence of criminal values turns out to be impulsivity and irresponsibility. These constitute the common target for interventions, as described in the risk-assessment tools and the programme manuals. Impulsivity is the first aspect of criminal values. In the DSM-IV, anti-social personality disorder is inferred stepwise from the observable behaviour: 'failure to plan ahead' indicates 'a pattern of impulsivity' (criterion A3), which in turn indicates a personality disorder. Impulsivity is also manifested by 'sudden changes of jobs, residences, or relationships' (DSM-IV 2000). In the same way, the HCR-20 and the PCL-R utilize a wide range of mundane acts and circumstances to establish impulsivity as part of the process of establishing an elevated risk for future violence and for psychopathy respectively. In the HCR-20, 'impulsivity' constitutes one of the dynamic risk factors. To determine whether the inmate is completely, partly or not at all characterized by impulsivity, the assessor passes a judgement on whether the individual reacts 'exaggeratedly or inadequately with regard to prevailing circumstances'. Another item in the same risk-assessment scale is formulated as 'plans lack feasibility', which measures a related attribute – the existence and the feasibility of plans for the future (Belfrage and Fransson 2000).

In the Cognitive Skills theory manual, the target for intervention is a specific pattern of behaviour which is said to be typical for offenders.

It includes 'a preference for an unstructured way of living with little planning or consideration for the future' and 'often recurring acts of impulsiveness and/ or aggression' (KVV 2002: 14). The behavioural pattern is also described in terms of a lack of self-control: 'a common characteristic of many delinquents is a lack of self-control, an apparent failure to self-regulate their behavior, and a tendency to behave impulsively' (Ross and Fabiano 1981: 38). In the psycho-pathy checklist, 'impulsivity' appears as item 14. A closely related item is 'need for stimulation/proneness to boredom' (item 3), which might be present if the individual is 'constantly starting and stopping new activities – such as school, jobs, relationships' (Hare 1991: 19). 'Poor behavioural controls' (item 10) and 'lack of realistic, long-term goals' (item 13) are other related items. The inmate is characterized by poor behavioural controls if 'he tends to respond to frustration, failure, discipline, and criticism with violent behaviour or with threats and verbal abuse' (ibid.: 23). The absence of realistic, long-term goals is established by means of a simple routine: 'Compare his plans for the future with his qualifications and employment or release records to determine whether or not they are realistic' (ibid.: 25). At least four of the total of 20 items in the psychopathy checklist are related to impulsivity, and many of the indicators of the impulsivity-related items concern the inability to hold down a steady job in prevailing labour market conditions.

Irresponsibility is the other central pole within criminal values. It is con-ceived in terms of a mixture of moral shortcomings and actual incompetence. Irresponsibility is about neglecting to do what one is expected to do, although it may also consist in a failure to assume responsibility for what one has actually done. To establish irresponsibility, one must take a close look at the mundane obligations of social life. This preoccupation is spelled out in detail in the psychopathy checklist. 'Irresponsibility' is item 15, and the description of this item is worth quoting in full.

> Item 15 describes an individual who habitually fails to fulfil or honor obligations and commitments to others. He has little sense or no sense of duty or loyalty to family, friends, employers, society, ideas, or causes. His irresponsibility is evident in a variety of areas including: financial dealings (a poor credit rating, defaulting on loans, failure to discharge debts, etc); behavior that puts others at risk (drunk driving, recurrent speeding, etc.); work behavior (frequently late or absent, careless or sloppy performance not attributable to lack of ability, etc.); business relationships (violating contractual arrangements, not paying bills, etc.); and relationships with family and friends (failing to provide financial support for spouse or children, causing them unnecessary hardship, etc.).
>
> (Hare 1991: 25)

Although, as an example, traffic violations are mentioned, there is undoubt-edly a bias towards economic commitments. Three out of the five areas have an immediate economic relevance – 'financial dealings', 'work behaviour' and 'business relationships' – and 'failing to provide financial support' is a prominent feature of irresponsibility in the area of family relations.

Economic irresponsibility recurs in the description of item 9, 'parasitic lifestyle', which focuses on 'financial dependence on others'. The inability to support oneself through regular work is of central importance: 'although able-bodied, he avoids steady, gainful employment; instead, he continually relies on family, relatives, friends, or social assistance' (ibid.: 22). In the DSM-IV, irresponsibility is one of seven criteria for anti-social personality disorder. In the specification of these criteria, the main focus is directed at employment. Irresponsibility 'may be indicated by significant periods of unemployment despite available job opportunities, or by abandonment of several jobs without a realistic plan for getting another job'. Apart from employment, the only other indicators mentioned are also of an economic nature. They are found under the heading 'financial irresponsibility', which 'is indicated by acts such as defaulting on debts, failing to provide child support, or failing to support other dependents on a regular basis' (DSM-IV 2000: criterion A6). In the Cognitive Skills theory manual, irresponsibility returns as a feature of the criminal lifestyle. The lifestyle to be targeted is, among other things, characterized by 'little effort or ambition to attain common goals regarding work or career' (KVV 2002: 14).

The positive values can be laid bare by inverting the postulated indicators. Self-control and responsibility are the standards according to which the crim-inogenic needs are established, targeted and measured. The opposite of impul-sivity is self-control – the ability to plan ahead, think decisions through, consider consequences, behave adequately in response to expectations and with regard to prevailing circumstances, having a structured way of living, an ability to accept criticism and frustration, and not being overcome by strong emotions. The opposite of irresponsibility is responsibility – the ability to take on responsibilities, fulfil commitments, pay the bills, be on time for work, have a good credit rating, respect speed limits, maintain steady employment, provide financial support for children, and accept responsibility for one's own actions.

It is apparent that responsibility and self-control, as correctional targets, are linked to traditional, work-centred norms of conduct. Ironically, the same norms stand in an ambivalent relation to a situation where entry-level jobs are mainly found in the service sector. The target-setting within the strategy is linked to values that are being called into question by developments in the labour market. Richard Sennett argues that 'at the lowest levels of fluid work, the realm of so-called McJobs – flipping hamburgers or clerking in stores' the value system has changed, and 'stability as such increasingly lacks moral prestige' (Sennett 2006: 75). Similarly, higher up on the occupational scale – 'in high-tech, finance, and the media' – delayed gratification is no longer organizing the career, and 'the steady, self-disciplined worker has lost his audience' (ibid.: 78). Risk-taking and shorter time frames are eroding the classic Protestant Ethic. Workers across the occupational scale are expected to be independent and creative (Oudhuis 2004; De Giorgi 2006). Consequently, the conceptions of self-control and responsibility that form the basis for interventions in prisons are questioned and potentially superseded in the current culture of employability. This leads to a paradoxical situation where socially accepted behaviour is branded as anti-social in the prison. Outside the prison, expressing one's emotions, involvement in a large number of short-term relationships, constantly starting and stopping new activities and egocentric reasoning – in short, almost any deviance from the traditional work-centred norms of self-control and responsibility – may be celebrated as expressions of creativity and independence. But inside the prison the same acts and attitudes are perceived to be indicators of anti-sociality and, as such, treated as targets for correction.

The precise meaning of acting responsibly and being self-controlled also depends on the position of the individual who is being assessed. The social position shapes what acts are taken to indicate the desired values of responsibility and self-control. This is simultaneously affirmed and denied within the cognitive-behavioural approach. On the one hand, the relevance of material circumstances is systematically denied. The inmate's position in the social structure is irrelevant. In the introductory one-to-one meeting of the Cognitive Skills programme, the message is unambiguous. The teacher is instructed to convey to the inmate that success does not only depend on 'education and social class' or 'access to labour market opportunities'; instead, the crucial difference is that 'successful individuals' have been able to 'master a set of thinking and reasoning skills'. Such skills can outweigh the impact of class background and career opportunities. Also, 'individuals from very poor conditions' have become successful thanks to the use of cognitive skills (KVV 2000: 17). The focus is on the available non-criminal options, however restricted these options are. The vision is restricted to becoming self-controlled and responsible under the prevailing circumstances, regardless of the nature of these circumstances.

On the other hand, the weight of the social structure is embraced. It is taken for granted that the position is subordinate and that the relevant situations are filled with conflicts and frustration. The Cognitive Skills programme asserts that many inmates 'have difficulties in relating positively to peers, teachers, parents, employers or other authority figures (including prison staff)', followed by a claim that 'the ability to act in social situations in such a way that one is accepted and met with positive reactions – rather than rejected and punished – demands that the offender develops an adequate register of cognitive and social skills' (ibid.: 161). This could be read as the core assumption of the rehabilitation strategy. The use of the words 'accepted', 'rejected' and 'punished' is not indicative of a relationship between equals. The inmate is the subordinate party. The responsibility lies with the inmate to act so as to avoid being 'rejected' and instead become 'accepted' by 'teachers, parents, employers or other authority figures'. Inmates commit crimes and are unable to maintain employment or relationships because they lack the necessary skills to cope with hardship and the expectations of their superiors. It follows that the actual targets for interventions are impulsive reactions in stressful situations and a failure to act responsibly in the marginal social position which prison inmates are assumed to occupy.

The correctional training intends to increase the ability to respond to everyday frustration and personal failure in a self-controlled and responsible way. Consequently, the Cognitive Skills programme includes role-playing scenarios such as:

> You want to ask your boss about a day off, but you notice that he seems tired and irritated when he arrives in the morning.

'You' refers to the inmate, who needs to get something important done on that particular day but its achievement depends on being given permission, as well as on the skills to handle the moodiness of 'your boss' (ibid.: 192). Besides 'your boss', three further figures recur in the scenarios, which are always fraught with trouble: 'your parole officer', 'your partner' and 'a friend'. Hence, the inmate will learn to handle everyday frustration in the workplace, negotiate conflicts with superiors, manage stress in close relationships and say 'no' to friends.

The cognitive-behavioural approach is firmly inscribed in the class structure; it moreover confirms the gender order. The target group is primarily male inmates. More than 90 per cent of the prison population is men, and the vast majority of programme participants are men. But programmes such as Cognitive Skills are also employed in prisons with strictly female participants. In the manual, the authors have made an effort to use a gender-neutral language, always speaking in terms of 'he/she'. But the behaviours to be modified are tacitly male, as can be taken from the choice of dilemmas and desired objects in the role-playing scenarios. The examples typically include cars and beer, a stereo or a demanding girlfriend. The programme is shot through with a specific conception of masculinity, which comes close to the colonial stereotype of men that are 'hypermasculine, violent and uncontrolled' (Kimmel 2001: 24). The inmates need to become better at coping with setbacks and frustration without resorting to uncontrolled aggression. Aggressive responses are frequently mentioned among the options in the role-playing scenarios. For instance:

> You ask your girlfriend to come with you to a party at one of your friends, and she says 'no'.

The first option is 'beat her up', the second one is 'break up and leave her', and the third is 'tell her to come along, end of discussion' (KVV 2000: 227).

Consequently, the programme aims at producing, not workers in general, but male workers, who can manage problems in close relationships, besides the stress at the workplace. The encouraged masculinity does not, however, coincide with the socially dominant masculinity. The typical man is purposeful, rational, risk-embracing and independent at the workplace (Whitehead 2002). That is a masculinity related to superiority. But the prison inmates are not to become purposeful, rational, risk-embracing and independent; instead, they will be self-controlled, responsible, flexible and reliable. The masculinity enacted in the role-playing scenarios is linked to subordination, and above all to the daily experiences of subordination at the workplace. The desirable competence involves a subaltern rather than dominant masculinity.

B
Targeting

As is indicated by the very notion of criminogenic *needs*, the target area is analysed as a lacuna. Criminality is seen as an absence of social skills and not as the presence of anti-social skills. The interventions consequently take the form of exercises to develop new skills rather than to eradicate old skills. Cognitive Skills is the Swedish designation for the most well-known of all cognitive behavioural programmes. It was developed in Canada by Elizabeth Fabiano and Frank Porporino, as the Reasoning and Rehabilitation Training Programme. Since the mid-1980s, it has been widely used in several countries in Western Europe and North America. At the turn of the millennium, it had been revised and supplemented by several other cognitive-behavioural programmes more specifically directed at substance abuse, violence or sexual offences. Cognitive Skills comprises 38 classes, delivered over a period of 13 to 19 weeks. Each session lasts two hours. The condition for participation is 'entrenched criminal cognition and conduct', which constitutes a very wide criterion. Inmates with 'obvious psychopathic characteristics', those with a low risk of reoffending and those 'without sufficient intellectual capacity' are the only ones who are explicitly excluded (KVV 2003a: 17). The recommended group size is four to eight participants. The teachers are regular prison officers who have completed a crash course in the theory and practice of the cognitive-behavioural intervention. When not teaching, they work as guards in the same prison. The programme teaches responsibility and self-control, in line with the targets set by the instruments used to detect psychopathy, personality disorders, cognitive deficiencies and future violence. Self-reasoning and role-playing are the preferred means of intervention.

Enacting subordination

The subordinate social position of the programme participants influences the choice of target – and the choice of tactics. This is visible in the use of role-playing, and along with it the focus on observable behaviour, the role of repetition, concrete tasks and unequivocal instructions. Role-playing in this context goes back to the 'psychotherapy for the poor' designed by Arnold Goldstein. His books (1973 and 1976) are frequently referred to in the Cognitive Skills manual. Psychotherapy for the poor was developed as a response to the failure of conventional, insight-oriented psychotherapy when applied outside the middle class. The lessons of the class-specific failure of psychotherapy would later be translated into the 'responsivity principle' of the cognitive-behavioural approach, according to which all programmes must be 'consistent with the ability and learning style of the offender' (Andrews and Bonta 1998: 245). Goldstein's approach was explicitly adjusted to what was perceived to be a specific learning style among 'lower-class patients' seeking psychiatric assistance. In particular, it was considered necessary to utilize.

> techniques responsive to such generalizations about lower-class patients as desire for authority and direction; preference for activity, rather than inspection; desire for structure and organization; and preference for concrete and objectively demonstrable explanations, rather than engagement in more symbolic activities.
>
> (Goldstein 1973: 17–18)

The diagnosed learning style reflects the subordinate status. 'Lower-class' psychiatric patients, and later prison inmates, needed to be told what to do. Their presumed 'desire for structure and organization', as well as their 'desire for authority and direction', *were* matched by structure, organization, authority and direction. In a programme setting, this translates into clearly defined roles and unequivocal instructions. Insight and reflection are made superfluous. The idea is that the skills cannot be taught by giving lectures, reading textbooks and discussing matters which are not 'concrete and objectively demonstrable'. Learning requires the activity of the body rather than the mind. For all these reasons, role-playing is the preferred means of intervention.

Impulsivity and irresponsibility are thought to give way to pro-social behaviour through the repeated practice of the correct reactions. Role-playing is more than just acting. 'Role-playing is not only acting, it is practice'; practice, more specifically, 'in using the skill in a situation which is as close to real life as possible' (KVV 2000: 165). The process is no different from the outcome: by actually doing right 'in a situation which is as close to real life as possible', the inmate will do the same thing in future situations, outside the prison. The crucial situations are those filled with conflicting interests and frustrations. It is in response to stress that the ability to act responsibly and in a self-controlled manner is put to the test. The majority of offenders are seen to react with aggression or, inversely, to avoid conflicts altogether and to 'devote themselves to different kinds of manipulative behaviours which often are illegal' in the absence of conflict management skills (ibid.: 212). The ability to manage stress presupposes a variety of more specialized skills, such as straightforward communication and learning to compromise. In the course of the programme, the inmates will learn how to compromise and express concerns non-provocatively, by trying out different strategies and correcting themselves while doing so in a variety of scenarios. In the class on 'straightforward communication', this is the first scenario:

> You have made a mistake at work. Your boss notices this, and yells at you that you are useless.

This role-play requires two actors. Both characters, the boss and the employee, are played by programme participants. The events unfold depending on the reaction of the inmate/employee, who is instructed to respond in one of three ways.

Aggressive: You get angry and say: 'I don't like it when you criticize me! Leave me alone.'
Non-straightforward: You say: 'I'm sorry. I was stupid. It will never happen again.'
Straightforward: You realize that you have made a mistake and say: 'I'm sorry, I will be more careful next time. But I don't think you need to yell at me.'

All participants must perform at least six times, acting as both the boss and the employee and experiencing what happens when they respond – or are responded to – in each of the three ways. Afterwards they will be asked what it felt like. When the participants are not acting but part of the audience, they are asked to observe and take notes – and in particular to pay attention to 'body posture, facial expressions and gestures as well as the verbal communication'. The scenes are also recorded on video, making it easy to take a closer look at details in the performances. Comments and reflections from the participants are encouraged. The teacher will wait until the end of the class to underline the benefits of 'straightforward' conflict responses (ibid.: 154–57).

'Compromising' is learnt in scenarios such as:

> Your employer suggests that you must dress in a more appropriate way for the job that you have. You cannot afford to buy the right kind of clothes.

This is a high-risk situation, where the progress achieved to date – getting a job – could quickly be obliterated. To solve the problem pro-socially, the

Table 2.1 Options and consequences

	Options	*Consequences*
1	Quit your employment.	You have no money and no job.
2	Explain the situation and ask for an advance on your wages.	Your employer understands the situation and waits to demand an improvement until pay day.
3	Steal the money so that you can afford to buy new clothes.	You will end up in difficulties.
4	Ask your employer to explain why your clothes are not appropriate.	You will receive an explanation.
5	Give him/her a good talking to.	You will be fired.

inmate must use at least two skills: thinking through the consequences and negotiating a settlement. The participants are first of all asked to write down the possible options. Together with the teacher, they will then discuss each option and its likely consequences. In this case, five pairs of 'options and consequences' are suggested (see Table 2.1).

It is left to the participants to decide which option they prefer. However, since it is assumed that a compromise is the best solution – that is, option 2 – the next step is to learn how to negotiate a settlement through role-play. One participant plays the employee ('the negotiator') and another the employer ('the counterpart'). The counterpart is asked to leave the room. The rest of the group will help the negotiator to come up with strategies. However, the negotiator has to go through the four steps of the 'negotiating process' – stating your own position ('I would like'), asking for the reaction of the counterpart ('What do you think?'), expressing the difference between the two positions ('use the word "difference"'), and possible options ('How would you feel about … ?'). The goal is to resolve the conflict of interests by reaching a negotiated settlement which satisfies both parties. The entire focus in this exercise is directed at the process and not the outcome. The role of the audience is to pay attention to divergences from the proper negotiating procedure. And if the negotiator jumps any step, the teacher will intervene and have him or her start all over again (ibid.: 216–26).

Role-playing is more than acting; also, it is not just doing. Role-playing is also about attitudes, values and beliefs. Ideology and practice are intertwined in the training programmes. Like all cognitive-behavioural therapies, the prison programmes are designed to affect thought *and* actions (McGuire 2000; Dobson and Block 2001). Slavoj Zizek has noted that the disciplinary procedures described by Foucault presuppose a notion of ideology as material praxis, where 'the "external" ritual performatively generates its own ideological foundation' (Zizek 1994: 13). Nowhere is this more apparent than in the role-playing associated with cognitive behavioural therapy. The classes provide a space where individuals act as flexible wage-labourers, responsible fathers and responsive parolees, while being addressed as flexible wage-labourers, responsible fathers and responsive parolees. The corresponding attitudes and beliefs about the world are communicated along with the behavioural instructions, and it is by actually conducting themselves as wage-labourers, for example, that the inmates will start to think about themselves as wage-labourers.

Rethinking frustration

Self-reasoning is the other preferred learning method. It is defined as 'what we think or say to ourselves' (KVV 2000: 268), and the exercises are directed at changing the content and focus of the conversation with oneself. Self-reasoning affects the cognitive aspects of behaviour. The individuals in the target group are simultaneously blamed for their actions and spurred on to act in a specific way. As such, it is an ideological technique that is productive rather than repressive. The very first class of the Cognitive Skills programme aims to instil 'the right attitude', the basic prerequisite for everything that will follow. The right attitude is a specific attitude towards one's own problems. To this end, the inmates are asked to complete a 'problem test' to 'investigate which situations might be a problem for you'. The test establishes to what extent, for example, I 'get mad when things don't turn out as I want them to' or I 'would like a better job', and thus to what extent these constitute a problem for the inmate. Are these things always, sometimes or never a problem? The possible problems are formulated in very general terms, and might apply to anybody. This is not unintentional, since one of the basic conclusions that should be reached during the class is that 'all human beings have problems and we are not defined or labelled by the number of problems we have'. So, in this respect, inmates are no different from anyone else; what does differentiate some people from others, however, is their way of handling problems. Some people 'see problems as "possibilities"'; they are able to 'take control' over their problems, and focus on what they themselves can do to bring about change (ibid.: 27–34).

The next stage is accepting 'ownership of the problem' in the sense 'that you take responsibility for your problems and acts' (ibid.: 46). This is directly related to the analysis of irresponsibility. The inmates are seen to have a tendency to blame their problems on others, but will now learn to accept responsibility for what they have done as well as for what they can do in the future. Responsibility is engendered by redefining the problems they face. Redefining problems as one's own is a process without an endpoint. There is no discrimination between different kinds of problems – socio-economic problems and personal frustrations are lumped together under the general heading of temporarily difficult situations. There are no limits to one's own responsibility and there are no significant others with any responsibility. All hardships literally belong to the individual, and *this* responsibility must be realized, accepted – and acted upon. On the other hand – and this is the promise: if the inmate accepts, and acts upon, this responsibility the problems will go away, or will at least become manageable. By proceeding step by step, using the available pro-social options and the skills being taught in the programme, the inmates will mitigate their own problems.

A specific set of self-reasoning skills is considered essential to increasing the likelihood of choosing the available pro-social options in the situations with which inmates are faced. In particular, 'responding to failure' is described as 'a very important skill for individuals convicted of crimes'. It is taken for granted that the participants are bad at coping with failure and must learn this skill from the very beginning. It is taught in five steps. The participants are asked to keep five considerations in mind when they are confronted with a failure, or what they perceive to be a failure. Each of the questions needs to be thought through: 'Decide if you have failed; think about what caused your failure; decide how you might do things differently if you tried again; decide whether you want to try again; try again, using another approach.' The skill is learnt through situation-bound self-reasoning. In the classroom, the participants are presented with specific situations and asked to practise the skill. For example:

> You had tried to stay sober (drug free) and thought you had made it, but in a weak moment you were persuaded by a friend to have a drink (a hit) – you were worth it, you needed it!

Having thought through the five steps, the participants will display their own self-reasoning in front of the class. In this way, the self-reasoning can be commented upon by the teacher and the rest of the participants. The reasoning can also be shown to be wrong, as there is always one appropriate way to handle a failure, in this case the relapse. The skill consists in focusing on one's own part in the failure and accepting responsibility. This implies persistence. The inmate is encouraged to try once more, using a different strategy (ibid.: 197–99).

Impulsivity is targeted through self-reasoning that strengthens self-control. The inmate's self-control is threatened by stress, and to manage stress it is essential to gain control over 'uncontrolled emotions' (ibid.: 240). Anger, in particular, must be contained. The following self-reasoning technique teaches anger management, in what is described as 'probably the most important exercise that you [the teacher] can have with them'. The participants are asked to visualize themselves standing in a queue for the latest James Bond movie. They have been waiting patiently for 15 minutes.

> You are hot, tired and hungry. Try to feel that.
> [10 seconds pause.]

Now, a guy your size – in a suit and waistcoat – slips into the queue just in front of you.

[15 seconds pause.]

You tell him, firmly but in a friendly tone, 'Hey you, there is a queue here!' He turns to you and says in a patronizing way: 'Fuck you!'

[No pause. The teacher immediately instructs the participants what to do:]

I want you to focus on your thoughts. What do you think? What do you say to yourself? Write it down – all your thoughts.

After a couple of minutes the participants are asked to read aloud what they have written on the paper. The teacher will encourage the inmates not to censor their answers but to provide 'truthful' responses such as:

I would think: I'm going to kick your ass – you fucking bastard.

The teacher is instructed to verbalize that scenario: the man 'falls to the ground with a bleeding nose and a broken jaw'. The inmates are then asked to think through the likely consequences when the police arrive on the scene. 'Who do you think the police will arrest – the guy in a suit and waistcoat or me who is on parole? Guess!' At this point, the idea of a 'mental switch' is introduced. The teacher extends on the above example of inappropriate self-reasoning and adds one word – 'but' – that will work as a mental switch.

BUT this guy is not worth it. He will not get at me. I have too much to lose. I will remain calm and composed.

In this way, the inmates learn to exercise self-control, or 'controlled self-reasoning' (ibid.: 266–72). The argument is not built on an ethical judgement saying that it is wrong to hit the man in the suit, but on the assumption of the class-bias characterizing the work of the police. The inmates are to be convinced on their own terms, and the teacher appeals to a conception that the police will never believe them, and for that reason this particular course of action is futile. By conceding that the class-biased nature of policing is not liable to change, the inevitability of the current social structure is tacitly invoked and used as an argument.

The training programme culminates in a series of exercises in creative and critical thinking. The exercises presuppose the right attitude, anger management through self-reasoning, the ability to negotiate a compromise, and other techniques that have been learnt during the programme. The habitual responses taught so far are now confronted with the element of change. To the extent that the exercises involve creativity, this refers to the ability to change one's perspective. The participants will learn to see things from the point of view of the established society and not from their own narrow point of view. The critical thinking is directed towards themselves and not the social context, with the explicit purpose of making the inmates adjustable:

> through critical analysis of their own reasoning, they will become more flexible and more willing to adjust to new circumstances and situations, and consider them to be challenges rather than further evidence of the unfairness, injustice and misfortune which come their way and which are beyond their control.
>
> (KVV 2000: 354)

By learning to uncover hidden agendas in magazine advertisements, for instance, skills in critical thinking are acquired that will make it easier for the inmate to respond to changes on the local labour market and to other 'new circumstances and situations'. The prevailing social conditions are reimagined as 'challenges rather than further evidence of the unfairness, injustice and misfortune which come their way'. The programme ends just as it started, on a positive note, conveying the message that everyone can become a winner. Some individuals have learnt to cope with extremely problematic social circumstances and become successful through the use of thinking and reasoning skills (ibid.: 17). The uneven nature of the playing field is acknowledged and simultaneously denied. If the harsh world of low-paid service jobs is affirmed during the exercises, it is denied as the prison inmates are motivated to programme participation.

Creating motivation *ex nihilo*

Participation is voluntary. In the end, the inmate can choose to abstain. But the decision is surrounded by efforts to motivate the inmate to participate. Two routes are pursued: extrinsic and intrinsic motivational tactics (Goldstein *et al.* 1998: 119). Extrinsic motivators are tangible rewards for programme participation. The web of incentives can – but need not – be formalized. The recommendation is sometimes turned into a requirement in the sense that services and less restrictive conditions of incarceration are made conditional on programme participation. BF, for example, 'shall complete programme activity in [name of prison] before transfer may be considered'. In this case, the recommendation for a given programme is noted down in the individual sentence plan as a condition for transfer to a more open prison. Usually, however, the recommendation is not laid down as a formal condition. Instead, the prison administration relies on the knowledge, which may be assumed to be widespread among the inmates, that programme participation generally pays off whereas non-participation might affect the conditions of incarceration negatively. The available services and the imposable restrictions are used to pressurize the inmate into participation – even if participation is not compulsory.

The external rewards are complemented by intrinsic motivational tactics. The motivation of the inmate has also been turned into a *direct* target for intervention. Unwillingness to participate is considered to be something that can and should be corrected. Motivational interviewing is the name given to the corresponding set of techniques, originally designed for use in the context of addiction treatment. Over the last decade, motivational interviewing has been transferred to correctional practice. The original author, William Miller, has argued that the technique is appropriate in a prison setting as it is particularly well-suited for 'clients with a low level of motivation, clients who are not ready to change, who are angry and who display a high level of resistance' (KVS 2002a: 46). Consequently, a substantial proportion of the Swedish prison staff have been educated to use the technique. Motivational Interviewing is regarded as the ideal complement to cognitive-behavioural treatment programmes for prison inmates, since it can create motivation for programme participation as well as enhancing programme effectiveness (Ginsburg *et al.* 2002).

Where there is no will to change, this will can be produced, without changing anything else. The assumption is that the will to personal change is already present in every inmate, but that it might be confused or mixed up with anti-social aspirations. By getting inmates to speak about their own goals and problems, it is possible to disentangle and reinforce the aspirations for a pro-social life.

> What we need to do is to encourage the client to talk. We want the client to tell us why he wants to change, what he wants with this change, and why it is important for him to change.
>
> (KVS 2002a: 35)

The inmate is encouraged to talk by a regular prison officer, who is instructed to suppress his or her usual instincts to confront and correct the inmate. Instead, the prison officer will establish a sense of companionship. The same officer who locks the cell door at night will now show respect and empathy, commend and support, and never tell the inmate what to do. The discussion proceeds *as if* there were no fixed goals or options. The inmates are enticed to disclose what they would do if they could.

> The client has interests and things he wants to do in life, which he hopes for, dreams about and cares for, and it is those things which will result in intrinsic motivation.
>
> (KVS 2002a: 38)

This basic motivation is utilized to produce the will to change. The empathetic prison officer will make the inmates see things differently and disentangle their dormant pro-social motivation by constantly referring back to what these individuals 'dream about and care for'. The inmates are to be convinced on their own terms. One of the guiding principles is to 'point out and underline the lack of correspondence between the client's goals and real life' (KVV 2003b: 14). That is, the role of the prison officer is to stress the inconsistencies, and thus the futility of pursuing the inmate's goals via the exercise of anti-social skills. At the same time, the inmates should be led to discover that their goals are within reach if they use the available pro-social skills and options. In this way, 'by drawing on the client's own perceptions, goals, and values', intrinsic motivation can be created and maintained (Miller and Rollnick 2002: 35).

Lack of motivation to participate in the programmes is interpreted as resistance. There are also other forms of resistance, of course; 'the variety of ways trainees seek to thwart, circumvent, object to, or resist participation' has been described as 'substantial' (Goldstein *et al.* 1998: 124). But the lack of motivation to take part in one's own personal transformation is seen as the root of all resistance. The absence of motivation constitutes the fundamental form of resistance. Conceptually, 'resistance stands in a contradictory relationship to motivation' (KVV 2003b: 14). This is consistent with the conception underlying the entire rehabilitation strategy. Like criminality, which is seen as an absence of social skills rather than as a presence of anti-social skills, resistance is analysed as a deficiency – as a lack of motivation. Within this conceptual framework, resistance cannot be an active choice. It is simply an absence of motivation to pursue pro-social courses of action, which in the first instance involves enrolling in the programme and participating in the classes. The assumption is spelled out in the original name of the special wing designed for the most troublesome inmates with substance abuse problems, those who refuse to take part in programmes, are violent, or sell drugs. It was originally called 'the wing for inmates who are difficult to motivate' (KVS 2002b). Words that would lead to associations with more overt forms of resistance – misconduct, disorder, and so forth – were not used. The name was later changed to the 'special motivational wing'. The emphasis on the lack of motivation, rather than on the acts of misconduct themselves, does not downplay the importance of resistance; it just reflects the view that the former is more fundamental.

There is no contradiction between encountering resistance and encouraging inmates to change their lives. On the contrary, techniques that increase motivation will at the same time decrease resistance. Motivational Interviewing is employed both to manage acts of resistance and to encourage a will towards personal transformation. The aspect of resistance management is most explicit when the level of motivation is close to zero. The technique is used on all types of prison wing. Yet on the special motivational wings, where no training programmes are available and the conditions of incarceration are harsher than on many other wings, the inmates are targeted exclusively with Motivational Interviewing (BRÅ 2005). The technique is applied to break resistance and awaken the dormant desire for an ordinary life. In this situation, as in other situations, success depends on the skills of the counsellor rather than on the convictions of the inmate. The question is not whether the inmate wants to change, but how such a will can be created in spite of displayed signs of the opposite. The ability to manage resistance is seen to be the decisive test for 'the true art of a counsellor' (Miller and Rollnick 2002: 110). Presumably, the motivation to change can be created *ex nihilo*, regardless of the circumstances, through the correct application of this set of discursive techniques.

C
Staying on target

A range of follow-up routines within the organization make sure that the exercise of power towards the target group stays on target. First of all, the motivation and the personal change of the individual inmate are monitored. The sentence plan documents the progress of the individual in terms of motivation and skills. Second, the compliance of prison officers is monitored. A system of video-surveillance combined with spot checks by programme inspectors is designed to detect teacher deviance from instructions in the programme manual. Third, the effectiveness of the intervention itself is evaluated, and confirmed through self-report questionnaires measuring attitudinal change within the target group.

Measuring change, monitoring compliance

The sentence plan is the main instrument to detect change at the level of individuals. It documents motivation as well as behaviour over time. Judging from the completed sentence plans in my sample, prison officers employ all kinds of cues to determine the degree of motivation for personal change. If the inmate does not assume responsibility for the crime, or voices concern about the prison sentence, this is a sign of persistent criminal values. In one of the sentence plans, an indication of criminal values was found in the attitude of the inmate who maintained that 'he has been treated unfairly and is innocently convicted'. On the other hand, a display of remorse, or acceptance of the punishment, indicates a will to overcome existing criminal values. Remorse is seen as the first step towards undertaking a wider reconsideration. BG, for instance, 'has many regrets about what he has done; in the future, [BG] plans to find a job and live a normal life'. In this case, the willingness to accept responsibility, displayed in the inmate's reasoning about the crime, extends to a wish for 'a normal life'. The inmates are also routinely asked about their perceived 'need for change'. The question is included in the form mainly to check the inmate's level of motivation.

But the preferred measure within the cognitive-behavioural approach is programme participation. Motivation to change is operationalized in terms of a willingness to participate in the assigned programme activity. It is through active participation in the training programmes that the inmate displays a determination to lead a pro-social life upon release. On the basis of the same assumption, programme participation also constitutes the primary measure of progress in terms of social skills. As the sentence plan is revised, it is possible to follow the progress of the individual through the traces of programme participation and, by implication, the progress in terms of increased social skills. BH, for instance, suffered from 'serious criminal thinking' according to initial assessment. Seven months later the following note was inserted in the sentence plan: *Våga välja*, a cognitive-behavioural programme against substance abuse, goes on and BH 'is making progress; he is conscientious and raises good points'. The mere fact that he was participating would have been taken as evidence that he was moving away from the 'serious criminal thinking' displayed earlier. In this case, however, BH not only participates but distinguishes himself by raising 'good points' and being 'conscientious', which indicates that he is well under way in acquiring pro-social skills and satisfying the criminogenic need selected in his plan. Should the progress fail to appear, documented for instance by notes on programme drop-out, the same routine enables adjustment of future interventions.

The conduct of teachers is closely monitored as well. Unlike previous correctional interventions, a lot of attention is devoted to the actual delivery of the cognitive-behavioural programmes. In one article, the aspect of implementation was referred to as 'the forgotten issue in effective correctional treatment' (Gendreau *et al.* 1999). This neglect has been corrected within the current rehabilitation strategy. The teachers are instructed to adhere to the manual and not improvise, backed by research showing the importance of universal delivery. Strict compliance to programme instructions is seen as essential for programme success, both by the authors of the Cognitive Skills programme and by the prison administration. In addition, mechanisms are in place to monitor compliance.

The prison service relies primarily on video surveillance to reduce the gap between the actual delivery of the programme and the instructions in the manual. The surveillance targets the teachers and not the inmates. As can be seen from the illustration of the classroom in Figure 2.1, the video camera is pointed towards the teacher. The six course participants are sitting to the side of the camera; their voices are captured on tape, but no other aspects of their conduct. All the classes given during the teacher's first two courses, and thereafter samples from individual classes, are recorded. The recordings are scrutinized by special instructors who monitor the programme integrity. The programme instructors cannot watch all classes but rely on spot checks; only a small sample of all recordings is actually being watched (KVV 2003a: 14). In this way, the panopticon has turned on the prison guards. The guards no

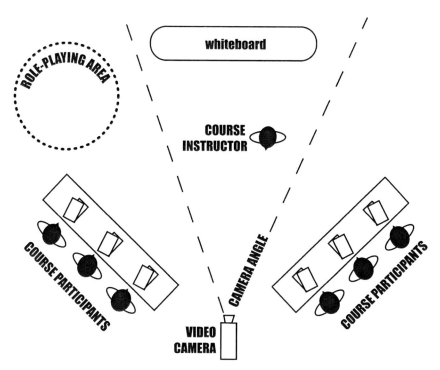

Figure 2.1 Teacher surveillance in the classroom

longer inhabit the central observation tower, as they did at the time of the birth of the prison (Foucault 1979a). In some respects, their position is similar to that of the inmates in the classic Benthamite prison. Just like them, the teacher-guards are not able to observe the inspector, nor do they know when they are being observed by the inspector. Similarly, the justification for the observation is the betterment of the individual, in this case the individual teacher-guard. The primary purpose is pedagogic. Using the exposed failures, the programme inspectors can suggest how the teachers can improve their performance. At the same time, the video recording operates as a control mechanism to secure strict compliance of the prison staff. The system of video recording, combined with spot checks by programme inspectors, serves both to detect non-compliance and to reinforce the motivation of teachers to comply.

The conduct of prison inmates is followed up through sentence plans whereas the conduct of prison officers is followed up through video surveillance. This makes it possible to see whether the strategy is on target inside the prison: whether individuals of the target group and members of the front-line organization participate in the exercise of power. But the existing auditing techniques do not cover the conduct of the target group outside the prison, and cannot say whether the interventions meet the targets in terms of enduring behaviour modification. Interestingly, the central target of wage labour is not followed up at all. The proposal of the National Audit Office to establish monitoring routines focused on the level of social inclusion, operationalized as 'legal income' (RiR 2004b), was never adopted. Hence, reconviction data is the sole behavioural indicator of programme effectiveness.

The approach carries a promise that it works in terms of reducing reoffending. In fact, it was called *What Works?* by its authors to emphasize the claim that according to the current state of research, *this* is what works, as opposed to other less successful interventions. Several studies have been performed with a straightforward focus on reoffending. Some of them have failed to show that the cognitive-behavioural programmes are effective in terms of reducing reoffending (Robinson 1995; BRÅ 2002; Falshaw *et al.* 2003). One meta-analysis shows moderate effects on reoffending (Wilson *et al.* 2005). Taken together, as Simon Merrington and Steve Stanley have commented, 'the evidence from rigorously conducted reconviction studies suggests that we are unlikely to see a major impact on reoffending rates, as promised by the *What Works?* literature, from programmes alone' (Merrington and Stanley 2004: 18). Auditing bodies have also noted the incomplete nature of this rehabilitation strategy. The Agency for Public Management pointed out that although reducing reoffending is 'probably the most important goal' of the prison service, 'the statistics on reoffending have not been developed to follow the rate of reoffending on a continuous basis and to relate this to the measures taken by the prison service' (Stats-kontoret 2003: 43). In addition, seven official evaluation studies conducted during the period have focused serious criticism on the outcome of the concerted efforts to reduce reoffending (BRÅ 1998, 2000, 2001, 2004, 2005; RRV 1999b; RiR 2004b). Such discouraging results have not affected the belief in the effectiveness of the cognitive-behavioural programmes. Within the strategy, their effectiveness is an axiom. The issue is not whether the programmes are successful, but rather, how to *make sure* that they are successful. What have been affected, however, are the routines of quality assurance. Programme effectiveness is established independently of reoffending rates.

As reconviction data cannot be – or at least, have not been – used to ascertain success, other standards have been found to prove the quality of the programme. The preferred standard in this regard is pro-social attitudes and values. The means of detecting changes of attitudes and values are self-report questionnaires. The Cognitive Skills programme contains its own follow-up routine. Initially, prior to the first lesson, the inmates are asked 50 questions mapping what is referred to as their 'cognitive behaviour'. This is done on an individual basis by the programme instructor. The questions range from 'What do you do when you feel depressed?' to 'Do you generally trust or distrust other people?' (KVV 2002: 120–25). The questions cover much the same ground as the programme. The answers are rated by the interviewer on a scale from 1 to 5. For instance, the question 'What do you do when you feel depressed?' constitutes one indicator of self-management. Answers such as 'never get depressed' mean bad self-management (1 point), whereas answers framed in such terms as 'think about why I feel this way' render the highest score (ibid.: 106). The same procedure is repeated after the completion of the programme. Any improvement in the score can be taken as evidence that the individual has profited from the programme. But the result is of no consequence for the individual inmates; the test is used to measure the programme's overall effectiveness.

The main instruments for evaluating programme effectiveness are the Eysenck Impulsiveness Questionnaire, the Sense of Coherence Questionnaire and the Criminal Sentiments Scale. Ever since the cognitive-behavioural approach was first implemented in Sweden in the mid-1990s, all three kinds of self-report questionnaire have been used repeatedly for this purpose. Taken together, they are considered to give a reliable indication of pro-social change. The design of the instruments is similar: the inmates are asked to take a position with regard to a set of propositions. The responses are anonymous. The questionnaires operationalize the norms at the heart of the theory of criminogenic needs, in particular self-control and responsibility. They capture the self-declared opinions of inmates on a wide range of issues, ranging from attitudes towards the criminal justice system to whether or not the inmate values his or her own life. The Eysenck Impulsiveness Questionnaire measures impulsivity, adventurousness and empathy. The questions are of a yes/no character, including 'Do you often buy things on impulse?'; 'Would you like to go scuba diving?'; and 'Do you feel sorry for very shy people?' (Eysenck et al. 1985: 619). The Sense of Coherence Questionnaire is designed to detect whether the individual perceives him or herself to be a part of the social context and to be in control of events in their own life. This is measured by questions such as 'When you talk to other people, do you have the feeling that they don't understand you?' The options range from 'never had this feeling' to 'always have this feeling' (Antonovsky 1987: 190–92). The final questionnaire, the Criminal Sentiments Scale, consists of propositions such as 'The law as a whole is sound'; 'Almost anything can be fixed in the courts if you have enough money'; and 'A cop is a friend of people in need' (Andrews 1984: 38–39). The test is designed to measure attitudes to crime and criminal identification. The programme is effective if the inmates show confidence in the criminal justice system and start to believe that the courts are honest and also that police officers are friends of people in need.

The questionnaires detect pro-social change. The key construct – pro-social orientation – is the combined measure of all three tests: 'a more pro-social orientation is indicated by a higher sense of coherence, empathy and attitudes

towards the judicial system as well as less impulsivity, adventurousness, tolerance towards crime and criminal identification' (BRÅ 2002: 18). Programme
participants have in fact shown improvements in terms of pro-social orientation
in the context of before and after tests. The results are seen as reliable indicators
of programme effectiveness. Although the measures themselves are far removed
from conduct, they are theoretically linked to pro-social behaviour. The stated
opinions of the inmates are said to 'mirror personality traits and attitudes' that
are correlated with criminality (ibid.). This chain – answers assumed to indicate
personality characteristics which in turn are assumed to underlie criminal conduct – enables the prison service to uphold a connection with the goal of
reduced reoffending, which is not visible in the reconviction data. Consequently, following five consecutive years of measurement, the prison service
could self-confidently assert that 'today, we can demonstrate with such certainty
that it [Cognitive Skills] works' (Chylicki 2000: preface). The programme was
later formally approved by an accreditation panel consisting of university pro-
fessors and prison officials. The panellists continuously rate programme delivery
and quality, and their decision means that the programme, according to 'available research', can be expected to reduce reoffending (KVS 2004c: 3). A mix of
administrative and scientific considerations thus confirms that the prison service
is on target.

Conclusions

Technologies of the self or discipline?

Cognitive Skills and Motivational Interviewing are prime examples of
productive power. This form of power presupposes the agency of those who
are targeted and must be understood in positive terms (P3). First of all,
participation is voluntary. The inmates formally apply for the courses and are
accepted following an interview. The participants are also free to leave at any
point. Further, the transformation is accomplished by the individual inmate.
From one perspective, it is almost as if the inmates were not in prison. An
observer in the prison classroom could just as well think that the participants
were employees engaged in the project of lifelong learning (Petersson 2003).
Moreover, the programme *works by appealing to the ambitions of the inmates*.
Participation is induced on the immediate promise of less restrictive conditions in the prison, as well as on the wider promise of social inclusion. The
programme is presented as the way back into society, and in a sense it is:
participation may be a first step on the road towards social inclusion, particularly when it opens up access to other services prior to and upon release.
Further, *the responsibility rests with the individual*, who is obliged to carry out
the actual work involved. The message that you will have to do most of
the work yourself is conveyed to the participants early on in the programme.
The role of the prison service is to facilitate the transformation – by

enhancing motivation and providing the required skill set. In addition, participation in the programme will *increase the individual's capacity to cope with difficulties*. Even if the living conditions upon release are unchanged, the inmate has been empowered to deal with them without further assistance, while pursuing available non-criminal options.

In a Foucauldian tradition, this is referred to with the concept 'technologies of the self'. These are thought of as techniques:

> which permit individuals to effect by their own means, or with the help of others, a certain number of operations on their own bodies and souls, thoughts, conduct and way of being, so as to transform themselves to attain a certain state of happiness, purity, wisdom, perfection, or immortality.
>
> (Foucault 1997: 225)

Technologies of the self are performed voluntarily by the individuals themselves, appeal to existing aspirations and enhance the skill set. That is, the techniques share all four of the characteristics attributed to Cognitive Skills above. Conceptually, technologies of the self are not only associated with autonomy, self-regulation and empowerment, but are also tied to subjection, constant self-surveillance and adjustment to conventional norms (Foucault 1985). However, *the emphasis* is on individual responsibility, personal aspirations and a lack of external restrictions – as opposed to the notion of discipline developed in *Discipline and Punish*, which stresses the very opposite: the body rather than the soul, coercion rather than agency, imposed objectives rather than genuine aspirations, and limited competence rather than personal growth. Both concepts describe power in action. Yet while 'discipline' refers to what is done to the individual, 'technologies of the self' designate 'the forms of elaboration, of ethical work [*travail éthique*] that one performs on oneself' (ibid.: 27; emphasis removed). The corollary of technologies of the self is 'government at a distance' whereby direct state intervention is made redundant. The vast majority of individuals are able to govern themselves as a result of a wide range of exercises through which they become good citizens. Citizens enter into loose and flexible alliances with governmental bodies and interest groups, and operate as partners in the reproduction of social order. There is no contradiction between the individual's self-interest and the reasons of state; on the contrary, government-led programmes are linked to the fears, needs and ambitions of the citizens who willingly participate (Miller and Rose 1990; Rose 1998).

However, it would be only partly accurate to describe Cognitive Skills as a technology of the self in a society where state power is exercised at a distance. A number of contradictory elements are also part of the programme: coercion, imposed objectives, close monitoring and limited competence. The individual inmate can refuse to participate, but this option is restricted.

Service provision and less restrictive conditions of incarceration are conditional on programme participation. So even if participation is not compulsory, *the web of incentives have been designed to encourage participation* in cognitive-behavioural programmes. Second, *the demands are placed on individuals from above* – by the head office and all the way down to the prison officer completing the sentence plan – with little consideration for the desires and ambitions that exist among the inmates. A general desire for social inclusion is posited to exist among the inmates – and this desire is appealed to – but no adjustments are made to individual preferences. The cognitive-behavioural approach is transformed into what Kevin Gorman has called 'one-size-fits-all interventions' (Gorman 2001: 6). What the individual inmate wants is irrelevant. Criminogenic needs are established, programmes are recommended and are then delivered in a uniform manner, regardless of the inmates' own perceptions of their particular needs. Third, while cognitive-behavioural programmes are one-size-fits-all, the demands, the incentives and the monitoring are individualized. The element of individualization, which is non-existent on the supply side, enters on the demand side. Far from governing at a distance, the state *confronts the individuals with very specific demands and close follow-up routines*. Finally, it is questionable *to what extent the programme empowers*. It contains exercises designed to create the prerequisite skills for maintaining work and relationships in the lower tiers of the labour market. This competence does not involve the ability to form associations, to plan one's own work, to engage with other members of society on an equal basis, or to cultivate leisure activities – or other abilities which might also be considered constitutive of empowerment at the level of individuals.

To conclude: the targeting includes elements of voluntary participation, individual responsibility, appeals to self-interest, and empowerment. At the same time, it contains elements of the opposite: coercion, imposed objectives, close monitoring and limited competence. In the Foucauldian tradition, the former characteristics are associated with technologies of the self, whereas the latter characteristics are associated with discipline. Both concepts are to a certain extent one-sided, and neither of them is therefore entirely accurate. A more complex concept is required to account for a productive power that incorporates a combination of contradictions. It would take into consideration the way that the strategy builds up a strong pressure around the individual to take part in programmes, but still relies on the individual choosing to do so. At one point it hands responsibility over to the individual to perform the change, and at another point removes this responsibility as it specifies the means and the steps that are to be taken. The power links the desire of subordinate individuals to the reasons of the state and the demands of the labour market. It targets behaviour, but speaks of thinking skills and values. It operates on a notion of the autonomy of the individual, while tying individuals to extremely limited social options. It simultaneously empowers and subdues; we are dealing with a combination of empowerment and subjection. Elements from both sides of this pair of opposites are always present. Productive power is voluntary and involuntary, responsibilizing and de-responsibilizing, authentic and imposed, involving freedom and necessity, empowerment and subordination.

As a combination of contradictions, productive power comprises techniques that are differently balanced. Cognitive Skills and Motivational Interviewing inside the prison are part of an abundance of cognitive behavioural and coaching practices spread across society. The techniques are remarkably similar in terms of therapeutic design (Furedi 2004). Yet they differ in other respects: there are do-it-yourself therapies online for everyone, company-sponsored coaching for executives, anger management for youth at risk, career coaching for students, and professional one-to-one therapy sessions for paying customers (Dahlstedt 2009). Some techniques are accessible on the market while other techniques are provided within state institutions. Some techniques are accessed individually while other techniques are dispensed to groups; some are sensitive to individual circumstances while others are manual-based; some promise to improve leadership while others prevent anti-social behaviour. In other words, some may be called technologies of the self whereas others are disciplinary.

The distinction appears to be related to successful inclusion in the labour market, and to whether the target group belongs to what Deleuze referred to as a control society or a disciplinary society. The statuses of the cognitive-behavioural interventions differ accordingly. In the first society, therapies and coaching are best described as technologies of the self. Participation is based on market incentives only, responsibility is fully individualized, and programmes appeal to self-interest. The individuals actively seek professional help, remaking themselves in the hope of improving their relative position in an inclusive society composed of a variety of markets. In the second society, however, therapies and coaching built along similar principles are best described as disciplinary. The inhabitants of this society are seen to be insensitive to market incentives and instead enrolled in institutions where the state governs at close range. They are collectively exposed to programmes that are manual-based and involve imposed objectives, a limited competence and constantly monitored teachers.

What is produced?

The entire strategy *could* be analysed from the standpoint that reducing reoffending is secondary to another, quite different function: diverting criticism and justifying increasing rates of imprisonment. Pat Carlen has shown that the cognitive-behavioural approach in Britain must be seen in this way – as ideology. In face of the constantly recurring criticism that prisons are counterproductive, it has managed to combine a neo-liberal agenda with a feminist emphasis on empowerment, thus winning over some of the critics and justifying the increasing rates of imprisonment. The approach has provided practitioners with a sense of mission and politicians with an argument that incarceration was partly for the inmate's own good (Carlen 2002). It may well be that the target of responsible and self-controlled wage-labourers is predominantly imaginary. As suggested by the employment and the reconviction rates of former prison inmates, the programmes are rarely successful in terms of behavioural change. On this reading, the prison is not a site where wage-labourers are actually constituted, but a showroom for the type of labour market opportunities and demands which await the inmates upon release (Hörnqvist 2008). Consequently, the interventions may be interpreted as repressive power, which in its ideological form operates by preventing insight, deflecting resistance and justifying an ongoing practice of another kind – in this case the practice of imprisonment.

Yet the cognitive-behavioural techniques in prison cannot be considered repressive simply because they are ineffective on their own terms. Power is the programmatic *attempt* to shape the behaviour in accordance with a set target. It follows that power is still power even if unsuccessful; and productive power is still productive even if unsuccessful. The set targets may not be achieved, but the organized and reflected attempts to shape the behaviour of individual inmates in accordance with the target are nevertheless carried through. So, in terms of the initial criteria, the interventions are productive (P4). But it remains to specify what 'productive' means in this context. If this form of power is productive, then what is produced? There are several possible answers. The techniques could produce citizens, constitute wage labour, incite motivation, generate actions, create skills or forge identities.

Foucault suggested that 'subjection' should be analysed 'as a constitution of subjects' (Foucault 1980: 97). The idea was elaborated in the governmentality literature, which paid attention to 'what forms of person, self and identity' were constructed (Dean 1999: 32). Training programmes similar to Cognitive Skills have been defined as 'technologies of citizenship' through which 'individual subjects are transformed into citizens' (Cruikshank 1999: 1). Similarly, Mary Bosworth has noted that, in contrast to the lively discussion on the nature of risk within the criminal justice system, there is agreement on the citizenship effect in contemporary post-Foucauldian analysis. The interventions are seen to be 'a primary means of creating accountable and thus governable and obedient citizens' (Bosworth 2007: 68). Accordingly, training programmes are considered successful to the extent that individuals 'come to experience themselves' as 'active citizens' (Dean 1999: 32).

The effect at the level of the personality is analytically central. This line of reasoning no doubt mirrors the assumptions as well as the ambitions of the rehabilitation strategy itself. Within the latter, a specific type of personality is projected to underlie the behavioural indicators. The criminogenic needs tend to appear in combination and reinforce one another. Anti-social values, attitudes, thinking patterns, emotional reactions and social skills are enduringly linked together into a specific type of personality (KVV 2002). At the other end of the spectrum, indicators of self-control and responsibility point towards an individual embodying all the values, sentiments, thought patterns and predispositions to act associated with an imagined model citizen. This figure is the very opposite of the anti-social personality of the typical offender. Citizens are seen to be different from most inmates in terms of who they are as persons, how they think and the values they hold. By implication, the necessary change is of a personal nature. Desistance presupposes a change from being one *kind* of person to becoming another kind of person. This basic conception of difference between the inmate and the citizen has been taken over in the Foucauldian tradition, along with a preoccupation with personal transformation. Yet what cognitive behavioural programmes actually do is perhaps more modest than constituting subjects, transforming subjects into citizens, or forging new identities or a particular kind of personality.

Cognitive Skills aims to modify some aspects of the behaviour of the inmate and produce a few new habits. The programme teaches basic skills related to the labour market and rudimentary reproductive functions. Even though the model citizen is invoked as a norm, the programme does not come close to turning inmates into citizens. The successful completion involves the accomplishment of a state of citizenship, which is reduced to the ability to follow the instructions of superiors, hold a relationship together, pay the bills on time and raise children. But this bundle of features is more reminiscent of Marx's figure of the wage-labourer than of Marshall's notion of the citizen. At best, basic employability is achieved; the programme will not lead the inmates 'to be accepted as full members of society, that is, as citizens' (Marshall 1977: 8). This conclusion does not underestimate the extent to which power is productive. But it shifts the attention from personality to conduct. The productivity does not depend on presumed personality effects; it is analysed strictly in terms of actions. Productive power produces actions – a motivation to act, and a capacity to act in certain ways. The attempts are undertaken to create behaviour in relation to the action-oriented targets within the strategy. In this strategy, Motivational Interviewing will create the motivation to act in ways consistent with the subordinate social position of the target group, whereas Cognitive Skills contains exercises designed to create a correspondingly specific capacity to act. Everything else is contingent. Wider aspects of the personality may be affected, or the intended effects on behaviour could fail to occur altogether. Conceptually, the interventions are productive in terms of actions, and only in this sense.

Chapter 3

Institutional order

Guiding repression through risk

The trend towards risk governance encompasses all sorts of organizations and both sorts of power. Increasingly, considerations of risk direct the programmatic attempts to shape behaviour on a day-to-day basis. The implications are different depending on context. In the global financial sector, risk governance involves self-regulation, standard-setting, and mutual trust (Alexander *et al.* 2006). But it may also imply the opposite: state regulation, fixed rules and distrust. Risk governance of institutional order in the prison is associated with the latter characteristics. Given that, generally, 'risk is the way organizations make sense of their environment and act upon it' (Ericson 2007a: 11), how does the Swedish prison service communicate risk to make sense of its environment and act upon security threats? This question will be pursued in this chapter. It assumes that a change occurred in the 1990s. In Sweden, as in many other countries, the introduction of risk technologies in the prison system involved a fundamental reorganization of repression. In their study on prison order, Richard Sparks, Anthony Bottoms and Will Hay note that 'the nature of the "game" has changed' following the implementation of techniques that appear 'to offer powerful tools for modernizing archaic practices' (Sparks *et al.* 1996: 94). As a consequence, the conditions of incarceration, as they come to form daily life for the individual inmate, are now the end result of a complex series of assessments and selections based on the risk of disorder. In this particular case, and in the case studied in the next chapter, the state's prerogative to use force is not triggered by actual rule violations, but by the anticipation of such violations. The assessed risk that somebody might violate a rule is sufficient ground for the use of force. In administrative practice, this involves a shift of attention from the rule violations themselves to a universe of high risk populated by a whole range of signifiers, factors and indicators.

The prison punishment is not the same for everyone. While the court determines the length of prison stay, the prison administration decides on any further use of force, that is, the specific deprivations of the inmate's liberty that are imposed *in addition* to the sentence. Taken together, they constitute the conditions of incarceration. By 'conditions of incarceration' I mean, first, the restrictions pertaining to the building where the inmate is placed. The physical security of the building, the fixed security systems attached to it such as fences, closed circuit television and detection systems, as well as the accompanying security regulations, restrict the inmates' freedom of movement and communication. Higher security translates into more restraints; being placed in a wing with a higher security level means more extensive restrictions on the ability to move and communicate. Second, there are restrictions pertaining to the individual inmates. Prisoners on the same wing may differ from one another in terms of restrictions on furloughs and other periods outside prison, or the possibilities of transfer to a prison with more open conditions. Finally, there is the varying frequency of physical controls, such as urine screening, cell inspections and body searches. Physical control routines differ widely within the prison system. The conditions of incarceration are constituted by this combination of restrictions pertaining to the wing, restrictions pertaining to the individual and physical control routines.

In general, a prisoner serving a long prison sentence and with many documented acts of misbehaviour is likely to be incarcerated under more closed conditions than a short-term prisoner with few reports of misbehaviour. But as will become apparent, many other circumstances are considered to be of significance for the risk assessment that underlies decisions. The resulting set of restrictions differs substantially from inmate to inmate. On the one hand, there are very open forms of incarceration. A prisoner placed in an open prison who is admitted into the work release system has a relatively high degree of freedom of movement and is not, or is only very seldom, subjected to intrusive physical controls. The prisoner can leave the prison during the daytime and is able to communicate freely with the outside world. At the other end of the spectrum, there are extremely closed forms of incarceration. High-risk prisoners are placed in maximum-security wings, with severe restrictions on their ability to associate with other inmates or to communicate with individuals other than members of the family. Urine screening, cell inspections and body searches are more frequent, and opportunities to spend periods outside prison may be completely withdrawn. Between these two extremes, there is a wide range of conditions of incarceration. One could speak of a spectrum of conditions of incarceration. Prisoners find themselves somewhere on this spectrum, depending on their combinations of restrictions. In practice, the conditions of incarceration, in the sense outlined above, are intertwined with access to amenities, treatment programmes and service supply which might also be regarded as part of the conditions of incarceration. Indeed, one could argue that the conditions of incarceration differ not only in terms of restrictions and controls but also in terms of inmate access to amenities and services. Yet the restrictions belong to a conceptually distinct category of repressive interventions. Decisions on restrictions, moreover, constitute part of a separate risk communication system. Determining the service provision, on the other hand, constitutes part of the rehabilitation strategy and of the risk communication system operating within that strategy.

The interventions must also be distinguished from the use of force that serves as punishment for rule violations. The conditions of incarceration are not a punishment for transgressions but constitute an administrative use of force grounded in a risk assessment of the individual inmate. There is a separate disciplinary system in the prison service that targets those who actually violate regulations (CPT 1992; KVVFS 2005). The disciplinary sanctions mainly involve postponements of the release date. In 2003, the prison service decided to prolong stays in prison by a total of 27,000 days distributed across 3,300 different occasions, as sanctions for disciplinary offences (KVS 2004a: 83). In each case, a decision is taken following an investigation of the rule violation, in which the inmate may dispute the accusations. The distinction between disciplinary sanctions and the conditions of incarceration is not always sharp. In particular segregation (solitary confinement) and forced transfer to another prison are located in something of a grey area between the two. Both interventions are frequently used; in 2003, 4,800 decisions were issued on segregation and 2,300 on forced transfers (ibid.: 83; SOU 2005a: 323). These decisions need not be based on a violation of the rules specific to the institution. Legally, segregation is not a disciplinary sanction. A prisoner may be placed in solitary confinement for administrative reasons, to preserve order, or on the basis of a risk assessment. Yet segregation is often perceived as a disciplinary sanction by inmates. 'Placement in the Unit PI at the Tidaholm Prison,' wrote the European Committee for the Prevention of Torture, 'was perceived as a punitive and often arbitrary measure by the vast majority of inmates interviewed on this subject' (CPT 2004: § 69). If the statement holds true, segregation works as an informal disciplinary sanction – as a punishment for unwanted actions that are not formally prohibited. The same applies to the use of forced transfers to another prison. Although not legally disciplinary sanctions for rule violations, they can be used in a way that is reminiscent of disciplinary sanctions.

In this chapter, I will first account for the way drugs, personality disorders and prison gangs are conceptualized as threats against prison order at the policy-level, and then the way these threats are broken down into guidelines and balanced against other administrative concerns to culminate in the goal of an individualized prison term. The drive to individualize repression questions a common theme in the literature on imprisonment: the warehousing of collectives. Entire social groups may be criminalized, but the prison service has not abandoned its interest in the individual. The section on targeting analyses the way in which the conditions of incarceration are in practice tailored around individuals. The process involves three steps: referral to a risk category, the individualization of the control level, and the accommodation of new information. The *management* of the risk of disorder is then followed up through the organization by statistical reporting routines and special auditing bodies. The prison staff are integrated in the governance of risks by means of a triple process that turns risk of disorder into rules for decision-making; makes the decision-making visible for inspection; and monitors the rule compliance of the decision-making retrospectively. In the concluding part, I will raise the question of what directs the use of power, arguing that it is one and the same thing throughout the strategy. The first-order control of the inmates as well as the second-order control of the staff is directed by the risk of disorder. Finally, I will discuss how the first-order interventions relate to the assumed characteristics of repressive power (R1–R4). The conclusion that risk rather than law directs the use of force calls the legal paradigm of repressive power into question.

A
Setting the target

The goal is conceived negatively. From a repressive perspective, the successful use of power results in obedience. Obedience is not perceived as action but as inaction: that is, as not performing acts that cross the line of the permitted. If, on the other hand, power is deployed unsuccessfully, transgressions are provoked. All actions performed by individuals in the target group amount to either obedience or disobedience. There is no middle ground. The prevailing power structure is conceptualized as a static order – as *status quo* – which is being reproduced through the lack of transgressions. By implication, institutional order in the prison service is reproduced as individuals refrain from acts laid down as transgressions of the rules specific to the organization. All transgressions are an immediate threat. They do not merely disturb the institutional order, thereby signalling that power has been deployed unsuccessfully; transgressions threaten the reproduction of the order as such. Even minor order disturbances tend to be perceived in terms of security – in the traditional sense of posing a threat to the very existence of the organization (Freedman 1992; Buzan *et al.* 1998). The relations of power are at risk if acts of transgression go unnoticed. 'Security is therefore not only about the exceptional,' Claudia Aradau and Rens van Munster remark on the repressive use of risk, 'but about everyday routines and technologies of security professionals' (Aradau and van Munster 2007: 98). For this reason, mundane activities of the prison staff are characterized under the general heading of security, involving an aspiration for an absence of existential threats to the organization rather than the presence of something positive.

Richard Sparks *et al.* have made the observation that 'the maintenance of order is a perennial problem for prison administrators and staff'. The perennial problem of upholding day-to-day order is distinguished from 'the special problem of the occasional complete or near-complete breakdown of order' (Sparks *et al.* 1996: 2; emphasis removed). From the point of view of a static conception of order, however, as well as according to central assumptions of policy-related research represented by researchers such as John DeIulio, Bert Useem and Peter Kimball, the prison provides a vivid example of the inherent connection between minute acts of transgressions and major institutional breakdown. Any disturbance can 'mushroom into a full-scale riot'; and if not immediately materialized, disturbances pave the way for a full-scale riot by undermining the administrative capacity to respond (Useem and Kimball 1989: 220). Prison riots are not different in kind from absconding, drug use and other violations of prison rules. What differs is the administrative capacity to manage the violations. The goal of preventing major prison riots, in which the inmates take over control of the facility, such as the 1971 Attica riot in New York, the 1990 Strangeways riot in Manchester or the 1994 Tidaholm riot in the Swedish city of the same name, is seen to presuppose the successful maintenance of order on a day-to-day basis.

Maintaining order means reducing order disturbances. In the Swedish prison service, order disturbance is a concept that encompasses a broad but well-defined range of activities. In legal terms, the kind of behaviour that constitutes order disturbances falls into two different categories: criminal acts and disciplinary offences. The first category comprises ordinary criminal acts, such as trading in drugs, interpersonal violence and extortion, which would also be actionable if they occurred outside the prison. Disciplinary offences, on the other hand, are specific to the prison setting. Absconding, refusal to work, damage, improper conduct and unauthorized possession of an article are among the 13 subheadings contained in the reporting forms (KVS 2002c: 7). These rule violations are related to security in two ways: in themselves and as they are mediated through inadequate management. Consequently, the target within the strategy is dual: on the one hand, existential threats within the target group and, on the either hand, inadequate governance of the organization, allowing the existential threats within the target group to unfold.

The changed clientele

Shanhe Jiang and Marianne Fisher-Giorlando distinguish three conceptual models to explain order disturbances. The first two focus on the prison environment. The 'deprivation model' stresses causes related to the conditions of incarceration and the 'situational model' primarily considers contingent circumstances and motives. The 'importation model', however, disregards the impact of imprisonment. It derives its name from the emphasis placed on what the inmates bring to the prison at the expense of how they are affected by the prison environment (Jiang and Fisher-Giorlando 2002). The Swedish prison service subscribes whole-heartedly to the importation model. The causes are literally located within the prison population. The risk of disorder is analysed as something arising exclusively from the inmates. Consequently, in the official reports on order disturbances, the focus is on the composition of the inmates. According to the government, the 'changed clientele' has made the task of preventing inmate misconduct 'increasingly complicated' (JuDep 2002). What is meant by the 'changed clientele' is elaborated in the threat assessments formulated by the head office and in other documents, from which there emerges a consistent picture of the nature of the perceived threat. The changed clientele is attributed to the growth over the last decade of three categories of prisoners: drug addicts, inmates with personality disorders, and prison gangs. These groups are perceived to be responsible for a large part of the order disturbances witnessed over the same period. Drug addicts, personality disorders and prison gangs permeate the management literature at all levels, from public inquiries, through strategic threat-assessments, to the administrative directives regulating the institutional placement of individual prisoners. Hence, these three categories of prisoner have been selected as constituting the risks that govern efforts to reduce order disturbances. Other categories of prisoners which have also received special attention from the prison service, such as sexual offenders, drink-drivers and economic criminals, are not viewed as constituting a risk.

Of all the selected risks, drugs constitutes the one that is most well-entrenched in the prison service. Drugs and drug users have constituted the single largest preoccupation of the criminal justice system since the 1970s, as reflected in the large number of drug users that are sentenced to prison (Tham 2003). A slight majority of all prison inmates are diagnosed as substance abusers. The threat posed to institutional order seldom needs much justification. A public inquiry stated in passing that 'drug addiction and drug trading in prisons result in a high level of anxiety, dissatisfaction, threats and other security problems for the inmates as well as the staff' (SOU 2000b: 224). No evidence was provided to corroborate this statement. The dangerousness of drugs is taken for granted. As a security threat, drugs have a dual character, simultaneously underlying both the profusion of minor infringements and the extraordinary, serious eruptions. Drug use is in itself an order disturbance. Four of the 13 subheadings contained in the reporting forms on prisoner misconduct relate directly to drug use. The combination of a high proportion of drug addicts, access to drugs, rules prohibiting the use of drugs, and frequent controls, make drug-related rule violations, sanctions and disputes endemic in many prisons. Although the threat assessments rarely make special mention of drugs, there are exceptions, as was the case when the special commission investigating a series of homicides in high-security prisons reached the conclusion that drugs were a decisive element. 'Both staff and inmates state that the drug trade is by far the most important cause of threats and violence among the inmate collective' (KVS 1998b: 11).

Both the operation of prisons on a day-to-day basis and analyses of spectacular events serve to ensure that drugs stay at the top of the security agenda.

By comparison with drugs, the risks associated with personality disorders and prison gangs are more recent. They were not mentioned among the grounds for differentiation in the extensive government inquiry on the prison system in the beginning of the 1990s (SOU 1993). Yet one decade later, prison gangs and inmates with personality disorders were firmly established as risks. One of the objectives of the Forensic Psychiatric Care Act, introduced in 1992, was to reduce the number of personality-disordered individuals sentenced to psychiatric care (Kullgren *et al.* 1996). As a consequence, a higher proportion of offenders diagnosed with mental health problems are sent to prison. This group, within the organization generally referred to as 'mentally disturbed', is perceived as highly problematic. The individuals are considered 'externalizing, easily insulted and exploitative', and as 'having difficulty participating in ordered activities, and repeatedly destroying the possibility of organized activity' (KVS 2004b: 13). Moreover, 'mentally disturbed [inmates] also tend to get excited and lose control over their actions during collective protests' (KVS 1998b: 38). The observations made by prison staff have been refined by forensic psychiatrists. Swedish psychologists and forensic psychiatrists have in a sense used the prison system as a scientific laboratory. Consequently, there is a voluminous body of research, arguing among other things that the diagnoses of psychopathy and anti-social personality disorder can explain violence and anti-social behaviour. Psychopaths in particular are prone to violence. 'Psychopathy,' say Henrik Andershed *et al.*, 'has in most scientific studies shown itself to be the single strongest predicator for recidivism (especially violent crime)' (Andershed *et al.* 2004: 5). The statistical correlations between the diagnoses and violent behaviour, along with a special focus on heinous crimes, have elevated the threat of personality disorder to such a level that extraordinary measures, such as the reintroduction of indefinite confinement, appeared motivated (SOU 2002).

The dangerousness of personality disorders is in part derived from a notion of otherness, whilst at the same time, paradoxically, the contrary also holds true. The disorder thus consists in a specific combination of difference and normalcy. While personality-disordered individuals are perceived to be very different from the rest of the population – which explains their ability to commit heinous crimes – they are at the same time difficult to differentiate, since they may appear to be well-behaved. Superficial charm, deceit and lack of guilt are among the core features of psychopathy (Hare 1991). The ability to manipulate and hide within the prison population makes psychopaths and other personality-disordered individuals all the more dangerous. As David McCallum remarks critically, 'they are more difficult to detect, require finer and more sophisticated tools and more specialist expertise to read the stigmata' (McCallum 2001: 98). With certain exceptions, such as 'grandiose sense of self-worth', most of the items on the psychopathy scale are referred to in terms of criminogenic needs within the rehabilitation strategy. Within this strategy, however, the same characteristics are not conceptualized as needs that can be changed but rather as personality traits that are resistant to change. In particular, those diagnosed as psychopaths are considered unreceptive to cognitive-behavioural interventions and as being likely to remain dangerous throughout their stay in prison.

Prison gangs are also a recent security threat. One report dated the emergence of the phenomena to the mid-1990s, when members of motorcycle gangs entered the prison system in the south of Sweden (KVS 2000). Within a few years, prison gangs were firmly established as a risk. Considering the weight assigned to them in policy terms and the extensive research on drugs and personality disorders, there is remarkably little research on prison gangs (Roxell 2007). Threat assessments are the prime source of information. At the turn of the millennium, the head office conducted two surveys into the extent and nature of the problem. The findings, which included the anecdotal evidence circulating among prison staff, was imbedded in a vivid narrative about young male offenders from immigrant backgrounds who have grown up in the poor suburbs of Stockholm and other big cities. This particular group was described as being 'without standards, dependent on gangs, violent and hateful', and its members were predicted to become 'our most troublesome inmates' (KVS 2002c: 5). Prison gangs are also closely linked to organized crime more generally, which threatens the country from the outside. According to the head office, imprisoned members of international criminal networks would bring 'habits and patterns from prisons in the former Eastern bloc', destined to 'cause us big problems in the future' (ibid.: 16). The foreign threat posed by organized crime is superimposed on the social threat from the suburbs. The prison is the physical location where this union takes place – where impoverished young men with no standards meet ruthless and resourceful criminal networks from the East. Local prison directors were concerned, and one of the surveys summarized their fears in the following manner:

> Most prisons mention that the gang members 'try to take over power in the prison and to control fellow inmates and the staff'. Other elements that are emphasized include threats and violence; solidarity among the inmates; that they are orderly, but 'you don't know what they are really doing'; that they influence staff decisions, file complaints, etc; organized criminality; the recruitment of new members; the domination of fellow inmates; that they are young; that they have foreign backgrounds; and that they spread their message.
>
> (KVS 2000: 11)

This characterization leaves no doubts as to why prison gangs have been selected as presenting a risk of disorder. Young male prisoners from poor circumstances join forces with more seasoned criminals from other countries and become an alternative centre of authority, threatening to disturb prison order in the most fundamental sense, by challenging the sovereign power of the prison administration.

Administrative breakdown and renewal

The risk of disorder is related not only to the disorderliness of the target group but also to the ability of the organization to exercise repressive power efficiently. Analysing why some American prisons experienced major riots in the 1970s and 1980s, Bert Useem and Peter Kimball conclude that 'the key factor has not been organization of the inmates but the disorganization of the state'. Each riot was seen to be preceded by an administrative breakdown.

> Inconsistent and incoherent rules for inmates and guards; fragmentation, multiplication of levels, and instability within the correctional chain of command; weak administrators, often "outsiders" to the system; conflict between administration and guards [were some organizational features that] sap the ability of the state to contain disturbances.
>
> (Useem and Kimball 1989: 218–19)

The risk technologies introduced in the 1990s promised a more efficient use of force towards the target group and enhanced control within the organization. They boosted the administrative capacity. From then on, the activity of the entire prison service could be streamlined along the risk of disorder.

In the Swedish prison service, the increase in numbers of drug users, prison gangs and inmates with personality disorders was placing 'completely new demands on the institution' (JuDep 2002). The problem was not so much the inherent disorderliness of the inmates as such but rather the inadequate application of force, given the inherent disorderliness of the inmates. The conditions of incarceration were perceived as being too lax and imprecisely applied, thus allowing dangerous criminals – drug users, prison gangs and personality-disordered inmates – to engage in acts of misconduct. In the official reports produced following major order disturbances in the form of large-scale riots, spectacular escapes and homicides, the head office has consistently emphasized the combination of ever more dangerous criminals and insufficient constraints and control routines (KVS 1995, 1998b, 2002c). This perceived security deficit spurred policy-level planning and the development of coercive interventions.

Security objectives do not reign supreme, however. The application of force is balanced against a range of countervailing considerations and circumstances. First, the basic legal principle is that the conditions of incarceration should be as little intrusive as possible. No prisoner should be incarcerated 'under more restrictive conditions than are demanded by security concerns in the particular case' (Proposition 1994/95: 27). A decision to place more rather than fewer restrictions on the individual prisoner must be justified. This is expressed, for example, in the guidelines concerning institutional placement: 'Since the main principle is placement in open prison, it is important, with respect to the legal security of the individual, to justify a decision that leads to placement in a closed prison or in a closed prison wing' (KVVFS 2004b: 1–2). Second, there are efforts to limit the harms caused by the prison term. The basic assumption underlying the current practice of imprisonment is that it has negative effects on the possible reintegration of the inmate. Gresham Sykes' famous thesis on the 'pains of imprisonment' found its way into the Prison Treatment Act, according to which the prison service is expected to 'counteract detrimental consequences of the deprivation of liberty' (SFS 1974: section 4). Intensified coercion and control may restrict the inmate's ability to commit rule violations but also increases the risk of negative side-effects. This has been described in terms of a conflict by the National Audit Office.

> There are currently certainly methods available which in principle enable a 100 per cent safe containment. There is however an obvious conflict between safe containment that isolates and stigmatizes, and the endeavour to achieve normalization and adjustment to a future existence without criminality.
>
> (RRV 1999b: 50)

Productive and repressive interventions in prison have different goals and stand in a tense, if not contradictory, relationship to one another. The most common metaphor used in official documents to describe the relationship is that of a balancing act. The National Audit Office speaks about 'a balancing act between safe containment and the inmates' motivation to change their attitudes towards crime or substance abuse' (ibid.: 50–51). And when the Ministry of Justice discussed the dual interests of the prison service – which involve 'a far-reaching security mentality' while at the same time safeguarding 'the possibilities for modification and change' – the conclusion was that 'often this is a matter of finding a suitable balance between these two interests' (JuDep 2000: 13).

Third, there is an economic dimension. The National Audit Office has criticized the prison service for keeping too many prisoners under conditions that are too restrictive, resulting in excessive spending. 'Many clients occupy unnecessarily secure, and therefore expensive, prison places' (RRV 1999b: 20). The precautionary mentality comes with a price-tag: 'every year, the prison service over-consumes security in the range of 80–165 million SEK [Swedish Krona]' (ibid.: 116). Fourth, the inmates themselves are expressing discontent at the over-consumption of security. Many inmates perceive restrictions and enhanced control routines as intrusive, incomprehensible and superfluous (KVS 1995, 1998b). The discontent is voiced through available organizational channels, such as the regular meetings between local prison management and inmate representatives, as well as in collective order disturbances such as strikes. The opinions of the target group cannot be simply disregarded, as policy-related research has shown that the imposition of restrictive conditions erodes the legitimacy of the prison administration, which in turn may exacerbate order disturbances (Wolf 1991; Olsson 2005).

Hence, security concerns must be balanced against legal safeguards, efforts to minimize harm, the goals of productive interventions, economic considerations and prisoner resistance. What makes the balancing possible is a common language of risk. The contradictory demands are translated into considerations of the risk of disorder. Control levels and restrictions, which could be opposed on legal grounds, can be negotiated via references to the specific risk associated with the individual. Likewise, the strategy-specific risk of disorder is the media through which security arrangements can be balanced against efforts to minimize the pains of imprisonment. Economic concerns may also be negotiated in terms of the same risk; secure and expensive conditions can be disputed as well as defended in terms of the risk posed by inmates. This negotiation is made possible by a conception of risk that is not seen as a uniform label applicable to broadly defined groups but rather as something that is finely grained and attributable to individuals. All institutional players can agree on the necessity of well-balanced decisions on the basis of reliable information of all the risk indicators of relevance in the individual case.

The government spoke of 'an individualized prison term' (SOU 2005a: 127). The journey through the prison system should as far as possible reflect the risk profile of individuals within the target group. That is the primary goal. It presupposed a second goal: the ability to direct organizational resources and activities to achieve the first goal. Indicators of high risk, or alternatively low risk, do not automatically translate into a specific set of conditions of incarceration. The placement of inmates is a complex administrative task. Decisions at the level of individuals have been a recurrent problem within the prison service. Efforts to identify drug addicts, to search for unauthorized objects, to legislate about release systems, or to build special prison wings have a tendency to evolve separately. The mere existence of institutionalized goals, operationalized risks, preferred means of intervention and auditing systems does not amount to effective risk management. Large quantities of information on the inmates, for instance, are crucial to the matching of individuals with conditions of incarceration. Yet large quantities of information on the inmates are not sufficient to refer individuals to prison wings. This also presupposes knowledge on the available options and on which places are free in which prison for various categories of inmate at a given moment, as well as functional routines for placement. Without appropriate routines, no strategy can work. In the late 1990s, for example, when the placement organization was dispersed around the country and the intake procedures demanded a referral from a psychiatrist, the special support wings designed for personality-disordered inmates were hard to fill because of the roundabout routines. The perceived security deficit was an organizational problem in the narrow sense. It was necessary to alleviate the mismatch between, on the one hand, the composition of the prison population, and, on the other, the conditions of incarceration. Risk was the element which enabled that fine-tuning of organizational activity.

B
Targeting

To reduce the risk of disorder, the prison service relies on administrative control organized around the conditions of incarceration. The approach resonates with research that stresses the central importance of containment and administrative control, as opposed to an elaborate sanctioning system or consensus-oriented management, to maintain institutional order (Useem and Kimball 1989; DeIulio 1991; Boin and Rattray 2004). One auditor voiced 'the need for differentiation' (Statskontoret 2003: 32) and, by doing so, also formulated the most fundamental policy assumption. 'Differentiation' is the magic word within the strategy. It refers to an analytical *and* physical division of the prison population. More specifically, differentiation stands for a risk-management approach comprised of three stages:

1   The identification of the individual (as belonging to a category) and a subsequent referral to *category-specific* conditions of incarceration. Routines for risk communication enable the prison service to develop special restrictions for drug users, personality-disordered inmates and prison gangs. Concomitantly, the number of special wings has grown considerably during the studied period; in 2004, half of all prison places were devoted to special categories of inmates.
2   *Individualizing* the conditions of incarceration. Decisions on the conditions of incarceration were made sensitive to individual differences across high-risk categories. The application of restrictions *over and above* the category-specific referrals was rendered possible by risk-assessment tools such as the placement form.
3   *Accommodating new information* and adjusting the conditions of incarceration, thus satisfying the ambition to individualize the prison term. The administrative guidelines based on the threat assessments as well as the placement form are ill-suited to capturing changes since they stress static factors. Instead, the sentence plan, a risk-assessment tool informed by the theory of dynamic criminogenic needs, transforms information on individual progress into a revised risk assessment.

The following presentation will reflect this movement from (1) the group to (2) the individual, and then, at the level of individuals, (3) over time.

Differentiating dangerous groups

Routine decision-making tends to proceed in a manner which involves a referral of the individual to a category, which then entails a certain outcome (Hawkins 2003). In frequently recurring decision-making situations, such as decisions on institutional placement or furloughs, only a few standard options are available in the majority of cases and there is little space for an individualized solution. The options are tailored not to individuals but to categories of individuals. The operationalization of drugs, personality-disordered inmates and prison gangs in the prison service exemplifies this. Differentiation tends to involve referral to group-specific conditions.

The risk management of drugs has settled into control routines that structure everyday life. These affect all units of the prison system and have led to a systematic differentiation of prison wings. Although drugs have been a security concern since the 1970s, the system of detection, control and special wings was not completed until recently. The search for traces of drug use has a substantial impact on both the daily activity of staff and the personal integrity of the inmates. In 2003, 93,000 urine screens were conducted, which means that, on average, every inmate was controlled once every third week. In the same year, 104,000 cells were subject to close inspections in the search for drugs and other unauthorized articles, meaning that, on average, every cell was controlled once a month (KVS 2004d). These figures may be viewed as an illustration of the extent to which the risk management of drugs has saturated the prison service. Beyond repeated physical controls, there are also other ways of identifying drug users. Almost all assessment forms and written documents on individual inmates contain a section on drug use. There are functional routines in place to pass on this information within the organization. A survey revealed that officials at the placement unit had information on the presence or absence of drug use in almost all cases. This information had been transmitted from the court verdict, from the investigation into the individual's personal circumstances conducted by the probation service or from the client-administrative computer register (BRÅ 2004). The extensive knowledge of the inmates' drug use laid the grounds for a systematic physical differentiation. More than one quarter of the total number of prison places is designated for drug users (KV 2005b). These places are then divided into three categories of prison wings, each with different conditions. Using the urine screens and the documented level of motivation to stop using drugs as the yard-stick, the inmate is placed in one of three categories. Initially, all diagnosed drug users are placed in 'motivational wings' with access to cognitive-behavioural treatment programmes and ordinary furloughs. Transfer to a 'treatment wing' is conditional on the inmate's good performance and negative urine screening results. Treatment wings have a higher level of service provision, and offer the possibility of periods outside the prison other than furloughs – in the form of the work release system, leisure activities and a possible transfer to a treatment centre in the community. On the other hand, upon signs of non-cooperation or continued drug use, the inmate may be transferred to a more restrictive wing, with little by way of amenities and rehabilitation. In prison wings for recalcitrant drug users, 'visits and periods outside the prison should be granted restrictively' (KVS 2002b: 14). Yet Motivational Interviewing is provided to awaken the dormant desire for something else.

Psychopaths cannot, according to the established view, be changed by treatment (Andershed and Skeem 2004), nor can they be identified by means of external signs or intelligence gathering. As a consequence, the threat posed by personality disorders has been managed by scientific detection and physical containment. Academic psychologists were given the task of singling out personality-disordered inmates – the superficially normal – from the rest of the prison population, while the prison service established wings that were specially designed for this category of inmates. When the central intake unit was opened in 1997, routines for identifying personality disorders on a regular basis were put in place for the first time. Prior to that, psychological investigations of the prison population were conducted from time to time in a non-standardized way, and with no administrative feedback routines establishing a connection between diagnosis and institutional placement. The task of forging this connection fell to the central intake unit. Prisoners sentenced to a term of at least four years are sent to this unit directly from the remand prison. The result is a systematic detection of personality-disordered inmates. Of all violent offenders examined during a seven-year period by psychologists using the psychopathy checklist and the diagnostic criteria for personality disorders, 58 per cent were found to have some kind of personality disorder. The close scrutiny of the individual reveals not only whether the inmate has a personality disorder but also of what kind; the correctional psychologists work with 11 different subtypes (Andershed *et al.* 2004). The routines for detecting personality disorders were accompanied by special support wings for this category, established in the same year as the central intake unit itself. The support wings house individuals who as a result of their 'externalizing and destructive behaviour cannot be managed in a normal wing' (KVVFS 2004b: 9). In the original directives, inmates with personality disorders were given special mention as the target group. These inmates are considered to be mentally disturbed but not in need of psychiatric care – they are not sick, if also not normal or simply violent, but rather a mix of everything. The intake procedures reflected this complexity and made a referral from a psychiatrist a requirement (KVS 2002c).

The current tactics employed to manage prison gangs can be summarized in three words: identify, monitor and disperse! The first objective is to distinguish the gangs and identify their members. In the special gang reports, the majority of prison directors reported the presence of gangs (KVS 2000, 2001). The total number of gang members was estimated to some hundreds.

The staff in the local prisons had identified members via mail controls, information from inmates, and external indicators such as tattoos and badges. A change in the legislation allowed the prison service to store information on possible gang affiliation at the individual level. Concomitantly, a central security register was created that augmented the opportunities for keeping track of gang members as they are being transferred from one prison to another. Given that gangs threaten to become an alternative centre of authority, once the prison service has identified gang members, all efforts are geared towards dissolving the gang. The head office intended to make it impossible for prison gangs to persist as organizations, and announced a firm determination to 'disturb their activities, restrict their options, and make sure that they do not expand their activities' (KVS 2002c: 10). In terms of the conditions of incarceration for the individual inmate identified as a gang member, this translates into frequent physical controls and close surveillance. Gang affiliation also places special restrictions on the institutional placement. According to administrative directives, the security register must be consulted before a prisoner who 'sympathizes with an extremist organization' is referred to a particular prison. In addition, the prison's 'geographical location' and its level of 'protection against release operations' must be taken into consideration (KVVFS 2004b: 8–9). Inmates associated with gangs are thus preferably placed under very closed conditions and dispersed across the country to restrict the possibilities of face-to-face communication with other proposed members. As opposed to the management of drugs and personality disorders, there were to be no special wings for gang members.

Warehousing collectives or curious about individuals?

Malcolm Feeley and Jonathan Simon were among the first to theorize the introduction of technologies of risk in the prison system. The new technologies were part of a 'new penology', in which a 'permanently dysfunctional population' would be warehoused in accordance with their levels of assessed risk (Feeley and Simon 1994: 192). Their influential thesis has since been criticized for neglecting the never-ending efforts to rehabilitate prisoners (Hannah-Moffat 2005). The analysis of productive interventions in the previous chapter supports that critique. In addition, Feeley and Simon's thesis on a new penology only partially captures the repressive use of power. Taken as an account of prison repression, it misrepresents the deployment of interventions. On their reading, individuals are targeted as part of a category, or as a bundle of risk indicators that is shared by a wider group of people. Interventions based on risk assessments 'target offenders as an aggregate in place of techniques for individualizing' (Feeley and Simon 1992: 450). The individual is treated exclusively as a member of a collective. Hence, knowledge of the individual, which goes beyond what is needed for a category-referral, would become redundant. This interpretation is perfectly consistent with the analysis presented so far in the chapter. The category-referral based on an assessment of collective threats goes some way towards providing a basis for understanding the design of conditions of incarceration. But technologies of risk have not replaced 'techniques for individualizing'. Drug users, personality-disordered inmates and prison gang members *are* treated as dangerous collectives. At the same time, there is a drive to individualize the conditions of incarceration over and above the category-referral, based on a detailed knowledge of the individual. Repressive power has by no means lost interest in the individual. The goal of a fully individualized prison term implies that every prisoner is surrounded by a specific set of restrictions.

The key invention was the introduction of the placement form and other easy-to-use risk-assessment tools in administrative practice. The 1990s witnessed a proliferation of forms for the collection, assessment and transmission of information on the individual inmate. A number of formal risk-assessment tools came to be used in the prison service: the HCR-20, the PCL-R, the DSM-IV. These instruments carry a promise of efficiency and accuracy, as they incorporate findings from scientific research identifying factors related to criminal conduct. The drawback, however, from an administrative point of view, is that the assessments have to be made by especially trained psychologists or forensic psychiatrists and that only a minority of the prison population – above all those who pass through the central intake unit – can be assessed in this way. But there are other administrative tools that operate in the same way as formal risk-assessment instruments: forms that can be completed by ordinary prison staff and which are applied to all prisoners. These tools – the placement forms and the sentence plans – may have a different scientific status but they perform the same function. Like their more advanced cousins, the placement forms and the sentence plans are used to structure the raw data on which decisions on the conditions of incarceration are based. Similarly, they register differences that affect the risk level of the individual. Taken together, the instruments constitute an administrative invention that facilitates the matching of individual prisoners and individual conditions of incarceration. This allows for a far-reaching individualization. At the same time, by documenting the information that can be used to justify the decisions taken on conditions of incarceration, it enables a far-reaching monitoring of prison staff.

The placement form and the sentence plan document all the information that is relevant to making decisions on placement, control levels and periods outside the prison. Administrative directives help the prison staff structure the vast amount of information. In the initial decision on the conditions of incarceration, two different kinds of information should be considered. The first comprises indicators of security threats, such as positive urine screens, self-declared drug use, tattoos, intelligence on gang membership, a high score on the psychopathy checklist, or a diagnosis of personality disorder. In addition, the risk classification of the prisoner is affected by features of the individual's history that are not reducible to the three collective threats distinguishable in the prison population. The traditional historical risk factors – such as age, gender, type of offence, sentence length, previous criminal record, frequency of reoffending and the inmate's history of misconduct within the prison system – are also significant. In the placement form, the criminal justice history of the individual is captured under headings such as 'type of crime', 'number of previous convictions', 'nature of previous criminality' and 'documented reports on misconduct during the last five years'.

The combined focus on collective threats and traditional risk factors is confirmed in the sample of sentence plans. The following quotations are used to assign a high-risk classification. They invoke, in turn, the stereotypical figures of a drug user, a psychopath and a prison gang member.

> [DB] must be placed in a closed prison for security reasons, on account of substance abuse and frequent recidivism, committing similar crimes.
>
> Severe criminal history and convicted on numerous occasions. [DC] has no workplace experience. [DC] is anti-social and has a psychopathic personality disorder.
>
> Long prison term, frequent recidivism, risk for absconding, for which reasons [BA] must be placed in a closed wing until at most 1 year remains prior to the date of conditional release.

Traces of drugs, organized crime and personality disorders indicate a high risk of order disturbances – and thus by extension of more closed conditions. However, as can also be extrapolated from these short excerpts, the motivations for high-risk status are never simply 'drug use', 'psychopathy' or 'prison gang membership'. Many previous convictions, a young age at first conviction, a long prison sentence and several reports on misconduct during previous prison terms will also contribute to a high-risk classification. The collective threats have not undermined the importance of the more traditional risk factors, such as age, gender, type of offence, sentence length and previous criminal record. In the individual case, the decision is based on a combination of indicators, where both traces of collective disorder and a long and troublesome history within the criminal justice system make a high-risk classification more likely. Inversely, the absence of drugs, criminal acquaintances and a psychiatric diagnosis indicate a lower level of risk, particularly if combined with a relatively clean criminal record and a stable social situation. DD is the typical low-risk prisoner.

> Old age at first conviction; has good support from the family. On leave of absence from work; has the possibility of returning to this previous employment when the prison sentence has been served. No criminal acquaintances or criminal values. No drug abuse.

DD is placed in an open prison despite having been awarded a long prison sentence. A low score on historical risk factors, and no indicators of collective threats, motivates few security precautions. Between the typical high-risk and the typical low-risk prisoners, there are all sorts of combinations of risk factors attributable to individuals. The placement form and the sentence plan make it possible to attain a high level of individualization. Consequently, prison repression is not uninterested in individual differences; on the contrary, it uses them to differentiate. The conditions of incarceration are delineated on the basis of risk assessments that are sensitive to group belonging as well as to differences between individuals.

Introducing the element of change

To add to the complexity, there is the element of change. The normal administrative procedure is to gradually lift the restrictions over the course of the inmate's stay in prison, moving towards more open conditions as the date of release comes closer. This change is to some extent quasi-automatic, since, generally speaking, the initial risk of disorder is considered to 'decrease with the passage of time' (KVVFS 2004b: 3). The idea that the individual will benefit from productive interventions aimed at rehabilitation has pervaded the prison system since its inception (Foucault 1979a; Duguid 2000). As a consequence of the in-built anticipation of positive change, the repressive interventions can be lifted gradually. But their removal is also conditional on the progress of the individual prisoner. Depending on events and circumstances during the prison stay, the risk level can be adjusted in either direction: upwards or downwards. The conditions of incarceration have been made sensitive to such changes in the risk level. But the element of change can only, to a very limited extent, be detected using risk-assessment tools that circulate information on security threats and historical indicators. All the prioritized indicators are seen to be static, with the exception of drug use. In order to make alterations of the conditions of incarceration justifiable, instruments must be used that can detect risk-related phenomena that may change. Therefore, the theory of criminogenic needs is picked up selectively within the disorder strategy – and transformed into indicators of the risk of disorder.

One must distinguish between the initial decision and all subsequent decisions. The risk assessment which determines the initial conditions of incarceration for the individual focuses on the traditional historical factors and on indicators of the collective threats. The sentence plan, on the other hand, is designed to inform subsequent decisions. Since the risk and need profile focuses on dynamic as opposed to static risk factors, it can detect an increase or a decrease in the risk level of the individual and the conditions of incarceration can be adjusted accordingly. In this context, dynamic risk factors are identical with criminogenic needs. The same type of phenomena is referred to under different headings; only the context is different. The word 'risk' is used in situations when decisions on restrictions are discussed, whereas the word 'need' is used when the topic is rehabilitation. This corresponds to the distinction between productive and repressive power. 'Risk' signals the use of force to enforce compliance and contain individuals, whereas 'need' signals training programmes to satisfy shortcomings and develop new skills. The contribution of the sentence plan in this context is less that of determining the risk of disorder, and rather that of monitoring whether the inmate has profited from the training, and thus whether the risk of disorder has been reduced. At the point of *adjusting* the risk level, the sentence plan – the cornerstone of the strategy that aims to bring about social inclusion and to reduce reoffending – turns into a component of the strategy to reduce order disturbances. In this way, the rehabilitation strategy not only governs productive interventions, but also encroaches on the disorder strategy. On condition that it translates itself into security considerations and uses the language of risk rather than need, it can affect the other strategy in operation in the prison service. The risk of reoffending and the risk of disorder, whilst they are elsewhere managed on separate organizational tracks, converge at the level of the individual inmate.

The convergence between the two risks is noticeable in the trajectory of individual conditions of incarceration, as documented in the completed sentence plans. The core of the sentence plan is the risk and need profile, in which the prison officer is requested to summarize all the available information on a given inmate. The summary should contain both a quantification of the inmate's risk level, in terms of low–medium–high, and a short narrative explaining how the officer arrived at this conclusion. Features indicating a high risk must be weighed against 'positive, protective factors' and 'the motivation of the client'. The concept of risk appears under two separate headings in accordance with the twin objectives of the prison service to reduce reoffending and to maintain institutional order. But the indicators of *changes* in the risk level tend to be the same; in the sample of completed sentence plans, the 'risk of reoffending' and the 'risk of misconduct' are, with few exceptions, not kept separate. Factors taken to imply a heightened risk of reoffending, such as reports of misconduct and an unwillingness to participate in programmes, are also taken as evidence of a heightened risk of order disturbances. Conversely, indicators of pro-social change indicate a reduced risk of disorder.

There is no easy answer to the question of what regulates the risk level of individuals. The sentence plan does not contain a preset vision of the process of risk reduction and permits a wide range of evidence to be used to adjust the risk level. Yet the cognitive-behavioural approach embodies a specific view on risk-level adjustment, which rests on the assumption that prisoners will reduce the risk they pose by participating in programmes that address criminogenic needs. On the basis of the same assumption, programme participation constitutes a reliable measure to establish a decreased risk. It can be used, along with other protective factors, to reduce the risk level, even when historical factors point in the opposite direction. A good example is DF, whose situation, according to the sentence plan, was characterized by multiple social problems, substance abuse, 'as well as an escalating problem of involvement in violent crime'. Hence, DF was seen as a high-risk prisoner when he started to serve his third prison term for a serious drug offence. However, one year later, his risk level was significantly reduced. Under the heading of 'positive, protective factors' the following revision is inserted: 'girlfriend and family who support [DF]. Accommodation exists, vocational training soon completed.' The motivation of the client is also seen as having improved, since he 'takes part in the motivational group; very anxious that his treatment and his pre-release plan will be of benefit to him and has plans for the future'. DF still scores high on almost all of the traditional historical factors, but this is outweighed by family support, accommodation, vocational training, programme participation and observed signs of motivation.

In the last example, all the dynamic factors pointed towards a reduced risk level. This is far from always the case, necessitating a choice as to which of the dynamic factors is the most important. Consider the following two examples. Both men have been placed in the same prison subsequent to convictions for economic crimes. In the first case, the risk was initially specified as medium, motivated by an 'early debut; [DG] has reoffended even though a considerable amount of time has elapsed between the offences'. Seven months later, this assessment was revised to low, with the following justification:

> During his prison stay, [DG] has exhibited a very good insight into his current as well as his previous offences. Further, [DG] exhibits no tendency towards criminal thinking. DG will most certainly be able to acquire and maintain employment after his prison term.

The risk level was reduced even though DG, in the meantime, was found to possess a SIM-card during a cell inspection, for which he received a warning. However, this disciplinary offence was overlooked; 'considering [DG]'s generally orderly behaviour in the prison, this can be seen as a singular occurrence and does not affect the previous assessment'. In the other case, DH is a well-educated prisoner initially classified as low risk, with the following justification:

> [DH] has behaved in exemplary fashion during the entire period from remand to prison. His references are very good from officials within the prison service, the police and other agencies concerned.

However, within two months of this assessment, DH was found guilty of a similar disciplinary offence as the incident involving posession of a SIM-card. A cellular phone was seized in his cell, and, as a consequence, his risk level was raised from low to medium. Both prisoners are perceived to be essentially well-behaved. Yet, in the first case, the risk level was reduced from medium to low, despite the disciplinary offence. In the second case, the risk level was *raised* from low to medium, as a result of a similar disciplinary offence. The two examples seem to contradict each other.

The assessment of risk is evidently influenced by more than knowledge of indicators as transmitted through the information-processing routines of the prison service. The forms and checklists have not replaced the agency of the decision-makers and the fact that they 'go about their task with a world-view' (Hawkins 2003: 204). The indicators of reduced or increased risk do not speak for themselves. To be significant, they must be integrated into a narrative that can justify a change in the conditions of incarceration. As Kelly Hannah-Moffat has shown in the context of Canadian parole board decisions on female prisoners, the function of indicators is to underpin a story justifying the decision that is taken. Programme participation, for instance, can justify a positive decision since it draws on the grand narrative on how risk is reduced in general. It enables board members to construct a story in which the inmates 'have benefited from the programs or gained insight and accepted responsibility for their offending' (Hannah-Moffat 2004: 379). Judging from my sample of sentence plans, the ordinary prison staff likewise appear to integrate indicators into a wider narrative. Ideally, the gradual transfer to more open conditions, which is routine as the prison term proceeds, should be accompanied by documented signs of progress that can be included in a story justifying the transfer to more open conditions. But it is hard to discern either a specific set of prioritized indicators within the sample, or one grand narrative of change. The cognitive-behavioural approach competes with commonsense notions of social inclusion through work and family relations, as well as with the cynicism motivated by information on traditional historical factors. To justify a transfer to more open conditions, the crucial point is that *some* indicators can be used to construct *some* form of narrative on personal change whereby the prisoner no longer poses a significant threat to the community, or to prison order.

Indicators of risk could also be used to tell the opposite story, justifying more restrictive conditions. The most common indicators of elevated risk are repeated acts of misconduct. This is almost tautological; recent order disturbances predict order disturbances in the near future. However, events that were already known at the time of the initial risk assessment can also be reinterpreted in the light of new information, justifying tighter restrictions. For example, one individual was characterized as a low- to medium-risk prisoner, an assessment that was motivated by the fact that '[DJ] behaves well on the wing, with few reports. He gives the impression that he really wants to look after himself during his prison term.' Seven months later, this assessment was changed.

High risk exists. [DJ] has been reported for unauthorized possession of articles, such as the blade of a scalpel and a sharpened screwdriver.

However, the motivation also pointed to the fact that 'he has committed crimes of a serious nature during previous prison terms'. The fact that DJ had reoffended in the course of previous stays in prison was nothing new. It had earlier been downplayed, but was now assigned importance in the face of the new reports of misconduct that had surfaced. So, indicators of a changed risk level may be combined with selected elements from the individual's history and with current circumstances to construct a narrative of the inmate who is making progress, or alternatively, a narrative of the inmate who is unchanged or worsening and still constitutes a substantial risk.

There are two fundamentally different strategies in operation in the prison service. One is productive and the other is repressive. In terms of organizational practice, the two strategies tend to operate within and beyond the prison service on almost entirely separate tracks. It is not just the targets or the preferred means of intervention that are different; the underlying visions, the organizational routines and the auditing system unfold along different tracks. But there are points of intersection and areas of conflict. In individual cases, or in terms of resource allocation, it is sometimes necessary to choose between order maintenance and rehabilitation. A transfer to more open conditions that is motivated in terms of rehabilitation may not be compatible with the assessed risk of disorder. In such cases, security concerns generally override other concerns. All change towards more favourable conditions depends on the outcome of an assessment of the risk for future misconduct. As is apparent in the rules that regulate the conditions of incarceration, security is the number one priority. The Swedish prison service is not unique in this respect. As Susan Clark Craig has observed: 'traditionally, the organizational effectiveness of prisons has been seen in terms of control, rather than rehabilitation, of inmates' (Clark Craig 2004: 92). However, interests of rehabilitation may be reformulated into considerations of risk. As evidenced in the sentence plans, the disorder strategy has absorbed elements from the cognitive-behavioural approach. The criminogenic needs are transformed into indicators of a changed risk of disorder, motivating a corresponding change in the conditions for the individual inmate. Observations formulated in the risk language of the rehabilitation strategy can be translated into the terms that govern the disorder strategy, and may thereby potentially trump the collective threats and historical risk factors. In this way, when decisions on adjustments of the conditions of incarceration are made, there is a selective appropriation of elements from the rehabilitation strategy.

C
Staying on target

Behind every restriction there is a decision. Behind every decision there is a risk assessment. Behind every risk assessment there is a selection of targets. Thus, ensuring that the deployment of conditions of incarceration stays on target is the same as making sure that the decisions made by members of the organization comply with the procedure for risk assessment. The decisions are taken both at the central level and at the local level. Decisions on institutional placement, the general level of physical control and longer periods outside the prison are made at the central administration whereas decisions on specific control measures and shorter periods outside the prison are made at the local prison. As decision-makers, the prison staff are integrated in the governance of the risks of disorder through a process that, first, regulates the decision-making relating to the conditions of incarceration in detail; second, makes the information on which the decision-making is based visible for inspection; and third, monitors that the decision-making complies to the detailed regulation. The governance targets the members of the organization, regardless of their position within it, above all as individuals. The performance of the organization itself is not continuously monitored. Instead, the management of disorder is subject to sporadic questioning from positions external to the strategy.

Monitoring the compliance of decisions

The legal grounds for subjecting inmates to differential restrictions and controls are provided by the Prison Treatment Act and the implementation regulations issued by the head office. The latter, in particular, closely regulates decision-making relating to the conditions of incarceration. Since the risk assessment is absolutely central, the regulation focuses on how it should be done. As can be expected (given the policy-level threat assessments and the traditional notions of security risks), drugs, personality disorder, prison gangs, sentence length, previous criminal record, frequency of reoffending and the inmate's history of misconduct are repeatedly stressed in the administrative directives regulating each type of decision along the spectrum associated with the conditions of incarceration: institutional placement, furloughs and all other periods outside prison.

The wording differs slightly, but the risk of order disturbance is always articulated in terms of drugs, organized crime and mental disorders. The following instruction is given to the official who is to make the choice between placements in open or closed prison wings. The assessment should take 'all the relevant facts' into consideration. After the initial, rather general formulations, the instructions become more specific. Placement in a closed prison wing in particular:

> concerns offenders who *might be suspected of abusing or handling narcotics* during the prison term, who may be assumed likely to escape from an open prison wing, or who could not be prevented from reoffending during a stay in an open prison wing. The offender *may be difficult to manage because of a mental disorder* or prone to violence and making threats. He *may have connections in the criminal sphere* which necessitate the

resources of a closed prison wing to prevent him from organizing criminal activity from within the prison.

(KVVFS 2004b: 7; emphasis added)

Similar formulations recur in the instructions written for prison officers responsible for making risk-based decisions on a daily basis. For instance, standard furloughs should be granted 'in spite of the general risk of misconduct which may always be presumed to exist'. After the enumeration of nine different risk factors, the following advice is given to officials who determine whether a prisoner should be granted a short-term furlough. It is not necessary to consult the sentence plan or the placement form: checking the inmate's conviction record is sufficient. 'Certain types of criminality' are taken to imply 'a significant risk' for continued criminal activity or 'a considerable risk' for misconduct. These are, once again, the security threats 'related primarily to *organized* or systematic *criminality*, but also to serious violent offences, in particular if these have been committed by alcohol- or *drug-abusers* or individuals with *mental disorders*' (KVVFS 2005: 34–35; emphasis added). In addition, the traditional indicators of risk of disorder, such as sentence length, previous criminal record, frequency of reoffending and the inmate's history of misconduct within the prison system, are frequently mentioned in the administrative directives. The historical indicators are not stressed as much as the recently found threats, but their weight needs to be considered nonetheless.

The increasing regulation of the decision-making procedure is accompanied by routines for documentation. Decisions on institutional placement, physical control and all periods outside prison are documented in written form. Minimum documentation consists of the decision itself, the grounds for the decision and the prison officer responsible. This information is open for inspection retrospectively. The information contained in the documented decisions, along with the information on the individual inmate drawn from other sources such as the sentence plan or reports on misconduct, makes it possible to reconstruct the risk assessment afterwards: the way different factors have been – and, equally important: should have been – weighed against each other. The organization has been made thoroughly auditable in this respect. It is possible to uncover the grounds and to identify the individual behind each decision. The large amount of information available on every inmate, in combination with the requirement that every decision must be signed by an individual officer, makes the decision-making auditable at the level of individuals.

The individual officers are caught in a transparency of a disciplinary type (Grossman *et al.* 2008). As their decision-making is made visible, it can be questioned. The systematic documentation of decisions in conjunction with the detailed directives for decision-making makes it possible to detect employee non-compliance. Non-compliance means that the risk has not been assessed in accordance with the guidelines and that relevant factors have not been taken into consideration. As a consequence, the risk is either underestimated or overestimated. Underestimating the risk posed by the individual is the more problematic when the prison service monitors the management of the risk of disorder. The monitoring is carried out on the assumption that staff deviance – an overly lenient interpretation of existing rules – will increase the frequency of order disturbances. There is also a concern for major order disturbances as a result of one individual error or a high frequency of order disturbances. The monitoring is internal in the sense that it never transcends the strategy and merely studies the application of force relative to the existing framework of rules. Whether the correct application of the rules actually reduces the level of order disturbances is not known, nor relevant, since there are no follow-up routines in place that could provide this information. It is, moreover, internal in the sense that it is almost exclusively performed by the prison service itself.

Minor, everyday deviations are recorded in a follow-up system organized around so-called quality councils. Quality councils take the form of a review of the implementation of coercive measures such as cell inspections, urine screens and decisions on furloughs, segregation and the postponement of release dates. The review culminates in a meeting between the local prison administration and lawyers from the head office. The lawyers will have examined the statistics prior to the meeting. Extraordinary figures, such as a high number of furloughs by comparison with other prisons, will alert interest. The lawyers may then proceed to investigate the files on individual inmates, looking for discrepancies between the regulations and the decisions taken by individual members of staff, as documented in the files. The results are presented at the meeting. Although, in theory, both an overly harsh and an overly lax implementation of the regulations can constitute grounds for criticism, the system of quality councils appears to be geared towards encouraging a stricter implementation of regulations. One prison, for example, which stood out in terms of granting a large number of furloughs, was criticized for:

> an overly broad interpretation of what may be considered reasons for granting special furloughs; for example, the meeting of writers, the end of term at a daughter's school, the completion of Ramadan, an early Christmas-morning service, and the purchase of food for the self-management program.
>
> (KV 2005c: 1)

Another prison was found wanting in terms of routines concerning reports on misconduct. The examining lawyer observed that late arrivals at the prison, following a period of furlough, were not always followed by reports on misconduct. The neglect to file such reports deviated from existing regulations (KV 2005d). Underreporting misconduct meant that actual order disturbances went undetected and, by implication, that any alterations of the restrictions on individuals, presumably necessary for preventing further order disturbances, could not be carried out.

The quality council covers the performance of the entire prison, yet the criticism may be broken down to focus on individuals. Individual prison officers can be held accountable for decisions based on a risk assessment. The decision is reprehensible not because of the way things turned out but because of the way the risk assessment was performed. An inmate may commit a serious crime during a furlough and the decision may still be correct. But there is a tendency for employees of the prison service to start managing the risks to themselves, rather than the risks perceived by the organization. This type of internal control system easily translates into 'an individualisation process which is driving risk experts and professionals to focus more on their personal, legal and reputational risks, rather than on the primary risks embodied in their formal mission' (Power 2004: 15). The monitoring of the management of the risk of disorder gives rise to a secondary risk management conducted by those who are exposed to the monitoring. The net effect of that risk management could be defensive adherence to procedure. At the same time, there is a residual space for employee discretion. The regulation does not reach every decision. As the above discussion shows, the reassessment of the risk of disorder, motivating a change in the conditions of incarceration, is incompletely regulated, and allows a wide variety of information to be considered. The employee can escape blame by constructing a narrative around the available indicators which justifies the decision made.

If the decision-making of individual members is closely monitored, there are no equivalent routines ensuring that the organization itself is on target. Within the strategy, no other institutional actor continuously audits the risk management of disorder carried out by the prison service. To a significant extent it is a closed system: identifying traces of the selected threats; elaborating a detailed set of rules regulating their management; applying more or less restrictive interventions on the basis of the combined knowledge of risks and rules; and monitoring the compliance of the staff – all is done by the prison service. The National Audit Office and the Agency for Public Management have attempted to audit the performance of the prison service in terms of maintaining order. But the audit organizations could not obtain sufficient information to assess the efficiency of repressive interventions. The performance targets related to order disturbances were found to be partial; there was no information on the economic cost of the security measures; and the impact of repression in relation to other goals of the prison service, such as rehabilitation, could not be estimated (RRV 1999b; Statskontoret 2003). So far, it has proved impossible to make the repressive performance of the prison service auditable in terms of efficiency. In addition, no state agency has been entrusted with the task to do so on a continuous basis. Without precise standards, relevant information and designated actors, there is little hope of effective monitoring.

The absence of external monitoring bodies does not mean that the performance of the prison service never becomes subject to inspection. In particular, the concern for negative media coverage serves as a mechanism to ensure that the prison service is on target. Most order disturbances and regular staff noncompliance fall below the radar. Yet the fraction of all order disturbances that reach the mainstream media affects the risk management of disorder within the organization. In Sweden, as in many other countries, prison *dis*order is immediately political. The extraordinary eruptions – riots, strikes, escapes and homicides – that occurred during the period examined in this study were followed up beyond the prison service, by the media and political representatives. Government commissions were appointed; after the prison riot in the maximum-security facility at Tidaholm in 1994 – when around 100 prisoners managed to gain control over large parts of the prison and burnt two buildings to the ground – and also after the prison breaks from four other high-security facilities ten years later (JuDep 1994; SOU 2005b). These incidents were portrayed and discussed at length in the media, and their political relevance was immediate. Following the prison breaks in 2004, for instance, the leader of the conservative party demanded the resignation of the social democratic Minister of Justice, who managed to stay in office; however, the director-general of the prison service was discharged. The influential players in the public debate did not necessarily express their concerns in the strategy-specific risk language, and some of them may have had an agenda that stretched well beyond a concern for prison order. The heated debate nevertheless contributed both to the exposure of deviations from the existing routines and to changes in these routines. Public inquiries, along with investigative journalists and news reporters, operate as a secondary follow-up system, ensuring that major order disturbances and their management will be closely examined. Ultimately, someone may be held responsible. Robert Keohane calls this 'external accountability'. The organization is not held accountable to the government that has delegated power to it, but to those who are affected by its performance (Keohane 2006). Through the media coverage of major order disturbances many actors perceive themselves to be affected by the operation of the prison service, which is held accountable to actors that are not part of the strategy.

Conclusions

What directs the use of power?

The strategy embodies a specific set of goals, visions, risks, routines and preferred means of intervention. The goal is to maintain institutional order, conceptualized as the non-violation of prison rules. The strategy is built around a vision of safe containment. The means of intervention are found in the design of the conditions of incarceration for individuals. The routines involve the placement organization, urine screens, the security register, the central intake unit, the quality councils, the sentence plan, the placement form, and so on. However, given this organizational infrastructure and the overall goal, what directs the use of power? The question concerns both the intra-organizational power and the power exercised towards the target group.

This chapter has tried to show that – and how – considerations of risk direct the exercise of power at each stage of the strategy. First of all, the risk of disorder is used to *set the target*, and to direct the actions of organizational members towards the target. The targets for repression are derived from an analysis according to which drug users, personality-disordered inmates and prison gangs threaten institutional order. The policy-level threat assessments are successively broken down – into special indicators of risk; into directives regulating furloughs, into guidelines regarding prison placements, into control tactics, and into the layout of the forms that circulate the information on individual inmates. The more traditional historical risk factors are not summarized into collective entities. Yet information on type of crime, sentence length, frequency of reoffending and misconduct during previous prison terms is nevertheless firmly ingrained in the strategy, operationalized in directives, tactics and forms, and attributed to individuals, who become targets for interventions.

Further, the risk of disorder directs the *targeting* at the level of individuals. On the one hand, there is a spectrum of conditions of incarceration; on the other, there are a large number of inmates. In addition, security objectives have to be balanced against countervailing considerations. Under these circumstances, risk is what makes the matching as well as the balancing possible at the level of individuals. Information on drug use and sentence length, on programme participation and institutional misconduct is translated into risk of disorder and guides the decision-making on institutional placement, level of control and other restrictions. As long as there is a traceable connection to the strategy-specific risk, all sorts of information can be used by the staff to justify a particular decision. For this reason, if reformulated into considerations of risk of disorder, information on the process of rehabilitation may also direct repressive interventions.

Lastly, the risk of disorder directs the efforts to *stay on target*. It is instrumental in controlling whether the actions of organizational members are linked to the target. Under conditions of vague performance targets, contradictory goals and uncertain outcomes, the risk of disorder has been made into something that is precisely regulated and communicated within the organization. As such, it makes organizational performance transparent down to the level of individual members. Through the existing routines for documentation and communication it is possible to follow traces of risk, on the one hand, and decisions on restrictions, on the other, in individual cases. The performance of the prison staff in this respect has been transformed into a matter of rule compliance, as indicators of risk are transformed into directives for decision-making. Deviance from the tightly regulated assessment procedure substantiating a decision can be exposed through a scrutiny of the documentation of risk-related information. The management of risk is followed up through all levels of the organization, by the quality councils examining the routines of local prison management, by internal investigations following special incidents, by statistical routines on disciplinary offences, and by periodic auditing by other state bodies. In this way, the performance of individual members is first made visible for inspection, and then evaluated in terms of rule compliance by means of the risk of disorder. The performance of the organization itself is simultaneously evaluated. The same follow-up practices circulate information on organizational performance and allow for changes in routines, in the allocation of resources and in the choice of tactics, changes that appear rational, or motivated, as they are linked to organizational goals through the risk of disorder.

Consequently, what directs the power is the same, irrespective of whether it is being exercised within the organization or in relation to the target group. The second-order control that structures the behaviour of individual members to make the first-order control possible, as well as the first-order control of individual inmates, is directed by the risk of disorder. The conditions of incarceration are shaped by communicating the risk of disorder; and the organization is governed by communicating the same risk. The intra-organizational power and the restrictions vis-à-vis the target group are thus guided by the very same, although the nature of the power is fundamentally different. While the monitoring of employees is disciplinary, and hence an instance of productive power, the conditions of incarceration are repressive.

Risk superimposed on law

The interventions towards individuals of the target group are repressive. According to Foucault, repressive power can be characterized by the assumptions (R1–R4) in the introductory chapter. The deployment of the conditions of incarceration matches the last three assumptions, whereas the first one – that the fundamental operation of power is to dictate laws – has to be modified following the analysis in this chapter.

The repression is mediated through conscious decisions (R2). The prison staff decide on the restrictions; and the decision presupposes an interpretation of prison regulation, of available options and of the information on the individual. The conditions of incarceration are not automatically applied. Further, the effect is either obedience or disobedience (R4). The ultimate aim is prison order itself – a passive obedience to prison rules. If the interventions are successful, the threats confronting the institutional order, which are seen to emanate from the inmates, will be deflected; conversely, failure will provoke order disturbances. The means and ends are firmly negative (R3). The preferred means of intervention – the conditions of incarceration – serve to maintain order, negatively, by preventing unwanted behaviour on the part of the inmates. As such, they are destructive, immediately removing the ability to act in certain ways, violating the private sphere, or frustrating the preferences of the individual. Actions are not produced, only prevented. The disorder strategy is thoroughly unproductive in relation to the target group. It strictly prevents some acts without directing the behaviour in alternative directions. In particular, the use of force is unrelated to the constitution of wage labour. Even if successful, the obedience that is being produced – compliance to prison rules – is not what is demanded on the labour market. A clean prison record does not imply employability. In line with Marxist state theory, repression within the prison has no economic function in terms of shaping the behaviour necessary for the reproduction of the capital relation.

In all these respects the disorder strategy constitutes a typical example of the repressive exercise of power. But the element of risk calls into question the legal paradigm of repressive power (R1). The legal framework in the prison service divides the actions of the target group into two categories: forbidden and allowed. Order disturbances are forbidden and everything else is allowed. In this sense, the announcement of the law *is* fundamental; it provides the platform for all further exercise of power. The law is the first operation and the final goal. Yet in neither capacity does it provide much guidance. The forbidden acts have not yet occurred and cannot be sanctioned. Instead, risk rather than law directs the use of force at the level of individuals. The conditions of incarceration are not based on a rule violation but on a risk assessment. The conditions are determined by the information available on the individual, as transmitted through risk communication routines of interlinked organizational units. The detected rule violations, on the other hand, activate a different type of repression, built around a separate sanctioning system involving postponements of the release date. This is a supplementary repression that corresponds to the legal paradigm. From the point of view of targets, risk is superimposed on a legal framework that cannot direct interventions. The overall goal of institutional order is conceptualized in legal terms as non-violation of the criminal law or of the rules specific to the institution. But this order cannot be a target of interventions precisely because it is an absence – an absence of transgressions. Instead, repression is directed towards bundles of risk indicators, derived from the analysed threats to institutional order. Risk thus links institutional order to the material targets for intervention.

The proposition that law provides the model for understanding repression must be relativized. Within this particular strategy, repression must be analysed as risk-based. It finds support in the law but is immediately based on risk. This has two important implications for the deployment of interventions: interventions are continuous and based on an appreciation of the individual. When law is the organizing principle, the interventions are dichotomous, and only actualized by rule violations. This creates a space which repressive power cannot reach. The law works as the external boundary for behaviour, and the individuals in the target group are left to their own devices as long as they do not cross the line of the permitted. When risk is the organizing principle, however, the interventions are continuous rather than dichotomous. All individuals in the target group are distributed along a continuum in terms of the relative degree of risk. There is no measure of freedom in Foucault's sense. Every position in the continuum corresponds to a level of coercion. The position depends on an appreciation of the individual based on all documented acts and circumstances, rather than on any one of a series of forbidden acts. Repression is thus relative to conlcusions about who the individuals are.

Chapter 4

Generalized control

Negotiating contradictory expectations through risk

The monitoring of airline passengers comprises an intrinsic part of the practical procedures involved in a border crossing. The process starts with the purchase of the airline ticket; the credit card payment involves monitoring, as does the check-in control of travel documents, passing through the detectors at the security control, the closed-circuit television surveillance in baggage handling areas, passport control, and walking through the customs zone. The traveller depends on having authorized access all the way. The screening process involves several state organizations, including the customs service and the police, as well as the data collection of private companies. The activities are linked to one another and form a 'surveillant assemblage', which 'relies on machines to make and record discrete observations' (Haggerty and Ericson 2000: 612). The relevant information is managed automatically, or semi-automatically. Although omnipresent, the control is unobtrusive. Most airline passengers will have no direct personal experience of it, except for the manual security checks at the airport. In all these respects, the power exercised towards airline passengers conforms to the control society model suggested by Gilles Deleuze (Deleuze 1990).

So far in this book, the theme has been the way power is exercised in the disciplinary society: towards individuals enrolled within institutions, on the presumption of social exclusion. In this chapter, I will change focus and look at how power is exercised in the control society: outside institutions, on the presumption of social inclusion. The programmatic attempts to shape the behaviour of airline passengers do not find support in the mechanism of enrolment that characterize the disciplinary society. The travellers are customers or citizens with a temporary relation to the controlling organizations. It is a generalized control, without a particular target group in social terms. Unlike the activity of the prison service and the public employment service, the monitoring is not directed at the socially excluded. The power belongs to the spheres of social inclusion; it is exercised on the presumption that the behaviour of those who are targeted does not need to be closely regulated or fundamentally changed. However, although airline passengers are part of the inclusive control society, where power is automatic, generalized and unobtrusive, the use of force is by no means excluded. On the contrary, the control of the control society may also be physical and repressive.

At the border, the customs service has wide-ranging coercive powers. Despite recurrent fears of an imminent loss of control over national borders, the Swedish border control agencies have in practice maintained their powers to monitor and control over the last decade. Upon joining the European Union in 1995, the sovereign nature of border control seemed to stand in opposition to the principle of the free movement of people and goods between member states. The border controls of one state could be seen as constituting a concealed restriction on the trade of other states. For this reason, a government inquiry proposed that there had to be some material circumstance that led the customs inspector to search the baggage or vehicle – the opinion or intuition of the inspector was not sufficient in itself (SOU 1994). Although the suggested degree of suspicion was the lowest possible in legal terms, the government rejected this regulation and established that 'an object can be singled out for control without there being any suspicion of a particular smuggling offence' (Proposition 1995/96: 57). As a consequence, basically no restrictions were introduced on the way the customs inspectors reach their decision to select an object for control. The law regulating the powers of the customs service to carry out controls states only that controls should not be conducted randomly (SFS 1996). The opposite of random controls are selective controls, which the customs service explains by enumerating all the possible ways in which a customs inspector may reach a decision. The controlled individual may have been identified through 'intelligence information', 'the knowledge, experience [or] intuition of the customs inspector', a 'drug sniffer-dog' or a 'risk profile' (TU 2003a: 79). It is hard to imagine a potentially questionable control selection that cannot be justified on one or more of these grounds, with reference to intelligence information, risk profiles, experience or intuition. Moreover, the customs inspectors do not have to mention any grounds for the decision to control. An inspector may ask a border-crosser to open up their baggage and then look inside for contraband such as drugs, weapons, alcohol, tobacco or child pornography, without having to specify the grounds for the decision.

The power to search is not limited to baggage and means of transport. A customs inspector also has wide-ranging discretion to examine the clothes, the body and certain body fluids of those crossing the border. Body searches require some degree of suspicion, since there must be 'reasons to assume' that the person is carrying contraband. Yet, in practice, this condition is easily fulfilled. Decisions as to which reasons qualify as 'reasons to assume' are left to the individual customs inspector. In a ruling from the Ombudsman of Justice dating from 1986, following a complaint made by a man and a woman who had been strip-searched in Lund, it was stated that the opinion of one customs inspector – that the couple seemed nervous – was to be considered as sufficient grounds for control (JO 1987). This interpretation was confirmed in another ruling from the Ombudsman of Justice, following a complaint from a man in Gothenburg in 1995. According to this ruling, a customs inspector's subjective judgement that a traveller 'looks nervous' may constitute sufficient grounds for a decision to search an individual's clothing or to carry out a strip-search (JO 1995: 3).

Since defining the precise meaning of 'selective control' is left to the individual inspector, anyone may be controlled on a wide variety of grounds. Based on no more than a hunch on the part of the customs inspector, a border-crosser may be subjected to controls ranging from a baggage search to a strip-search and urine testing. The requirement of 'reasons to assume' does not restrict the use of force in practice. Just as Sophie Hydén and Anna Lundberg said about the practice of the police to stop and control an individual's identity and residence permit inside the country: 'anything, alternatively nothing at all' can be vindicated as a reason for conducting a control (Hydén and Lundberg 2004: 94). Yet the use of coercion *is* restricted, since only a small proportion of all border-crossers are subjected to physical control. In the year 2003, of a total of approximately 59 million border-crossers, only 125,000 individuals were singled out for customs control (TU 2004b: 17). Thus, on average only one of every 500 border-crossers is singled out. Considerations of risk determine who will be subject to control. Every inspector determines whether to control this passenger or that passenger, based on an assessment of the likelihood that the passenger is carrying contraband. This assessment is a risk assessment. Hence, *some* notion of risk will inevitably guide the individual customs inspector at the gate when deciding to conduct, or refrain from conducting, a control. The question is that of what form this notion might take.

Reducing illegal trade is a primary goal in the customs service. Yet the control activities must be balanced against the principle of non-interference in the regular flow of goods and passengers across the border. In the section on target-setting, I will show that this conflict is resolved through the goal of fewer and more accurate controls. This is followed by an analysis of the control selection at the level of individuals, focusing on the range of possible indicators of risk, which is limited by poor information but, lately, has been extended through the use of set profiles in relation to the booking information compiled by private transportation companies. As a consequence, the controlled individual is reduced to an impersonal bundle of risk indicators. To ensure that the customs service stays on target, the documented input and output of the control activity is evaluated by other state organizations in terms of efficiency. All aspects of the organization are made responsive to the same considerations of risk as those that guide the selection of objects. In drawing conclusions, I will discuss the legal paradigm of repressive power from the point of view of the marginal role played by conscious decisions (R2), both on the part of those who exercise power and on the part of those over whom power is exercised. I will also once more pick up the theme of risk governance, this time not simply to claim that risk directs the activity throughout the customs service. Risk, moreover, works as a common language through which different and contradictory expectations are brokered within the organization.

A
Setting the target

For something to be visible – and manageable – as a risk in the customs service, it has to resonate with the control routines of the service. This is a necessary but not sufficient precondition, necessary since trafficking and refugee smuggling, for example, are ruled out on formal grounds. The customs service is only allowed to control individuals in search of goods; powers relating to the control of individuals as individuals – their identity, right to stay in the country, and so on – remain in the hands of the police. But it is not a sufficient precondition, since the trade in rare animals and plants, for example, is perfectly commensurate with the customs service's control routines, without these being considered high-risk commodities. The selected risks are those that resonate with the control routines of the customs service as well as with dominant security concerns beyond the customs service, such as political agendas on drugs and corporate interests in intellectual property rights. During the period examined, drugs, alcohol, cigarettes and pirate copies satisfied both conditions.

High-risk commodities

Around 50 products are associated with import and export restrictions, violations of which are criminalized. However, not all restrictions are enforced with the same determination; some commodities are searched for much more intensely than others. The prioritization is justified in terms of risk: the most wanted commodities are seen as high risk while the neglected commodities are perceived as low risk. Since the end of the 1990s, attempts have been made to assess respective risks in terms of the harmfulness of the different commodities and the extent of the trade in a given commodity. The concept of 'benefit to society' was introduced to make the efforts of the customs service calculable in terms of the harm the seized products would have caused to 'society' had they not been seized. This counterfactual harm was operationalized in economic terms; for example, every gram of heroin seized had a postulated value of 3,000 SEK. This amount was thought to be on a par with the negative economic consequences of heroin use, which would have had to be covered primarily by public sector actors (SOU 1998). The concept of 'benefit to society' was developed into a full-scale risk classification model, when penal value was added as a factor in the equation, along with a conception of the level of trade that could be tolerated. In theory, and using heroin as the standard, it was made possible to risk-classify all prohibited commodities (TU 2004a).

The risk classification model aspires to produce an unprejudiced evaluation of the magnitude and the probability of the threat. Nothing but the inherent harm and the estimated prevalence of the product is taken into consideration. Yet the model presupposes a prior selection of risks. There is very limited information on some of the prohibited commodities, precisely because they are not considered to be risks in the first place – resulting in few controls, few seizures and hence little knowledge. To take one example, the customs service suspects that the Convention on International Trade in Endangered Species of Wild Fauna and Flora is repeatedly being violated, but finds the quantities of the trade 'hard to estimate' (TU 2004a: 18). Similarly, the illegal trade in ecologically harmful waste and pharmaceuticals has not been classified in terms of risk because of lack of knowledge within the organization. In fact, because of insufficient information, only a minority of prohibited commodities are risk-classified *at all*. On the other hand, there is an overwhelming amount of knowledge on the risk-classified commodities, above all drugs, since they have been prioritized – and seized – for many years. Any attempt to analyse the risk level in terms of the estimated prevalence of certain commodities will necessarily have a circular character, since it will inevitably be affected by the same control priorities that it seeks to guide.

The control priorities are politically determined. The annual government instruction provides a general, but at the same time unambiguous, description of the framework within which risks have to be understood by the customs service. Drugs are to be given 'the highest priority' (Regeringen 2003c: 2–3). The customs service has been characterized as 'a leading element in the coalition of forces against drugs being built up in society' (SOU 1998: 13). Its particular contribution consists in preventing narcotic drugs from entering the country, thereby reducing the supply on the Swedish market. The long-standing predominance of drugs is reflected in the number of pages and the level of detail devoted to the description of the trade in each and every criminalized narcotic substance in the customs service's national threat assessment. In the threat assessment published in 2004, 119 of 320 pages are devoted to an in-depth description of the trade in narcotic drugs. There is little need to dramatize the risk by elaborating on the harmful consequences of the illegal drug trade. The high-risk label assigned to drugs is firmly institutionalized. It is enough simply to mention the number of seizures, the smuggling networks actually detected and their modus operandi.

If drugs are the number one enemy, alcohol and tobacco are next in line. Illegal imports of alcohol and cigarettes are to be given 'high priority' according to the government instructions (Regeringen 2003c: 3). As with drugs, there is a close correspondence between the government agenda and long-standing customs' control routines. The detailed knowledge of the illegal trade in alcohol and cigarettes, as displayed in the threat assessments, indicates an extensive control practice. But unlike drugs, the amount of resources devoted to the control of illegally imported alcohol and tobacco has also been questioned within government. One public inquiry suggested that a lowering of tax duties would be more effective than control measures as a means of reducing the illegal trade in alcohol (SOU 2004). If the tax were lowered, the trade would become less profitable, making control measures redundant. However, during the period examined, the traditional selection – first drugs, then alcohol and tobacco – was still in effect.

An important change is the emergence of organized crime as a risk in itself, as distinct from individual acts of smuggling. Increasingly, the customs service has come to focus on the business structures involved in smuggling. The reorientation was operationalized in the form of a special performance indicator called 'A-matters'. A-matters comprise very big seizures, for instance over 0.5 kg of heroin or more than 100,000 cigarettes (TU 2003a). The shift of focus towards larger seizures and the underlying business structures is reflected in the statistics. In the early years of the 2000s, the number of drug seizures dropped significantly at the same time as there was an increase in the total amount of drugs seized (TU 2004c). The tactics employed build on an understanding of organized crime which resembles the spectrum-based theory of enterprise formulated by Dwight Smith in the 1970s. Smith claimed that criminal organizations and regular corporations operate on the same principles along a 'spectrum of legitimacy' (Smith 1980). Organized crime is an economic activity that obeys the laws of the market, although located at the illegitimate end.

This interpretation is consistent with the official EU definition, adopted by the Swedish customs service, according to which organized crime comprises business associations involved in extra-legal activities. The threat assessments issued from head office describe extensive similarities between organized crime and regular corporations. The business associations engaged in smuggling are seen to be 'run along the same lines as legal companies' (TU 2003a: 109). Specifically, they need to 'enter into contracts, find markets, purchase transportation services and other services, and reinvest their capital in the same way as legal companies' (TU 2004a: 273). And the basic operation involves exploiting business opportunities. The overriding drive is to make money, in much the same way as for the shareholders of a regular company: 'the goal of the members of these groups and crime organizations is primarily that of attaining the maximum amount of economic gain' (TU 2003a: 92). Moreover, illegal business organizations strive to make well-informed decisions concerning potential economic losses. Every shipment is an investment, and as the future gain of an investment is uncertain, risk assessments are necessary. The analysts at the head office see their own function mirrored in their opponent: 'organized crime makes constant "threat assessments" about the Swedish customs service's level of presence and ability to conduct controls' (ibid.: 4).

In themselves, the analysed similarities between illegal and legal trade are of major importance for the customs service, since its task is to do the very opposite – to distinguish between legal and illegal trade. But they are interesting also from another point of view. Ironically, the similarities and the many interconnections with legal trade become an argument for the urgency of disrupting illegal business associations. All the resemblances make organized crime appear more ominous – more calculating and harder to detect. Ordinary companies can hide illegal business organizations. Organized criminal networks are involved in a wide range of business activities at both ends of the spectrum of legitimacy: smuggling and extortion as well as legal trade. At the time of the EU enlargement in 2004, this was perceived primarily as a foreign threat. Criminal organizations based in Poland, the Baltic States and Russia, thought to operate relatively freely because of widespread corruption and insufficient state control, are, according to the customs service, about to diversify, spread and increase their activities over and across the Swedish border. This involves a substantial up-grading of the risk level that is attributable not so much to the increased possibility of large-scale trade in contraband, of which there are few direct indications, but more to the nature of the threat (TU 2003a, 2004a).

Organized crime is at times framed as an existential threat. The networks are conceived to have the capacity to subvert the criminal justice system through a combination of threats and corruption. As an antagonistic enemy that endangers core state functions, organized crime fulfils the government criteria to be managed within the domain of national security (Proposition 1998/99; J. Eriksson 2004). Consequently, a process of securitization is under way which, if successful, will extend the range of options available for dealing with events and individuals associated with organized crime, eventually 'claiming a right to use whatever means are necessary to block a threatening development' (Buzan *et al.* 1998: 21). Securitization implies a reliance on the use of force with the aim of excluding, dispersing and exterminating the existential threat. The tendency to consider organized crime as an existential threat not only extends the range of repressive options but also affects the process of risk selection.

The well-established connections to organized crime keep alcohol and tobacco high on the customs agenda, despite public tolerance manifested in the widespread consumption of illegally imported alcohol and cigarettes. And when it comes to establishing new risks, such as intellectual property infringements, the links to a securitized phenomenon are decisive. Anything which can be shown to be connected to organized crime will almost automatically be selected as a risk. At the turn of the millennium, following initiatives from concerned multinational corporations as well as EU-level working groups on counterfeiting, violations of intellectual property rights came to be elevated to the high-risk category. The customs service described the trade in pirate copies as 'a global problem which is no longer only about money but primarily about security, life, and health', said to cause an annual loss of 200,000 jobs within the European Union (TU 2001, 2002: 44). The vivid depiction of the threat is typical for risks which are not yet firmly institutionalized as such (J. Eriksson 2004). At the same time, there is nothing particular about the imported commodities themselves. In 2002, the seized products included above all clothes and cellular phone shells. A large number of toys, wallets, handbags and perfumes were also confiscated (TU 2002). Hence, the trade in pirate copies illustrates the double challenge of organized crime. While being a security threat, the business is virtually indistinguishable from legitimate economic activities. This particular trade, which is part of something that should be facilitated, namely foreign trade, should be disrupted. The customs service must do both; stop the trade in pirate copies without stopping foreign trade in general.

Balancing behind a veil of ignorance

The practical task for the customs service is to reduce the trade in drugs and other prioritized contraband. However, the customs service does not conduct controls of all shipments and passengers entering and leaving the country in order to inflict the maximum possible damage on illegal trade. There is a range of other considerations to be made as well. Combating drugs and organized crime is not the only goal. As Katja Franko Aas has noted, 'contemporary governments seem to be caught between two contradicting impulses: on the one hand, the urge towards increasing securitization of borders, and on the other hand, the awareness of global flows for sustaining the present world economic order' (Franko Aas 2005: 199). There is an inherent conflict between the control activity of the state, which by its very nature impedes trade, and the export- and import-oriented industries that depend on fast transports across borders. This is a delicate problem, which gives rise to a dilemma for the customs service.

On its own terms, the customs service states its mission in the following way:

> We shall offer flexible customs routines within the rules of foreign trade, an easy border crossing for travellers and an efficient border protection.
>
> (TU 2004c: 4)

The use of words like 'flexible', 'easy' and 'efficient' reflects the contradictory nature of the mission. The customs service is responsible for *all* goods entering and leaving the country. Organizationally, it is split into one section dealing with legal trade and another dealing with illegal trade. This corresponds to a double task: collecting taxes on legal trade and preventing illegal trade. Both tasks are carried out simultaneously, in a manner which is supposed to interfere as little as possible with legal trade and as much as possible with illegal trade. The customs service is to facilitate one type of trade while disrupting another. The two goals are not necessarily compatible, since legal and illegal trade are intertwined in practice and distinguishable only at the juridical level. Every train, plane, truck or ferry may carry legal as well as illegal commodities. Indeed, any means of transport might be involved simultaneously in both legal and illegal trade. Moreover, the import or export of *legal* commodities might also be illegal. Under certain circumstances, presenting false information when declaring goods – or not declaring them at all – is a crime. This is considered to be a major threat in itself, since companies that provide false information concerning the value of declared goods inflict a substantial economic loss on the state (TU 2004a).

The conflict between the control activity of the state and the export and import of private industries is also manifested in the existing performance indicators, which are fraught with contradictory expectations. The performance indicator 'benefit to society' was introduced with reference to the needs of the public and the corporate world. Business and the population at large were conceived to 'demand not only a simple and efficient treatment of all honest companies and passengers, but also an efficient selection of those who cheat' (SOU 1998: 135). But, here, the adjective 'efficient' is used in two opposite senses – 'efficient treatment' means 'no control' whereas 'efficient selection' means 'control'. This underlines the contradictory mission of the customs service. Business interests push towards less control while security concerns push towards greater control. And efficiency considerations mean that the front-line employees have to control *less and more at the same time* – singling out for control fewer 'honest companies and passengers' and more 'of those who cheat'.

The contradictory mission is also reflected in the 'hit percentage' target. Rather than simply demanding a high number of seizures, the government expects a high number of seizures in relation to the total number of controls. This translates into the performance indicator hit percentage, as the ratio between the number of seizures and the number of controls. The ratio should be as high as possible. A high hit percentage implies that few legal shipments are controlled, while many illegal shipments are controlled, or at least that many of the controlled shipments turn out to be illegal. The very construction of the target involves a compromise between the respective interests of minimum interference in legal trade and maximum interference in illegal trade. Increased accuracy in combination with the noticeable trend towards a decreasing number of controls constitutes a way of simultaneously accommodating both free trade interests and security objectives (Regeringen 2003c; TU 2004c).

The contradictory expectations are resolved in the goal of making few but accurate selections. In practice, risk is the medium through which control selections are negotiated. Features of the trade are reformulated as indicators of risk. Assessments of what characterizes illegal trade and assessments of what constitutes legal trade are translated into a common risk continuum. Potentially all border-crossers are categorized with regard to the probability of being involved in, first and foremost, large-scale drug smuggling. The high-risk category is of special interest, since by definition this is where most seizures can be expected. But the low-risk categories are equally important. The goal of increased accuracy presupposes the existence of reliable indicators and detection routines regarding both high-risk and low-risk passengers. The entire focus is thereby shifted to the means by which the selection is made.

The ability to make risk assessments presupposes information. In the absence of information there is no possibility of calculating the risks. But the control activity is fundamentally structured by the opposite: lack of information. The only way to determine whether a shipment is illegal is to actually conduct controls. There are of course exceptions when intelligence information provides good reason to believe that a particular shipment is illegal. But in the overwhelming majority of cases, where qualified intelligence is lacking, there is no way of knowing before conducting a control. Thus, without knowing in advance which trade is legal and which is illegal, the customs service is confronted with the twin tasks of minimum interference in legal trade and maximum interference in illegal trade. To complicate things further, the available information on the individuals passing through customs is very limited, and little information is extracted from past seizures and transmitted within the organization.

There is basically only one way of knowing that a passenger is a courier, namely by performing a customs control, and this is exactly what the customs service has been doing throughout its history. If the couriers share any identifiable common characteristics, these will be the ones that have been detected in connection with past seizures and transmitted in the forms being used within the customs organization to report seizures. The collected knowledge is summarized in the national threat assessment, which depicts the typical courier, presented by type of contraband. Heroin smugglers are described in the following way: 'Two-thirds of them are men, and in the majority of cases they are Swedish citizens', and 'most of them were born in the 1970s' (TU 2004a: 194). Much the same is also said about the detected khat smugglers. 'The average khat-courier is a Swedish or Danish man around 30 years of age' (ibid.: 16). Amphetamine smugglers are slightly more multinational: 'Swedes, Poles, Lithuanians and Danes are the most common nationalities.' They were in their thirties and the male dominance was even more pronounced: 'only 10 per cent are women' (ibid.: 146). And again, regarding ecstasy, the couriers are 'primarily found in the category of young men' who are of 'predominantly Swedish nationality' (ibid.: 180–82).

The profiles of couriers are obviously very rudimentary. What can be said about the average drug smuggler, based on the information accumulated in the customs organization, seems to be the following: Swedish citizen, male and around 30 years old. Evidently this profile is of limited value in practice, as there are a lot of Swedish men in their thirties passing the border every day who are not couriers. Why is there no more detailed knowledge of couriers? The answer to that question is administrative. There are no routines for collecting more in-depth knowledge about the couriers that are detected. The current forms used for reporting seizures contain a series of questions regarding the goods found, the quantity, the means of transportation and where the goods were hidden. But as regards the person transporting the goods, age, sex and nationality constitute the only information that customs inspectors are requested to submit, and thus the only information that can be processed within the organization. Trying to construct a profile from only these three characteristics does not make sense. The customs service is at a loss for an answer to the question regarding who is a courier. Information on age, sex and nationality is far from enough to single out which passengers should be controlled.

The customs service is thus faced with two dilemmas. Without impeding the flow of legitimate commodities and passengers across the border, the customs service is expected to minimize the risk of individual acts of smuggling and disrupt the illegal business structure behind the drug trade. This dilemma is resolved in the goal of increased accuracy of controls. But an accurate control selection is undermined by lack of information to make risk assessments that score better than random controls. This is a second dilemma that fundamentally structures the control activity of the organization. What John Rawls said about 'the principles of justice', which are 'chosen behind a veil of ignorance' (Rawls 1973: 12), also applies to customs controls.

B
Targeting

The lack of information affects the foundations of risk management. If contradictory security agendas and corporate free trade interests are negotiated through risk, the goal of accurate risk assessments is endangered by poor information. For this reason, all types of information that can be used to calculate the risk of smuggling are valuable – from the most rudimentary statistical information to qualified intelligence. There is also a marked trend towards more data collection and processing in the customs service. During the period examined, the organization has significantly increased the amount of information available; a push which has information which has been reinforced by organizational reforms. There has been a reallocation of resources not only from customs clearance to crime control, but also within the crime control branch itself, towards intelligence and analysis. New legislation has been enacted, regulating the increasing use of information technology and the growing number of computerized registers. Of particular importance was the systematic access to the booking information of transportation companies.

The focus in this section is the selection of indicators. The indicators are what the customs are looking for – not the contraband, since this is hidden and by definition not visible. The amount of information available on each individual, in combination with the information passed on from earlier seizures, circumscribes the range of possible risk indicators. Within the range of possible indicators, some are preferred over others and the selection of indicators structures the final selection of the individuals actually being controlled. The preferred indicators separate the controllable from those who are not to be controlled. The question of which *individuals* are selected in practice lies outside the scope of this chapter.

The selection of indicators depends on the precise nature of the risk assessment. There are two ways of reaching a decision to control: performing an informal risk assessment, or performing a formal one. The former is when the customs inspector looks for signs indicating that the passenger might be smuggling, basing the decision on personal and professional experience. The latter involves the employment of fixed risk profiles to determine the control selection. The quest for accuracy entails a predisposition to use fixed risk profiles. But a large proportion of all risk assessments are still of an informal nature. To get a better idea of what indicators enter into the customs inspectors' assessments and what indicators are contained in the risk profiles, interviews were conducted with customs staff at one Swedish airport (Eriksson 2005). The interviews were used to expand the very limited information on the selection of indicators contained in written documents.

Informal assessments and formal profiles

The limited amount of available information significantly structures informal risk assessments, including the choice of indicators. A customs inspector has little time to decide; the initial time frame is a matter of a seconds. The customs inspector has to make a first decision while observing a lot of passengers walking through the customs gate with their luggage. The inspector can extend the time, postpone the final decision and increase the amount of available information by stopping a passenger, checking the ticket and asking questions regarding possible transits, hotels and the purpose of the journey. This questioning may last up to one minute. After extracting some basic information about the journey and observing the individual's demeanour, the decision will be taken as to whether to conduct a control or let the individual pass. Consequently, the possible range of risk indicators is fundamentally restricted by what the passengers might display and what the customs inspector can observe during the short encounter at the gate. Recently the customs service has extended the use of plain-clothes inspectors with the objective of making better-informed decisions. These inspectors observe the passengers as they disembark, pick up their luggage and proceed to the customs gate, thereby increasing the amount of information available (TU

2004d). But the range of risk indicators is still the same. The indicators will of necessity relate to individual demeanour and exterior signs of social status, since not much else is displayed and can be observed at the gate.

Class, race, gender and age easily become equivalent with indicators of risk. In the USA, Robert Kraut and Donald Poe conducted an experiment with a mock customs control, where both professional customs inspectors and laymen selected individuals for control. The experiment showed that 'the travellers were most likely to be searched if they were young and lower class, appeared nervous, hesitated before answering, gave short answers, avoided eye contact, shifted their posture, and had taken pleasure trips' (Kraut and Poe 1980: 784). Interestingly, the assessments of the professional customs inspectors did not differ from those of the laymen. Although the existing literature on actual customs controls is limited, it indicates that common-sense notions – structured by class, race and gender – of what constitutes normal behaviour and normal passengers structure the selection of indicators in the absence of more substantial information (Galbraith 2004; Heyman 2004). The normal was also repeatedly invoked as the standard when the inspectors explained what they were looking for at the Swedish airport. As one interviewee stated, inspectors are looking for 'that which differs, and that can be anything, I'm afraid; for example, if a lot of white people have walked by and then a black person comes, you make it simple'. The conception of 'that which differs' comprises multiple aspects, ranging from pre-judiced views of people out of place to more trivial examples of extraordinary behaviour. 'It is not normal to declare 2 litres of alcohol,' another customs inspector said, 'no ordinary Svensson [average citizen] does that, and if you are going to select a person, this in some way would fit the picture.' On this reading, *anything* that diverges from the dominant norm becomes an indicator, which may be used to separate people into a high-risk category.

The customs inspectors seem to make use of implicit profiles, or stereo-types, made up of sets of indicators. Although it was often pointed out in the interviews that you can never really tell – anybody might be a courier – some people appear to be excluded. Passengers were divided into stereo-typical low-risk and high-risk passengers. On the one hand there are the low-risk business people, who are relatively shielded from control. 'Those office people,' one inspector said, 'are hard to carry out controls on,' adding that 'they bring nothing but paper'. At the other end of the risk spectrum, there is the typical drug user. 'The junkie' is described by the same inspector as a 'young guy, almost like a bum, rather worn out, and not at all well-kempt,' followed by a comment that operating with this kind of stereotype is a trap – 'you seldom find anything'.

The mark of true craftsmanship was the ability to spot the tiny signs of illegality hidden in the legitimate flow of passengers. 'That which differs' was conceived of as a combination of subtle divergences which may be recognized by the trained eye of the customs inspector relying on intuition and experience. Some customs inspectors voiced an ambition to get beyond a stereotypical categorization of passengers based on demeanour. This involved a search for the less obvious.

> It may be a person walking close to three other persons like I said, 50-year-old men in a suit, and then a person comes who is around 30, still well dressed, but without a suitcase, and with another kind of bag, who does not fit in that company. You have to find *those people*.

Looking for odd combinations was accompanied by a search for traits that recalled memories from past seizures. Discussing the intricate matter of singling out drug swallowers, which involves justifying a decision to detain a passenger for several days, one customs inspector stressed the need to rely on one's own judgement. Finding it hard to articulate the criteria in some other way, the inspector referred to past seizures, stressing the importance of 'experiences from previous occasions when you made seizures on individuals in the past'. This is inevitable, since in the end there is nothing else to fall back on. The interviewed inspector was making a virtue out of necessity. Because of the lack of written documentation of other customs inspectors' experiences, customs officers *have to* rely on their own experiences. The interviews illustrate the fundamental condition that the range of possible indicators is limited and that individual inspectors are left to their own devices. For structural reasons, the indicators will of necessity relate to demeanour and exterior signs of social status. For administrative reasons, the inspectors are forced to rely on their own judgement, based on recollections of previous seizures and assumptions as to what constitutes deviance from the norm.

In the 1990s, the age-old practice of informal assessments at the point of entry was supplemented by a system of formal risk profiles utilizing information technology. The formalization of risk made the selection less dependent on the passengers' demeanour and the customs inspectors' commonsense notions of normality, and was seen as the main route towards the organizational goal of increased efficiency (SOU 1998; TU 2003a). State-of-the-art information technology that allows for a more accurate classification of passengers at the low and high ends of the risk spectrum will at the same time improve efficiency in terms of producing a higher hit percentage and larger seizures with less use of control resources. This is the promise of risk profiles.

The indicators included in the risk profiles are very different from those used in the context of informal risk assessments because of the different kind of information being utilized. The risk profiles are built on, and applied to, information available to customs prior to arrival. This kind of information is not readily available to the customs service, and has to come from sources outside the organization. For this reason, the transfer of personal data on individuals about to enter the country has been made statutory for transportation companies. All companies that 'forward goods, passengers or vehicles to or from Sweden' must 'transmit information on the passengers regarding name, route, baggage and co-passengers, and the mode of payment and booking' (SFS 1996: section 15). The communication routines are most developed for airline passengers. The customs service is supplied on a regular basis with booking information by airline companies, either by having access to the company's computers or online via their own computers. Apart from the information on name, route, baggage and co-passengers, and the mode of payment and booking, the airline companies can decide to supply further information contained in the booking, such as when the booking was made, telephone number, possible hotels, any rebooking and the particular travel agency used. As Colin Bennett, who has traced the steps from the purchase of an airline ticket to arrival, has noted, the personal information that travels along with the passenger can 'reveal an enormous amount about our travel preferences' (Bennett 2005: 118). Many companies have agreed to supply this kind of additional data.

The booking information constitutes the data from which risk profiles are constructed. Guided by the threat assessments, customs inspectors who work exclusively with the task of profiling extract a set of indicators from the booking forms. Although the selection of indicators is fundamentally constrained by their kind of information the airline companies have chosen to extract from their customers for commercial purposes, the customs service has used a substantial proportion of the total number of possible variables to construct risk profiles. Typical indicators include:

- Mode of payment (for example: cash)
- Telephone number (for example: unregistered cellular phone)
- When the booking was made (for example: close to departure)
- Baggage (for example: few bags)
- Travel agency (for example: used previously by detected smugglers)
- Rebooking (yes/no)
- Co-passenger (yes/no)

No variable is in itself a relevant indicator of risk. For instance, many people who book their flights close to departure are ordinary business people. Taken individually, the indicators have little significance; it is all about the combination of indicators. And the combinations may vary, since there are different profiles in use. The risk profile of cocaine couriers from one part of the world differs from the profile of steroid couriers from another part of the world. But the underlying principle is always the same. The profile consists of a set of variables, extracted from the booking information, where every variable is designated a specific value.

Once the profile is constructed, the booking information becomes the data to which risk profiles are applied. This undertaking involves two steps of selection. The total amount of data made available by the airline companies is immense. Moreover, the task of running through the information is time-consuming since it has to be done manually. Thus, it is not possible to check the bookings of all passengers arriving, and in practice, only certain flights are subject to scrutiny. This is the initial selection: flights from certain countries, primarily those known to produce or transit drugs, are considered high risk, while other flights are considered low risk. The next selection is among the passengers arriving on the high-risk flights. If a passenger matches the profile when the bookings are scrutinized by the profilers, the customs inspectors at the gate are notified. The passenger is then singled out for control upon arrival. The second selection is quasi-automatic: it is triggered when the booking information on the passenger matches the profile – where a match is defined as scoring on a predetermined number of indicators, say six out of a total of nine indicators comprising a particular profile. Further information on the individual passenger is unnecessary: it is sufficient to know that he or she fits the profile. Any suspicion or information relating to a particular shipment, drug or illegal business association is superfluous. That which is assessed is neither the person, in terms of character or credibility, nor the possible relations between a person and an act or an organization. In this way, the formalization of risk assessments significantly affects the control selection. The more profiles are being used, the more the selection will be geared towards those individuals who match the specific criteria. Further, the more details the risk profiles contain, the more limited the selection. Eventually, the size of the controllable population would be limited to the number of individuals corresponding to the characteristics enumerated in all of the profiles.

The use of risk profiles operates on the basis of both knowledge and ignorance. A vast amount of information on all the indicators is circulated. Yet this knowledge is remarkably detached from the individuals crossing the border. The individuals who are singled out are unknown. When the control selection is made within the flow of border-crossers, the person is not being assessed, and visible signs of nervousness or social status are disregarded. The individual is stripped of individuality and reduced to a disparate bundle of impersonal indicators of risk. The control selection is based on a set of impersonal conditions such as mode of payment, number of luggage pieces and possible rebooking. The repression is fundamentally uninterested in individuals. The wealth of information that accompanies the individual from the purchase of the ticket to the final destination is never assembled into a notion of personality. It is simply matched with risk profiles to make a decision. Consequently, an individual is being sorted out for physical control based on circumstantial data rather than on knowledge – or even a notion – of that individual. This is a basic feature of the society of generalized control. As David Lyon points out, it has become commonplace to use information only distantly related to individuals 'to determine who should be targeted for special treatment, suspicion, eligibility, inclusion, access' (Lyon 2003: 20). In this context, when circumstantial data are processed by the customs service, 'special treatment' ranges from luggage inspection to detention.

C
Staying on target

The control selection is structured by security concerns and business interests, as negotiated in a common language of risk, under circumstances characterized by poor information. Overall performance is determined by how well the customs service resolves this dilemma. The management of security concerns and business interests under a veil of ignorance is followed up in terms of efficiency. Efficiency audits by the National Audit Office are the main mechanism employed to ensure that the customs service stays on target.

The correlation between control and seizure

As opposed to the public employment service and the prison service, there is no system for monitoring the front-line employees within the customs organization. The performance of individual inspectors cannot be evaluated in terms of compliance or efficiency. There are no detailed regulations as to precisely when to intervene, or how to perform the risk assessment, against which the customs officials could be held accountable. And attempts to measure efficiency by means of performance indicators such as the hit percentage have foundered since, according to the National Audit Office, this encourages manipulation. By reducing the total number of controls, individual customs inspectors can increase the hit percentage: that is, they can make themselves seem more efficient when in fact they are not (RRV 2001b).

Only the performance at the organizational level is audited to ascertain that the repression is on target. To find a standard for measurement, attempts have been made to sharpen the concept of efficiency. The problem once again is associated with the limits of the available knowledge. How can the auditors know that the risks are being managed efficiently? The National Audit Office has pointed out the basic problem in measuring performance in terms of efficiency. The only available indicator of output is the number and volume of seizures. But since it is impossible to know the total amount of imported contraband, the efficiency of the customs service is, in one sense, fundamentally unknowable: 'variations in the number or the volume of seizures may depend on changes in the efficiency of border protection *or* changes in the volume of smuggled products' (RRV 2001b: 62; emphasis added). An increasing amount of seizures might just as well be the result of an increase in illegal trade, which means that the customs service might appear more efficient while in reality it had become less efficient. More seizures are compatible with a diminishing share of the total trade in prohibited commodities. This basic uncertainty is also expressed in the National Audit Office's criticism of 'benefit to society', which is the other existing performance indicator besides hit percentage. 'Benefit to society' focuses only on the volume of the seizure and does not evaluate 'whether the seizure has an effect on the organization behind the crime', and hence contributes to reducing the illegal trade (ibid.: 56).

At the same time, while the impact on the illegal trade is impossible to measure because of a fundamental lack of knowledge, there is still plenty of information on how the risks are handled. And *this* information is open to inspection – and can be used by the auditors to evaluate efficiency in another sense, leaving aside the impact on the actual trade. The monitoring focuses strictly on the measurable input and output of control activity. There are statistics on the number and volume of seizures and statistics on the number of controls carried out, which can be broken down to evaluate the performance of sub-units within the organization. One type of information may be compared with the other, and questions can be asked regarding the correlation between seizures and controls. The National Audit Office evaluated the efficiency of the customs service by juxtaposing on the one hand information on the number of seizures, and, on the other, information on the deployment of personnel at different places and points in time. It was concluded that at many border crossings the risk of smuggling was not taken into account sufficiently in the planning of customs work. The number of inspectors on duty was to a large extent determined by rigid work schedules and the personal preferences of the customs inspectors regarding, for example, vacation times. At one location highlighted in the report (see Figure 4.1), the auditors found 'almost no correlation between the number of control hours per weekday and the number of seizures per weekday' (RRV 2001b: 35). While

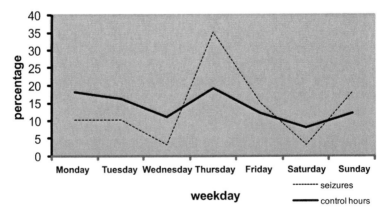

Figure 4.1 The correlation between control hours and seizures

most seizures were made on Thursdays, this was not reflected to a sufficient extent in the input of control hours: that is, the number of people working on Thursdays. The auditors would have preferred to see a closer connection between the allocation of customs control inspectors and the known risks of smuggling. More personnel were to be deployed in relation to those border crossings, points in time and means of transport that were associated with the highest risk of smuggling.

This is an internal follow-up system in the sense that it exclusively considers information on the input and output of the control activity – without reference to anything beyond the immediate scope of the customs service. There is no need to go beyond the statistics to ensure that the customs service is on target. In this way, using the risk of large-scale trade primarily in drugs as the standard, potentially everything could be evaluated. The division of labour, the decisions on prioritized flows, the choice of control strategy and the deployment of personnel can be evaluated as to whether the correlation between control and seizures has improved. Although there is no continuous monitoring, the head office or state audit organizations can, when called for, scrutinize the risk-relevant information retrospectively to see whether the chosen course of action is on target. The flow of risk-related information also allows for a future-oriented streamlining of the customs service. As 'risk assessments should direct where customs controls take place', as well as 'when the border control is manned' (RRV 2001b: 9), the organization as such is made responsive to the same considerations as the selection of objects. By using information from the input and output of past control performance, all aspects of the organization may be reorganized in terms of risk. Thus, stressing the observation of Bridget Hutter and Michael Power, risk can be used to change the organization as such. Within this strategy, it 'functions as an "organizing" category for management in general, a concept in whose name organizing and re-organizing is done' (Hutter and Power 2005: 9). In this sense, risk serves as the medium for organizational self-correction.

Conclusions

Repression beyond conscious decisions

The power exercised by the customs service is repressive. It involves the use of force (R3), and aims at nothing but compliance with laws regulating the import and export of commodities (R4). In line with the assumption that power proceeds from the law (R1), the point of departure employed in this chapter was an account of the framework of rules surrounding the control activity. But although the interventions find support in these rules, they do not provide much guidance as to how customs controls are deployed in practice. So in this case, just as in the last chapter, considerations of risk rather than legal definitions are the central organizing principle. The analysis of customs control further questions the legal paradigm of repressive power. Given the two counter-examples, it cannot be assumed that repressive power always conforms to the conventional paradigm.

The assumption that repressive power is mediated through conscious decisions (R2) is called into question from two perspectives. From the perspective of those over whom power is exercised, conscious decisions are basically irrelevant. No one in the target population is confronted with a choice prior to the use of force. Border-crossers are never confronted with a situation where they can choose a legitimate as opposed to an illegitimate course of action that is connected to the possible future repressive reaction. As the customs service points out in the flyer handed out upon a completed inspection, 'you can be controlled even though you do the right thing' (TU 2003b). Border-crossers are not confronted with a binary regime. There is no way to be on the safe side, since neither an observed transgression nor even a material suspicion of a transgression is a necessary prerequisite for the use of force. Border-crossers may be subjected to controls ranging from baggage search to urine testing to detention, regardless of their degree of rule compliance. They may be perfectly aware of what goods are allowed and prohibited and make use of that information when deciding on what to bring on the trip. But *this* decision is irrelevant to the indicators being used by the inspectors to trigger controls. The airline passengers are targeted on the basis of how well they match informal stereotypes or formal risk profiles. Notions of normality and irregularity divide those who are to be controlled from those who are to be exempted. Legal criteria are absent when this line is drawn, as are elements of conscious decisions, past or present, on the part of the target population. Whether the control selection is based on appearance or circumstantial data, the indicators of risk are derived from circumstances beyond conscious decision-making, unless, of course, you are familiar with the composition of risk profiles and stereotypes, and make use of that knowledge to manipulate the booking information and your appearance to avoid control.

The assumption that power is mediated through conscious decisions also has to be nuanced with respect to those who exercise power. The control selection relies on conscious decisions made by a customs inspector at the point of entry. But the space for conscious decision-making – the element of deliberation and discretion – is being narrowed down following the trend towards automatic control. The introduction of information technology circumvents the discretion of front-line employees. The risk-profiling of booking information tends to eliminate the need for a conscious decision to initiate a repressive intervention. High-risk passengers are quasi-automatically selected when the information is screened. The selection is not fully automatic, as the screening is done manually and the notified customs inspectors at the gate can choose to abstain from controlling passengers that match the profile. Although the repressive power still relies on human agency, it is inscribed in a system where decision-making is being designed out by information-processing techniques that make deliberation and discretion redundant.

A common language accommodating contradictions

State power is not the business of a single organization; rather, it is organized in strategies that stretch well beyond, in this case, the customs service. To understand the control of border-crossers, one cannot restrict one's focus to the customs service. Policy priorities are selected through public inquiries, influenced by business lobby groups, and established by the government in its yearly instruction on control priorities; efficiency audits are performed by government oversight bodies, and risk-related information is transmitted by transportation companies. All these activities are connected to the control activity of the customs service, through information flows in the widest sense – expectations, demands, commands, assessments and audits. But the demands and expectations do not point in the same direction. The dominant interests of border control and smooth foreign trade are not immediately compatible; instead, they are negotiated and *made compatible* within the customs service. During the period examined, risk constituted the common language through which different and contradictory expectations were brokered. This common language does not erase the contradictions but makes different priorities and goals negotiable. Security concerns, corporate interests and managerial reforms are framed as considerations of risk, which are consistent with the communication and control routines of the customs service. Dominant security agendas – above all, zero-tolerance drug policies and initiatives to combat organized crime – are translated into considerations of high risks of illegal import. Corporate interests and free-trade agreements are articulated in terms of less intervention in low-risk cross-border flows. Managerial reforms to increase organizational efficiency are transformed into the goal of better management of both high-risk and low-risk flows.

The artificial language of risk is used to guide the activity of the customs service. It directs many if not all aspects of organizational performance, including resource allocation and control selection. Decisions on policy-level priorities, as well as the choice of interventions at the level of individuals, are articulated in terms of the risk of illegal imports. Above all, the risk of large-scale drug smuggling is used to assign resources to certain flows, evaluate work schedules and create risk profiles. In this way, the risk language not only negotiates different organized interests over and above the customs service, but also mediates between ground-level activity and policy-level planning within the organization, transforming it into a body that is auditable and governable in terms of an identical set of risks. Drug smuggling and organized crime are established as the main targets, balanced against the objective of minimum interference in legal trade, broken down into performance targets such as hit percentages and A-matters, and concretized as an individual who matches a number of risk indicators inferred from the booking information. And in the other direction: by reviewing information on the input and output of control, such as the correlation between control hours and number of seizures, the management of the risk of illegal import is translated into feedback routines that connect the selection of border-crossers with the governance of the organization.

As a result, contradictory expectations are translated into a common lingua that enables communication between the various actors in the strategy. The risk of illegal import is the language through which all institutional players make themselves understood. If a certain actor does not express its concerns in the artificial language, it would unplug itself from the communication system of the customs service, and as a consequence would not be understood. To be effective, requests and expectations must be put forth in the strategy-specific risk language. By implication, strategies have an outside. There are unplugged actors, who have not transformed their interests into the common lingua of the customs service, or who have attempted but failed. During the period examined, examples included political groups that resisted the criminalization of pirate copying, or suggested a lower tax as the best way to reduce illegal importing of alcohol. This is also where an analysis in terms of risk encounters its own limits. The concept of risk can negotiate some contradictions, but not all of them. The concept of risk is crucial to understanding how strategies operate. Yet it is ill-suited to capturing the element of struggle that originally went into the strategy, and that continues to accompany it from the outside. This element is particularly worth mentioning since it is consistently neglected in this book.

Chapter 5

Conclusions

The distinction between productive and repressive power is usually taken for granted within a Foucauldian tradition. In the introductory chapter, the tacit assumptions were disentangled from historical narratives and made explicit in eight basic propositions reflecting Foucault's own as well as later work within the tradition. To what extent does that conceptualization of productive and repressive power need to be modified? Based on the case studies, four of the eight assumptions, (P3–P4) and (R1–R2), must be changed in order to account for the complexity of both forms of power. There are, however, no reasons to revise the other four assumptions, (P1–P2) and (R3–R4). In Table 5.1, the italicized text indicates what will be modified.

Productive power revisited

Foucault was first to conceptualize productive power. The shift from repressivity to productivity involved something of a Copernican revolution in the study of power. Over the last decades, the focus has become galvanized into a set of conceptions of which some proved useful in the case studies. This is above all true of the assumptions that power is organized around norms and that effects are produced regardless of intentions and consent. In other respects, this study represents a critique of the current Foucauldian mainstream. In particular, two themes in the critique stand out; that the elements

Table 5.1 Revisions needed in the conceptualization of productive and repressive power

	Productive Power	*Repressive Power*
The organizing principle	norms	law or risk
The element of decisions	disregarded	presupposed or circumvented
The means used	self-chosen and imposed	negative
The effect	only actions	obedience

of coercion, imposed objectives and close monitoring are overlooked and, further, that there exists a basic ambiguity regarding the productivity of power which must be resolved.

P1
Power is organized around the norm

The productive interventions in the public employment service are guided by employability needs, whereas criminogenic needs provide the direction in the prison service. In both cases, the needs are a mix of research findings and moral values: that is, they are norms in the Foucauldian sense – 'a mixture of legality and nature, prescription and constitution' (Foucault 1979a: 304). Normative assumptions are articulated together with detected or stipulated deficiencies among the targeted individuals and are presented in terms of risk factors to be corrected by interventions.

P2
The effects are achieved regardless of intentions and consent

In the prison service, the inmates learn to handle everyday frustration in the workplace, to negotiate conflicts with superiors and to manage stress at home in role-playing scenarios. Similarly, in the public employment service, the long-term unemployed learn to conduct job interviews or to call potential employers by acting as job applicants in role-plays. The interventions subvert the level of conscious decision-making. The participants will learn how to manage stress and how to get work regardless of what the targeted individuals think of this competence. The effect is 'obtained directly through the mechanics of training' (Foucault 1979a: 180); it relies only on the decision to start the programme or go to the classes. And *this* decision is subverted through interventions that target the motivation to participate. Participation in the activity guarantee is secured through the system of monetary sanctions, and in the prison service the web of incentives is reinforced by motivational interviewing to encourage participation.

P3
Power is a combination of empowerment and subjection

The third chapter ended with a call for a more complex concept of productive power. The cognitive-behavioural training programmes found in prisons could be analysed neither as technologies of the self nor as discipline in the classic Foucauldian sense. They were found to share characteristics associated with technologies of the self, such as voluntary participation, individual responsibility, appeals to existing aspirations and empowerment. At the same time, the programmes contained elements of the opposite: coercion, close monitoring, imposed objectives and limited competence. Hence, a more complex notion is required which takes into account that the interventions rely on constraints to participate as well as the choice to do so; that they hand over the responsibility to the individual to change but take it away by specifying the means and steps to be taken; that they link the desire for social inclusion to harsh labour market demands; and that they operate on a notion of the autonomy of the individuals while embedding them in a constraining social structure. The corresponding conceptualization must allow for a combination of contradictions. Productive power involves elements of empowerment as well as subjection – means that are at the same time voluntary and involuntary, tactics that are responsibilizing and authoritarian, goals that are authentic and imposed, and results that are beneficial and detrimental to the targeted individual.

The concept of productive power must allow not only for a combination of contradictions but also for a variation in the relative strength of each element. On the one hand, there are interventions that are voluntary rather than involuntary, that appeal to desires rather than imposing objectives and that govern at a distance. On the other hand, there are interventions where the elements of coercion, imposed objectives and governance at close range are more pronounced. The difference is gradual as elements of both pairs of opposites are always present. Productive interventions may also differ in further respects. The cognitive-behavioural techniques, which are built along similar principles, represent a variety in two additional respects. Some techniques are purchased on the market while others are provided within state institutions. Moreover, some techniques are accessed individually and are sensitive to individual circumstances while others are dispensed to groups and tend to have a one-size-fits-all character. The former is associated with technologies of the self whereas the latter is associated with discipline. In all these respects – voluntary versus involuntary, individual responsibility versus close monitoring, genuine aspirations versus imposed objectives, empowerment versus limited competence, market solutions versus state institutions, and individualized versus collective – the productive interventions studied in this book are situated at the disciplinary end of the spectra.

The distinction between technologies of the self and discipline could be related to Deleuze's idea of two societies (Deleuze 1990). This involves a shift of focus from particular institutions to the question of what can be said about the interventions that more generally confront individuals. Are we living in a disciplinary society or in a society where the productive interventions are more like technologies of the self? The answer depends on who 'we' are. Both societies can be seen to exist simultaneously. Depending on the status of the target group, and in particular on its employment status, individuals belong to one society or the other. The control society exists for those who are socially included, whereas those excluded from the world of work are part of the disciplinary society. In the former society, activity is based on market incentives, responsibility is individualized and programmes appeal to ambitions regarding career opportunities. Direct state intervention is not necessary. The inhabitants of the disciplinary society, on the other hand, are seen to be insensitive to market incentives and are instead enrolled in state institutions where they are closely monitored and exposed to programmes providing basic skills. The productive interventions may be immediately entwined with repressive power also dispensed by the state, as in the case of the activity guarantee. The state acts as a last resort, should the power exercised elsewhere fail to produce the qualifications, expectations and routines necessary for wage labour.

P4
Power produces actions

Productive power is by definition productive. But there is a fundamental uncertainty as to what power produces. The most central aspect of productive power also happens to be the one that is most often misrepresented. It is far from always clear what is actually being produced. In one interview, Foucault said that power produces 'knowledge', 'things', 'pleasure' and 'discourse' (Foucault 1980: 119); in another, that 'the individual' was one of the 'prime effects' of power (ibid.: 98). The ambiguity also surfaces in the govern-mentality literature, where new entities were added to the list of phenomena produced in and through power. Nikolas Rose and Peter Miller have argued that 'shared interests are constructed' and 'common modes of perception are formed' (Rose and Miller 1992: 184). Mitchell Dean high-lighted 'the formation of identities' (Dean 1999: 32). Pat O'Malley has suggested a focus on how 'we' are transformed into 'subjects' (O'Malley 2004: 27). There is a persistent interest in personal transformation. Mary Bosworth focu-ses on the creation of 'citizens' as the central dimension (Bosworth 2007).

It may well be the case that the exercise of power has wide-ranging effects – gives rise to knowledge, pleasure, discourse, subjects, citizens, identities, interests and modes of perception. But such interpretations are either indeterminate or border on metaphysics. The assumed effects are often just assumed and beyond the reach of evidence, or simply implausible. It is unlikely that productive power in general, and at least not the interventions analysed in this book, constitutes subjects, transforms subjects into citizens, forges new identities or creates a particular kind of personality. If we want a more direct route to the effects of power, I would suggest a focus on beha-viour rather than on what is supposed to underlie behaviour. On this read-ing, power produces actions in accordance with a set target. No assumptions are being made about further effects. That would be 'a study of power', using Foucault's expression, 'at the point where it is in direct and immediate rela-tionship with that which we can provisionally call its object, its target, its field of application' (Foucault 1980: 97). The focus on behaviour avoids speculative arguments, while at the same time going to the heart of the matter. Power is about influencing the conduct of others. To exercise power is to affect relevant areas of the subordinated individuals' behaviour, not to create identities or a special kind of person. Productive power is productive in this sense, and only in this sense. It produces actions – a motivation to act and a capacity to act in certain ways.

Repressive power revisited

Within the tradition, starting with Foucault himself, there is a tendency to disregard repression and over-value the productive dimensions of power. The governmentality approach would reinforce the neglect of physical force. The relative irrelevance of repression operated as a basic assumption. As Roy Coleman has remarked, it 'assumed rather than demonstrated the absence of coercion' (Coleman 2004: 9). The need to study repressive power was dismissed along with Marxism and state theory in general (Melossi 2006). Since repression has traditionally been associated with the state, and since the principal focus of the governmentality literature is directed at power *beyond* the state, the analysis of repression was inevitably pushed to the margins. Consequently, a database search using the term 'repressive power' generates numerous hits where it is revealed immediately in the abstract that the author intends to elaborate an analysis of power in contradistinction to a simplistic notion of power as repression. What characterizes the 'other' form of power is not elaborated. The nature of repression has never been discussed in its own right within the Foucauldian literature. Yet what would happen if this either–or thinking – that power is seen as either productive or repressive – were to give way to a detailed study of both productive and repressive power? To realize the full potential of a Foucauldian approach it is necessary to study both forms of power on their own terms. Only in that way is it possible to reach a non-simplistic notion of the repressive aspects of power. The analysis of the interventions presented in this book entails a revision of the conventional Foucauldian notion of repression. In particular, the pivotal role of risk and the circumvention of decision-making challenge the legal paradigm.

R I
Power is organized around law or risk

Law divides actions into two categories – permitted and prohibited. This operation provides the platform for the exercise of repression. It points out which actions are to be reduced to a minimum. In this sense, law is fundamental in all case studies. At the same time, it is relatively absent in organizational practice. Law as the only model for understanding the exercise of repression must be questioned. The design of conditions of incarceration or the deployment of customs controls does not conform to the legal paradigm. In these cases, risk directs the use of power: it sets the organizational target and guides the actions of front-line members, who tailor interventions around individuals in the target group. While the activity finds support in the law, it is essentially shaped by communicating the risk of disorder, or of illegal import. Hence, repression does not always unfold according to a legal paradigm.

I would suggest a risk-based paradigm of repressive power as a supplement to the existing legal paradigm. The exercise of repression can be organized around risk or around law. In this book there are examples of both, although interventions that conform to the risk-based paradigm have received most attention. When law is the organizing principle, interventions are actualized by rule violations, and only by rule violations. In the public employment service, for instance, the repression proceeds from the legislation on unemployment insurance, which is transformed into individual rules, directing the sanctioning in practice. Equally in the prison service, the sanctioning system is organized as external boundaries for behaviour, where only reported violations are investigated and punished. When risk is the organizing principle, on the other hand, interventions are continuous. All individuals in the target group are distributed along a continuum in terms of the relative degree of risk. Every position in the continuum corresponds to a level of coercion; or, if the risk is below a certain threshold, corresponds to no intervention at all, as the selection to customs control shows. The repression is shaped by the communication of risk-relevant information rather than by the detection of rule violations. In practice, the relationship is one of competition: repression is organized either around risk or around law. The guiding principles are mutually exclusive. Conceptually, however, the relationship between the legal and the risk-based paradigm is supplementary. Repressive power that cannot be understood according to one paradigm might be understood according to the other.

R2
Power presupposes or circumvents conscious decisions

According to the legal paradigm, repressive power is always mediated through conscious decisions. Those who are exposed to power are told what to do, and then think how to respond. They have a choice, and decide on actions that are either permitted or prohibited. Those who exercise power apply existing rules, an operation that equally presupposes conscious decisions. According to the risk-based paradigm, however, the same element is contingent. Risk-based repression tends to ignore the decision-making of individuals within the target group and to circumvent the decision-making of those who immediately exercise the power. Individuals within the target group are targeted on the basis of who they are, or rather on the basis of the bundle of risk indicators they present and whether that bundle match existing risk profiles. Decisions on rule compliance are irrelevant. Border-crossers, like prison inmates, are not confronted with a situation where they choose a course of action that may or may not trigger a repressive reaction. The element of decision-making is also contingent with respect to those who exercise power. In the case studies, there are several examples where risk-based repression is dependent on a decision of front-line employees. For instance, the decision to control or not to control is fully in the hands of customs inspectors as long as it is based on informal risk assessments. At the same time, the space for discretion is narrowed down following the trend towards automatic control. The online reporting routines in the public employment service and the risk-profiling of booking information in the customs service tend to eliminate the need for a decision to initiate a repressive intervention. The intra-organizational regulation and monitoring further shrinks the space for discretion. The discretion of front-line employees in the prison service, for instance, is circumscribed by detailed directives for which decisions are to be made under which circumstances, and the follow-up routines that monitor compliance. Although the repression still relies on human agency it is inscribed in a system where decision-making is circumvented by information-processing techniques, detailed regulation and close monitoring.

R3
Power may be understood in strictly negative terms

There is no need to modify the assumption that repressive power is essentially destructive. The impact on the targeted individuals is negative. The financial support is withdrawn from the unemployed who remain inactive; the physical integrity of selected border-crossers is violated; high-risk prison inmates are subjected to intrusive controls and their freedom of communication is curtailed. The mediated effects of repression may be positive. Repressive power is exercised on the pretext of a greater good; the inflicted harm is considered justified in relation to other, positive outcomes. But the immediate effect is strictly negative.

R4
The effect of power is either obedience or disobedience

There is also little need to modify the assumption that obedience marks the successful use of repressive power. In the prison service and the customs service, the repressive interventions do not produce specific acts, but make individuals refrain from engaging in specific acts, namely those that cross the line of what is permitted. Yet the term 'obedience' takes on a slightly new meaning in the public employment service. Depending on the conditions specified in the individual action plan, failing to apply for the required number of jobs and not attending training programmes may constitute rule violations. The activation strategy thus inverts the relationship between activity and passivity. Usually, repression is triggered by actions and obedience is passive. But in this case, obedience is active and disobedience is passive. It appears that repression also may produce specific acts. In this respect, the exercise of repressive power takes on features of productive power.

Strategies and risk revisited

In the introductory chapter, a distinction was made between programmatic and non-programmatic power. Reflection and organization were seen to be the decisive aspects. The power analysed in the case studies is no doubt programmatic. It is calculated rather than spontaneous, organized rather than unorganized, and recurring rather than singular. The rights and the resources to exercise power in relation to a target group have been conferred on to the members of an organization. They are caught in a web of directives, routines, communication, monitoring, evaluations, expectations and relations of accountability that shapes their deployment of productive as well as of repressive interventions. It follows that the interventions must be analysed together with the organizational context. But this context tends to be overlooked within the Foucauldian tradition, although the programmatic exercise of power constitutes the centre of attention. While a keen interest in the programmatic interventions themselves has been accompanied by research into discursive rationalities and historical trajectories, the organized nature of power is only rudimentarily conceptualized in the Foucauldian literature.

The concept of strategies is one way of ameliorating the neglect of the organizational dimension and of simultaneously satisfying the need to find tools to make sense of the range of meso-level phenomena that may account for the reproduction of social order. Can the programmatic exercise of power be understood as a strategy – that is, as a process with three stages in which the targeting of the unemployed, prison inmates and border-crossers is preceded by target-setting and integrated in successive controls of the employees? The argument for the usefulness of the conceptual approach is embedded in the account of how interventions are deployed. It must ultimately be left to the reader to decide whether the concept of strategies can successfully account for the two dimensions of calculation and organization that distinguish the programmatic deployment of productive as well as repressive interventions.

If strategies designate organized attempts to shape behaviour in a three-stage loop, risk is the complementary concept, which captures the element of calculated and negotiated direction over and above the organizational exigencies. The idea of 'governing through risk' builds on the assumption that risk has a special status due to its capacity to negotiate and guide organizational activity towards goals. While legal restrictions, available information, political expediencies, fiscal limitations and technical possibilities inevitably influence the exercise of power, it is being directed in terms of risk.

Risks provide a calculated and negotiated direction in all three stages of the strategies examined. First of all, risks are used to set the target. Risks are closely linked to the organizational goal. In the customs service, preventing illegal imports is one major organizational goal; hence, risk is articulated in terms of illegal imports. At the same time, risks are communicated in strategies that extend beyond the customs service and involve other actors whose demands and expectations point in sometimes very different directions. The conflict between enforcement and economy has been one common feature throughout. The customs service is torn between the dominant interests of border control and smooth foreign trade; the public employment service must enforce activity requirements without choking the labour market with control functions; and the prison service must balance security concerns against public finances and considerations of rehabilitation. The demands are not immediately compatible, and must be made compatible within the organization. In the cases examined, risk constituted the common language through which different and contradictory expectations were brokered. Conflicting expectations, differences in opinion and available information were rephrased as considerations of risks, which were consistent with the goals and the routines of the front-line organization. There is no inherent limit to what can be translated to fit the risk communication system operating within a strategy. Considerations of efficiency, security, sovereignty, rehabilitation, due process, welfare, cost efficiency, free trade and business interests have all been framed in terms of risk. The artificial language of risk does not erase the contradictions but makes different priorities negotiable within the confines of front-line organizations of the state.

Second, risks guide the targeting. The targets point out what it is about the individuals that needs to be changed to efficiently – that is, balanced against other considerations – minimize the risk of long-term unemployment, of reoffending, of disorder and of illegal imports. They are traced by indicators of risk that are established through a mix of political ideals, administrative experience and scientific research. Beyond these similarities, there are also differences in terms of how productive and repressive interventions are guided. The targets of the productive interventions are composed of deficiencies, conceptualized as employability needs and criminogenic needs, which are to be satisfied through training and therapies that produce the corresponding competence and motivation. In the repressive strategies, on the other hand, rather than guiding the interventions themselves, the risks guide the targeting by determining which intervention is appropriate. The targets consist of a physical presence: material threats such as drugs, psychopaths or organized crime that must be dissolved or contained. Reports on institutional misconduct as well as booking information have been translated into indicators of risk that guide decisions on repressive interventions, determining when and what types of interventions are activated in practice.

Finally, risks guide the intra-organizational power which ascertains that the productive and repressive interventions are on target. In all the studied cases, the first-order targeting was linked to a range of control mechanisms within and beyond the organization. In the public employment service, the intra-organizational power was integrated in a layered control structure.

Above the control of the unemployed, conducted by case managers, there was the control of the case managers, conducted by other members of the organization; and beyond the organization there was the control of the organization, conducted by other state organizations. Employees in all positions are affected; although in particular those who are positioned in the intersection between the organization and the target group. Risk provides the main route to uncover the central dimensions of employee compliance and performance. Whether indicators of drug use have been duly considered in risk-based decisions on furloughs is, for instance, one measure of employee compliance within the prison service. The management of the risk of disorder is being assessed in terms of the same risks that guide the first-order targeting. The monitoring is built around the visibility produced by the circulation of risk-related information. In the prison service, the performance of the prison officers was first made visible, through video-recordings of their teaching or by the construction of forms documenting their decisions; and then assessed in relation to the directives on how to execute programmes or on how to make decisions. As a result, a system of disciplinary surveillance is established that intervenes only if irregularities are detected, and shapes the behaviour of front-line employees in one particular direction: towards deploying productive and repressive interventions in accordance with organizational rules and goals.

The efforts to stay on target also involve control mechanisms that focus on the organization itself, as opposed to the individual member. All the studied organizations are from the outset inscribed in a network of control extending from other parts of the state. Audit institutions and policy-oriented research institutes continuously monitor performance from a vantage point outside of the front-line organization. The artificial language of risk facilitates the activity of auditing bodies, and makes organizational performance transparent under conditions of vague performance targets, contradictory goals and poor information on outcomes. In the customs service, risk was used to evaluate resource allocation and policy priorities by comparing the input and output of past interventions with the known risk of smuggling. In this way, the organization is made responsive to the same risks that guide the first-order targeting. The strategy-specific risks are used to reorganize the organization itself, influencing it towards adopting routines and policy priorities that enhance the efficiency – the primary objective balanced against other considerations – of interventions. The multiple layers of control are the organizational prerequisite for the complex mix of productive and repressive power towards the target group. Taken together, the various elements of strategies contribute to the reproduction of power relations that are at heart unequal, contentious and unstable.

Bibliography

Ackum Agell, S. (1996), 'Arbetslösas sökaktivitet', *Aktiv arbetsmarknadspolitik*, SOU 1996:34. Stockholm: Fritzes.

Åkesson, J. (2004), *Jobbsökarens handbok – hur du marknadsför din kompetens*. Uppsala: Uppsala Publishing House.

Alexander, K., Dhumale, R. and Eatwell, J. (2006), *Global Governance of Financial Systems: The International Regulation of Systemic Risk*. Oxford: Oxford University Press.

AMS (2003), *Förmedlingsarbete med ökat sökandeansvar. Åtgärdsprogram för förbättrad sökaktivitet.* Stockholm: Arbetsmarknadsstyrelsen.

——(2004a), *Enhetlighet, rättssäkerhet och effektivitet i Arbetsförmedlingens arbete samt Mål för Arbetsförmedlingen.* Stockholm: Arbetsmarknadsstyrelsen.

——(2004b), *Åtgärdsprogram för stärkt enhetlighet och rättssäkerhet i arbetslöshetsförsäkringen.* Stockholm: Arbetsmarknadsstyrelsen.

——(2005a), *Årsredovisning 2004.* Stockholm: Arbetsmarknadsstyrelsen.

——(2005b), *Arbetsmarknadspolitiska program. Årsrapport 2004*, Ure 2005:1. Stockholm: Arbetsmarknadsstyrelsen.

AMSFS (2001), *Arbetsmarknadsstyrelsens föreskrifter om individuella handlingsplaner*, AMSFS 2001:11.

AMV (2001) *Metodstöd för handlingsplaner*, 2001-09-04. Stockholm: Arbetsmarknadsverket.

—— (2004) *Handlingsplan metodstöd*, 2004-12-22. Stockholm: Arbetsmarknadsverket.

Andershed, H. and Skeem, J. (2004), 'Psykopati: Aktuell teori och forskning', in L. Lidberg and N. Wiklund (eds.) *Svensk rättspsykiatri. Psykisk störning, brott och påföljd.* Lund: Studentlitteratur.

Andershed, H., Forsman, M., Johansson, P. and Johansson, B. (2004), *Riksmottagningen 1997–2003: En beskrivning av långtidsdömda män i Sverige.* Kumla: Kriminalvården.

Andrews, D. (1984), *Criminal Sentiments and Criminal Behavior: A Construct Validation.* Ottawa: Ministry of the Solicitor General.

Andrews, D. and Bonta, J. (1998), *The Psychology of Criminal Conduct.* Cincinnati: Anderson Publishing.

Antonovsky, A. (1987), *Unraveling the Mystery of Health.* San Francisco: Jossey-Bass.

Aradau, C. and van Munster, R. (2007), 'Governing Terrorism through Risk: Taking Precautions, (un)Knowing the Future', *European Journal of International Relations,* 13: 89–115.

ARM (1999), *Kontrakt för arbete: rättvisa och tydliga regler i arbetslöshetsförsäkringen*, Ds 1999:58. Stockholm: Arbetsmarknadsdepartementet.

Bäckman, O. (2006), 'Sysselsättning och arbetsmarknad', *Social rapport 2006.* Stockholm: Socialstyrelsen.

Baker, T. and Simon, J. (2002), 'Embracing Risk', in T. Baker and J. Simon (eds.) *Embracing Risk: The Changing Culture of Insurance and Responsibility*. Chicago: University of Chicago Press.

Belfrage, H. and Fransson, G. (2000), *HCR-20: Bedömning av risk för framtida våld*. Sundsvall: Rättspsykiatriska regionkliniken.

Bennett, C. (2005), 'What Happens When You Book an Airline Ticket? Surveillance, Globalization and the Regulation of International Communications Networks,' in E. Zureik and M. Salter (eds.) *Global Surveillance and Policing: Borders, Security, Identity*. Cullompton: Willan.

Bergeskog, A. (2001), *Labour Market Policies, Strategies and Statistics for People with Disabilities*, IFAU Working Paper 2001:13. Uppsala: Institutet för arbetsmarknadspolitisk utvärdering.

Bernstein, P. (1996), *Against the Gods. The Remarkable Story of Risk*. New York: John Wiley & Sons.

Black, D., Smith, J., Berger, M. and Noel, B. (1999), *Is the Threat of Training More Effective Than Training Itself? Experimental Evidence from the UI System*, Research Report No. 9913. Ontario: University of Western Ontario.

Boin, A. and Rattray, W. (2004), 'Understanding Prison Riots: Towards a Threshold Theory', *Punishment and Society*, 6: 47–65.

Boltanski, L. and Chiapello, È. (2005), *The New Spirit of Capitalism*. London: Verso.

Bosworth, M. (2007), 'Creating the Responsible Prisoner: Federal Admission and Orientation Packs', *Punishment and Society*, 9: 67–85.

BRÅ (1998), *Frigivning från fängelse*, BRÅ 1998:6. Stockholm: Brottsförebyggande rådet.

——(2000), *Från anstalt till livet i frihet. Delrapport 1: Inför muck*, BRÅ 2000:20. Stockholm: Brottsförebyggande rådet.

——(2001), *Från anstalt till livet i frihet. Delrapport 2: Efter muck*, BRÅ 2001:2. Stockholm: Brottsförebyggande rådet.

——(2002), *Att lära ut ett nytt sätt att tänka: utvärdering av Cognitive Skills-programmet i kriminalvården 1995–2000*, BRÅ 2002:11. Stockholm: Brottsförebyggande rådet.

——(2004), *Förberedd för frihet? Slutrapport från utvärderingen av förstärkta frigivningsförberedelser åren 2001–2003*. Stockholm: Brottsförebyggande rådet.

——(2005), *Kriminalvårdens särskilda narkotikasatsning*, BRÅ 2005:3. Stockholm: Brottsförebyggande rådet.

Brown, P. (2001), 'Skill Formation in the Twenty-First Century', in P. Brown, A. Green and H. Lauder (eds.) *High Skills*. Oxford: Oxford University Press.

Brown, P., Hesketh, A. and Williams, S. (2003), 'Employability in a Knowledge-Driven Economy', *Journal of Education and Work*, 16: 107–26.

Burchell, G. (1996), 'Liberal Government and Techniques of the Self', in A. Barry, T. Osborne and N. Rose (eds.) *Foucault and Political Reason*. Chicago: University of Chicago Press.

Buzan, B., Wæver, O. and de Wilde, J. (1998), *Security: A New Framework for Analysis*. Boulder: Lynne Rienner.

Carlen, P. (2002), 'New Discourses of Justification and Reform for Women's Imprisonment in England', in P. Carlen (ed.) *Women and Punishment: The Struggle for Justice*. Cullompton: Willan.

Castel, R. (2003), *From Manual Workers to Wage Laborers: Transformation of the Social Question*. New Brunswick: Transaction Publishers.

CEC (2001), *Making a European Area of Lifelong Learning a Reality*. Brussels: Commission of the European Communities.

Chylicki, P. (2000), *Cognitive Skills i svensk kriminalvård 1999. Rapport 4.* Norrköping: Kriminalvårdsstyrelsen.

Clark Craig, S. (2004), 'Rehabilitation versus Control: An Organizational Theory of Prison Management', *The Prison Journal*, 84: 92–114.

Coleman, R. (2004), *Reclaiming the Streets: Surveillance, Social Control and the City.* Cullompton: Willan.

CPT (1992), Report to the Swedish Government on the visit to Sweden carried out by the European Committee for the Prevention of Torture and Inhuman or Degrading Treatment or Punishment (CPT) from 5 to 14 May 1991. Strasbourg: Council of Europe.

——(2004), Report to the Swedish Government on the visit to Sweden carried out by the European Committee for the Prevention of Torture and Inhuman or Degrading Treatment or Punishment (CPT) from 27 January to 5 February 2003. Strasbourg: Council of Europe.

Cruikshank, B. (1999), *The Will to Empower: Democratic Citizens and other Subjects.* Ithaca: Cornell University Press.

Dahlstedt, M. (2009), *Aktiveringens politik: demokrati och medborgarskap för ett nytt millenium.* Malmö: Liber.

Dean, M. (1999), *Governmentality: Power and Rule in Modern Society.* London: Sage.

De Giorgi, A. (2006), *Re-thinking the Political Economy of Punishment: Perspectives on Post-Fordism and Penal Politics.* Aldershot: Ashgate.

Delander, L., Thoursie, R. and Wadensjö, E. (1991), *Arbetsförmedlingens historia.* Stockholm: Allmänna förlaget.

Deleuze, G. (1990), *Negotiations. 1972–1990.* New York: Colombia University Press.

DeIulio, J. (1991), 'Understanding Prisons: The New Old Penology', *Law and Social Inquiry*, 16: 65–99.

Dobson, K. and Block, L. (2001), 'Historical and Philosophical Bases of the Cognitive-Behavioral Therapies', in K. Dobson (ed.) *Handbook of Cognitive-Behavioral Therapies.* New York: Guilford Press.

Dreyfus, H. and Rabinow, P. (1982), *Michel Foucault: Beyond Structuralism and Hermeneutics.* Brighton: Harvester.

DSM-IV (2000), *Diagnostic and Statistical Manual of Mental Disorders.* Arlington, VA: American Psychiatric Association. Task Force on DSM-IV.

Duguid, S. (2000), *Can Prisons Work? The Prisoner as Object and Subject in Modern Corrections.* Toronto: University of Toronto Press.

Ekström, V. (2005), *Individens eget ansvar och samhällets stöd: en utvärdering av "Skärholmsmodellen" vid Jobbcentrum Sydväst.* Stockholm: Socialtjänstförvaltningen.

Ericson, R. (2007a), *Crime in an Insecure World.* Cambridge: Polity Press.

——(2007b), 'The Architecture of Risk and Power', *British Journal of Criminology*, 47: 955–68.

Ericson, R. and Haggerty, K. (1997), *Policing the Risk Society.* Toronto: University of Toronto Press.

Eriksson, J. (2004), *Kampen om hotbilden.* Stockholm: Santérus Förlag.

Eriksson, L. (2004), *Arbete till varje pris. Arbetslinjen i 1920-talets arbetslöshetspolitik.* Stockholm: Stockholms universitet.

——(2005), 'Tulltjänstemäns riskbedömningar vad gäller resande'. C-uppsats, Stockholm: Stockholms universitet.

Eysenck, S., Pearson, P., Eating, G. and Allsopp, J. (1985), 'Age Norms for Impulsiveness, Venturesomeness and Empathy in Adults', *Personality and Individual Differences*, 6: 613–19.

Falshaw, L., Friendship, C., Travers, R. and Nugent, F. (2003), *Searching for 'What Works': An Evaluation of Cognitive Skills Programmes*, Home Office Research Findings No. 206. London: Home Office.

Feeley, M. and Simon, J. (1992), 'The New Penology: Notes on the Emerging Strategies of Corrections and its Implications', *Criminology*, 30: 449–74.

——(1994), 'Actuarial Justice: The Emerging New Criminal Law', in D. Nelken (ed.) *The Futures of Criminology*. London: Sage.

Foucault, M. (1977), *Language, Counter-Memory, Practice*, ed. D. Bouchard. Oxford: Blackwell.

——(1979a), *Discipline and Punish*. Harmondsworth: Penguin.

——(1979b), *Power, Truth, Strategy*, eds. M. Morris and P. Patton. Sydney: Feral.

——(1980), *Power/Knowledge: Selected Interviews and Other Writings 1972–1977*, ed. C. Gordon. New York: Pantheon Books.

——(1982), 'The Subject and Power', in H. Dreyfus and P. Rabinow, *Michel Foucault: Beyond Structuralism and Hermeneutics*. Brighton: Harvester.

——(1985), *The Use of Pleasure. The History of Sexuality: Volume 2*. Harmondsworth: Penguin.

——(1988), *Politics, Philosophy, Culture: Interviews and Other Writings, 1977–1984*, ed. L. Kritzman. New York: Routledge.

——(1989), *Foucault Live*, ed. S. Lotringer. New York: Semiotext(e).

——(1997), *Ethics: Subjectivity and Truth. Essential Works of Foucault, 1954–1984 Volume 1*, ed. P. Rabinow. New York: The New Press.

——(1998), *The Will to Knowledge. The History of Sexuality: Volume 1*. Harmondsworth: Penguin.

——(2003a), *'Society Must Be Defended'. Lectures at the Collège de France 1975–1976*, eds. M. Bertani and A. Fontana. New York: Picador.

——(2003b), *Abnormal. Lectures at the Collège de France 1974–1975*, eds. V. Marchetti and A. Salomoni. New York: Picador.

——(2006), *Psychiatric Power. Lectures at the Collège de France 1973–1974*, ed. J. Lagrange, Houndmills. Basingstoke: Palgrave Macmillan.

——(2007), *Security, Territory, Population. Lectures at the Collège de France 1977–1978*, ed. M. Senellart, Houndmills, Basingstoke: Palgrave Macmillan.

——(2008), *The Birth of Biopolitics. Lectures at the Collège de France 1978–1979*, ed. M. Senellart, Houndmills, Basingstoke: Palgrave Macmillan.

Franko Aas, K. (2005), '"Getting Ahead of the Game": Border Technologies and the Changing Space of Government', in E. Zureik and M. Salter (eds.) *Global Surveillance and Policing. Borders, Security, Identity*. Cullompton: Willan.

Fredriksson, P. and Holmlund, B. (2003), *Improving Incentives in Unemployment Insurance: A Review of Recent Research*, IFAU Working Paper 2003:5. Uppsala: Institutet för arbetsmarknadspolitisk utvärdering.

Freedman, L. (1992), 'The Concept of Security', in M. Hawkesworth and M. Kogan (eds.) *Encyclopedia of Government and Politics*. London: Routledge.

Fröberg, D. and Persson, K. (2002), *Genomförandet av aktivitetsgarantin*, IFAU Rapport 2002:2. Uppsala: Institutet för arbetsmarknadspolitisk utvärdering.

Furedi, F. (2004), *Therapy Culture: Cultivating Vulnerability in an Uncertain Age*. London: Routledge.

Galbraith, R. (2004), *Raped by U.S. Customs: Strip Searches and the War on Black Women*. Ann Arbor: University of Michigan.

Garland, D. (2001), *The Culture of Control*. Oxford: Oxford University Press.

——(2003), 'The Rise of Risk', in R. Ericson and A. Doyle (eds.) *Risk and Morality*. Toronto: University of Toronto Press.

Garsten, C. (2004), '"Be a Gumby": The Political Technologies of Employability in the Temporary Staffing Business', in C. Garsten and K. Jacobsson (eds.) *Learning to be*

Employable: New Agendas on Work, Responsibility, and Learning in a Globalizing World. Basingstoke: Palgrave Macmillan.

Gendreau, P., Little, T. and Goggin, C. (1996), 'A Meta-Analysis of the Predictors of Adult Offender Recidivism: What Works!' *Criminology*, 34: 575–607.

Gendreau, P., Goggin, C. and Smith, P. (1999), 'The Forgotten Issue in Effective Correctional Treatment: Program Implementation', *International Journal of Offender Therapy and Comparative Criminology*, 43: 180–87.

Giertz, A. (2004), *Making the Poor Work. Social Assistance and Activation Programs in Sweden.* Lund: Lunds universitet.

Gilbert, N. and van Voorhis, R. (eds.) (2001), *Activating the Unemployed.* New Brunswick: Transaction Publishers.

Ginsburg, J., Mann, R., Rotgers, F. and Weekes, J. (2002), 'Motivational Interviewing with Criminal Justice Populations', in W. Miller and S. Rollnick (eds.) *Motivational Interviewing: Preparing People for Change.* New York: Guilford Press.

Goldstein, A. (1973), *Structured Learning Therapy: Toward a Psychotherapy for the Poor.* New York: Academic Press.

——(1976), *Skill Training for Community Living: Applying Structured Learning Therapy.* New York: Pergamon Press.

Goldstein, A., Glick, B. and Gibbs, J. (1998), *Aggression Replacement Training: A Comprehensive Intervention for Aggressive Youth.* Champaign, IL: Research Press.

Gomm, R., Hammersley, M. and Foster, P. (2000), 'Case Study and Generalization', in R. Gomm, M. Hammersley and P. Foster (eds.) *Case Study Method.* London: Sage.

Gordon, C. (1991), 'Introduction', in G. Burchell, C. Gordon and P. Miller (eds.) *The Foucault Effect: Studies in Governmentality.* London: Harvester Wheatsheaf.

Gorman, K. (2001), 'Cognitive Behaviourism and the Holy Grail: The Quest for a Universal Means of Managing Offender Risk', *Probation Journal*, 48: 3–9.

Goul Andersen, J. and Jensen, P. (eds.) (2002), *Changing Labour Markets, Welfare Policies and Citizenship.* Bristol: Policy Press.

Grossman, E., Luque, E. and Muniesa, F. (2008), 'Economies through Transparency', in C. Garsten and M. Lindh de Montoya (eds.) *Transparency in a New Global Order: Unveiling Organizational Visions.* Cheltenham: Edward Elgar.

Haggerty, K. and Ericson, R. (2000), 'The Surveillant Assemblage', *British Journal of Sociology*, 51: 605–22.

Hannah-Moffat, K. (2004), 'Losing Ground: Gendered Knowledges, Parole Risk, and Responsibility', *Social Politics*, 11: 363–85.

——(2005), 'Criminogenic Needs and the Transformative Risk Subject: Hybridizations of Risk/Need in Penality', *Punishment and Society*, 7: 29–51.

Hardt, M. and Negri, A. (2000), *Empire.* Cambridge, MA: Harvard University Press.

Hare, R. (1991), *The Hare Psychopathy Checklist – Revised.* Toronto: Multi-Health Systems.

Hawkins, K. (2003), 'Order, Rationality and Silence: Some Reflections on Criminal Justice Decision-making', in L. Gelsthorpe and N. Padfield (eds.) *Exercising Discretion: Decision Making in the Criminal Justice System and Beyond.* Cullompton: Willan.

Hemerijck, A. (2002), 'The Self-Transformation of the European Social Model(s)', in G. Esping-Andersen (ed.) *Why We Need a New Welfare State.* Oxford: Oxford University Press.

Henman, P. (2004), 'Targeted! Population Segmentation, Electronic Surveillance and Governing the Unemployed in Australia', *International Sociology*, 19: 173–91.

Hertzberg, F. (2003), *Gräsrotsbyråkrati och normativ svenskhet. Hur arbetsförmedlare förstår en etniskt segregerad arbetsmarknad.* Stockholm: Arbetslivsinstitutet.

Hetzler, A. (2004), 'Rehabilitering och de långtidssjukskrivna', in R. Lindqvist and A. Hetzler (eds.), *Rehabilitering och välfärdspolitik*. Lund: Studentlitteratur.

Heyman, J. (2004), 'Ports of Entry as Nodes in the World System', *Identities: Global Studies in Culture and Power*, 11: 303–27.

Hirsch, J. (2005), *Materialistische Staatstheorie*. Hamburg: VSA-Verlag.

Hjertner Thorén, K. (2005), *Municipal Activation Policy: A Case Study of the Practical Work with Unemployed Social Assistance Recipients*, IFAU Working Paper 2005:20. Uppsala: Institutet för arbetsmarknadspolitisk utvärdering.

Hobbes, T. (1985 [1651]), *Leviathan*. Harmondsworth: Penguin.

Honneth, A. (1991), *The Critique of Power*. Cambridge, MA: MIT Press.

Hörnqvist, M. (2004), 'Risk Assessments and Public Order Disturbances: New European Guidelines for the Use of Force?', *Journal of Scandinavian Studies in Criminology and Crime Prevention*, 5: 4–26.

——(2007), *The Organised Nature of Power: On Productive and Repressive Interventions Based on Considerations of Risk and Need*. Stockholm University: Department of Criminology.

——(2008), 'The Imaginary Constitution of Wage Labourers', in P. Carlen (ed.) *Imaginary Penalities*. Cullompton: Willan.

Hutter, B. and Power, M. (2005), 'Organizational Encounters with Risk: An Introduction', in B. Hutton and M. Power (eds.) *Organizational Encounters with Risk*. Cambridge: Cambridge University Press.

Hydén, S. and Lundberg, A. (2004), *Inre utlänningskontroll i polisarbete*. Linköping: Linköpings Universitet.

IAF (2004), *Arbetsmarknadsverkets handläggning av försäkringsärenden samt utbetalningen av statsbidrag till arbetslöshetskassorna*. Katrineholm: Inspektionen för arbetslöshetsförsäkringen.

——(2005a), *Tillämpning av regelverket för lämpligt arbete. Delrapport med utgångspunkt från de individuella handlingsplanerna*. Katrineholm: Inspektionen för arbetslöshetsförsäkringen.

——(2005b), *Anvisning till aktivitetsgarantin eller förlängd period med arbetslöshetsersättning*. Katrineholm: Inspektionen för arbetslöshetsförsäkringen.

——(2005c), *IAF 2004. Första årets verksamhetsberättelse*. Katrineholm: Inspektionen för arbetslöshetsförsäkringen.

IAFFS (2004), *Inspektionen för arbetslöshetsförsäkringens föreskrifter om tillämpningen av 11 § lagen (1997:238) om arbetslöshetsförsäkring gällande lämpligt arbete*, IAFFS 2004:3.

Jacobsson, K. (2004), 'A European Politics of Employability: The Political Discourse on Employability of the EU and the OECD', in C. Garsten and K. Jacobsson (eds.) *Learning to be Employable: New Agendas on Work, Responsibility, and Learning in a Globalizing World*. Basingstoke: Palgrave Macmillan.

Jessop, B. (2001), *Regulation Theory and the Crisis of Capitalism*. Cheltenham: Edward Elgar.

——(2008), *State Power*. Cambridge: Polity Press.

Jiang, M. and Fisher-Giorlando, M. (2002), 'Inmate Misconduct: A Test of the Deprivation, Importation, and Situational Models', *The Prison Journal*, 82: 335–58.

JO (1987), *Fråga om disciplinärt ansvar vid felaktig tullkontroll*, Diarienummer 1161–1985. Stockholm: Justitieombudsmannen.

——(1995), *Anmälan från Dan Lahti mot Tulldirektionen i Västra Götaland*, Diarienummer 798–1995. Stockholm: Justitieombudsmannen.

Johansson, H. (2001), 'Activation Policies in the Nordic Countries: Social Democratic Universalism under Pressure', *Journal of European Area Studies*, 9: 63–77.

Johansson, T. (2006), *Makeovermani: om Dr Phil, plastikkirurgi och illusionen om det perfekta jaget*. Stockholm: Natur och Kultur.

JuDep (1994), *Upploppet på Tidaholmsanstalten 22 juli 1994*, Ds 1994:140. Stockholm: Fritzes.

——(2000), *Från anstalt till frihet*, Ds 2000:37. Stockholm: Justitiedepartementet.

——(2002), *En ny kriminalvårdslag*, Dir 2002:90. Stockholm: Justitiedepartementet.

Junestav, M. (2004), *Arbetslinjer i svensk socialpolitisk debatt och lagstiftning 1930–2001*. Uppsala: Uppsala universitet.

Kemshall, H. (1998), *Risk in Probation Practice*. Aldershot: Ashgate.

——(2003), *Understanding Risk in Criminal Justice*. Buckingham: Open University Press.

Kendall, K. (2004), 'Dangerous Thinking: A Critical History of Correctional Cognitive Behaviouralism', in G. Mair (ed.) *What Matters in Probation*. Cullompton: Willan.

Keohane, R. (2006), 'Accountability in World Politics', *Scandinavian Political Studies*, 29: 75–87.

Kimmel, M. (2001), 'Global Masculinities: Restoration and Resistance', in B. Peas and K. Pringle (eds.) *A Man's World?* New York: Zed Books.

Kraut, R. and Poe, D. (1980), 'Behavioral Roots of Person Perception: The Deception Judgments of Customs Inspectors and Laymen', *Journal of Personality and Social Psychology*, 39: 784–98.

Kullgren, G., Grann, M. and Holmberg, G. (1996), 'The Swedish Forensic Concept of Severe Mental Disorder as Related to Personality Disorders', *International Journal of Law and Psychiatry*, 19: 191–200.

KV (2005a), 'Vår vision', www.kvv.se (accessed 14 June 2005).

——(2005b), *Kriminalvårdens årsredovisning 2004*. Norrköping: Kriminalvården.

——(2005c), *Internkontroll avseende utevistelser från långtidsavdelningen vid Anstalten X – slutrapport*, KVS Region Stockholm 2005-09-28.

——(2005d), *Rapport ang. kvalitetsgranskning av utevistelser från Anstalten Y*, KVM Stockholm Söder, 2005-01-17.

——(2006), *Programsammanställning. Avslutade program 2003 – juni 2006*. Norrköping: Kriminalvården.

KVS (1995), *Oro och upplopp på fängelserna – ett förslag till motverkan*. Norrköping: Kriminalvårdsstyrelsen.

——(1998a), *What Works*. Norrköping: Kriminalvårdsstyrelsen.

——(1998b), *RSS-rapporten. Orsaker till hot och våld mellan intagna: förslag till åtgärder*. Norrköping: Kriminalvårdsstyrelsen.

——(2000), *Kriminella gängbildningar: en pilotundersökning om gängbildningar vid landets anstalter*. Norrköping: Kriminalvårdsstyrelsen.

——(2001), *Kriminella gängbildningar: undersökning om gängbildningar vid landets anstalter 2001*. Norrköping: Kriminalvårdsstyrelsen.

——(2002a), *What Works III*. Norrköping: Kriminalvårdsstyrelsen.

——(2002b), *Insatser mot narkotika. Forskningsbaserad narkomanvård – ett förslag till handlingsplan*. Norrköping: Kriminalvårdsstyrelsen.

——(2002c), *Intagna som kräver extra resurser avseende säkerhet och omhändertagande*. Norrköping: Kriminalvårdsstyrelsen.

——(2002d), *Q-BoM. Kvalitetssystem för Brotts- och missbruksrelaterade Program*. Norrköping: Kriminalvårdsstyrelsen.

——(2004a), *Kriminalvård och statistik 2003*. Norrköping: Kriminalvårdsstyrelsen.

——(2004b), *'De psykiatriska modulerna' – handlingsplan för ett förbättrat omhändertagande av psykiskt störda intagna*. Norrköping: Kriminalvårdsstyrelsen.

——(2004c), *Ackreditering av Brotts- och Missbruksrelaterade program i svensk kriminalvård*. Norrköping: Kriminalvårdsstyrelsen.

———(2004d), *Kriminalvårdens redovisning av drogsituationen 2003*. Norrköping: Kriminalvårdsstyrelsen.

KVV (2000), *Reasoning and Rehabilitation (reviderad upplaga). Utdrag ur Handbok för undervisning i
Cognitive Skills*. Norrköping: Kriminalvårdsverket / T3 Associates Training and Consulting Inc.

———(2002), *Cognitive Skills Teorimanual*. Norrköping: Kriminalvårdsverket.

———(2003a), *Cognitive Skills – Manual för programmets genomförande*. Norrköping: Kriminalvårdsverket.

———(2003b), *Cognitive Skills – Manual för utbildning av programledare*. Norrköping:
Kriminalvårdsverket.

KVVFS (2004a), *Kriminalvårdsstyrelsens föreskrifter och allmänna råd placering av dömda i
kriminalvårdsanstalt*, KVVFS 2004:19.

———(2004b), *Kriminalvårdsstyrelsens föreskrifter och allmänna råd om planering av kriminal-
vårdspåföljd m.m*, KVVFS 2004:15.

———(2005), *Kriminalvårdsstyrelsens föreskrifter och allmänna råd för verkställighet i anstalt*,
KVVFS 2005:2.

Kyvsgaard, B. (2006), 'Virksomme og uvirksomme programmer og behandlingstiltag', in
B. Kyvsgaard (ed.) *Hvad virker – hvad virker ikke? Kundskabsbaseret kriminalpolitik og praksis*.
København: Jurist- og Økonomforbundets Forlag.

LAN (2004), *Insatser för aktivering och motivering av arbetssökande*, Anbudsinbjudan. Stockholm:
Länsarbetsnämnden i Stockholms län.

Lemke, T. (1997), *Eine Kritik der politischen Vernunft – Foucaults Analyse der modernen Gouverne-
mentalität*. Berlin: Argument.

Lernia (2004), *Insatser för aktivering och motivering av arbetssökande*, Anbud 2004-06-07.
Stockholm: Lernia.

Levitas, R. (2005), *The Inclusive Society? Social Exclusion and New Labour*. Basingstoke: Palgrave
Macmillan.

Lindqvist, R. (2000), *Att sätta gränser. Organisationer och reformer i arbetsrehabilitering*. Umeå:
Borea bokförlag.

Lindqvist, R. and Marklund, S. (1995), 'Forced to Work and Liberated from Work.
A Historical Perspective on Work and Welfare in Sweden', *Scandinavian Journal of Social
Welfare*, 4: 224–37.

Lipietz, A. (1988), 'Accumulation, Crises, and Ways Out: Some Methodological Reflections
on the Concept of "Regulation"', *International Journal of Political Economy*, 18: 10–43.

Lødemel, I. and Trickey, H. (eds.) (2001), *'An Offer You Can't Refuse': Workfare in International
Perspective*. Bristol: Policy Press.

Luhmann, N. (2006), *Organisation und Entscheidung*, 2nd edn. Wiesbaden: Verlag für Sozial-
wissenschaften.

Lundin, M. (2000), *Tillämpningen av arbetslöshetsförsäkringens regelverk vid arbetsförmedlingarna*,
IFAU Stencil 2000:1. Uppsala: Institutet för arbetsmarknadspolitisk utvärdering.

Lyon, D. (2003), 'Surveillance as Social Sorting', in D. Lyon (ed.) *Surveillance as Social Sorting*.
London: Routledge.

McCallum, D. (2001), *Personality and Dangerousness: Genealogies of Antisocial Personality Disorder*.
Cambridge: Cambridge University Press.

McDonald, C., Marston, G. and Buckley, A. (2003), 'Risk Technology in Australia: The Role
of the Job Seeker Classification Instrument in Employment Services', *Critical Social Policy*,
23: 498–525.

McGuire, J. (2000), *Cognitive–Behavioural Approaches: An Introduction to Theory and Research*.
London: HM Chief Inspector of Probation.

McKinlay, A. and Starkey, K. (1998), *Foucault, Management and Organization Theory: From Panopticon to Technologies of Self*. London: Sage.

McQuaid, R and Lindsay, C (2005), 'The Concept of Employability', *Urban Studies*, 42: 197–219.

McQuaid, R., Green, A. and Danson, M. (2005), 'Introducing Employability', *Urban Studies*, 42: 191–95.

Mäkitalo, Å. (2002), *Categorizing Work: Knowing, Arguing, and Social Dilemmas in Vocational Guidance*. Göteborg: Göteborgs Universitet.

Marshall, T. H. (1977), *Class, Citizenship and Social Development*. Chicago: Chicago University Press.

Marx, K. (1954 [1867]), *Capital. Volume 1*. Moscow: Progress Publishers.

Maurutto, P. and Hannah-Moffat, K. (2006), 'Assembling Risk and the Restructuring of Penal Control', *British Journal of Criminology*, 46: 438–54.

Melossi, D. (2006), 'Michel Foucault and the Obsolescent State', in A. Beaulieu and D. Gabbard (eds.) *Michel Foucault and Power Today*. Lanham: Lexington Books.

Merrington, S. and Stanley, S. (2004), '"What Works"? Revisiting the Evidence in England and Wales', *Probation Journal*, 51: 7–20.

Meyer, J., Drori, G. and Hwang, H. (2006), 'World Society and the Proliferation of Formal Organization', in G. Drori, J. Meyer and H. Hwang (eds.) *Globalization and Organization: World Society and Organizational Change*. Oxford: Oxford University Press.

Miller, P. (1987), *Domination and Power*. London: Routledge and Kegan Paul.

Miller, P. and Rose, N. (1990), 'Governing Economic Life', *Economy and Society*, 19: 1–31.

——(2008), *Governing the Present: Administering Economic, Social and Personal Life*. Cambridge: Polity.

Miller, W. and Rollnick, S. (2002), *Motivational Interviewing: Preparing People for Change*. New York: Guilford Press.

Nilsson, A. (2002), *Fånge i marginalen*. Stockholm: Stockholms universitet.

——(2005), 'Vad är nytt med "det nya klientelet"?' *Nordisk Tidskrift for Kriminalvidenskab*, 92: 147–61.

OECD (1998a), *The Battle against Exclusion*. Paris: Organisation for Economic Co-operation and Development.

——(1998b), *Early Identification of Jobseekers at Risk of Long-Term Unemployment*. Paris: Organisation for Economic Co-operation and Development.

Olsson, C. (2005), *Bärsärkarna: en kvalitativ beskrivning och analys av upplevelser från intagna och personal vid incidenter av upploppskaraktär under 2004*. Norrköping: Kriminalvårdsstyrelsen.

O'Malley, P. (2004), *Risk, Uncertainty and Government*. London: Glasshouse Press.

Ong, A. (2006), *Neoliberalism as Exception: Mutations in Citizenship and Sovereignty*. Durham, NC: Duke University Press.

Oudhuis, M. (2004), 'Work as an Arena for Disciplining Mind, Body and Emotions: The Volvo Bus Plant Case', in C. Garsten and K. Jacobsson (eds.) *Learning to be Employable: New Agendas on Work, Responsibility and Learning in a Globalizing World*. Basingstoke: Palgrave Macmillan.

Parsons, T. (1937), *The Structure of Social Action*. New York: McGraw-Hill.

Peck, J. and Theodore, N. (2000), 'Beyond "Employability"', *Cambridge Journal of Economics*, 24: 729–49.

Persson, K. and Johansson, E. (2000), *Friare användning av arbetsmarknadspolitiska medel*, IFAU Rapport 2000:1. Uppsala: Institutet för arbetsmarknadspolitisk utvärdering.

Petersson, K. (2003), *Fängelset och den liberala fantasin*. Norrköping: Kriminalvårdsstyrelsen.

Power, M. (2004), *The Risk Management of Everything*. London: Demos.

——(2007), *Organized Uncertainty: Designing a World of Risk Management*. Oxford: Oxford University Press.

Procacci, G. (1998), 'Against Exclusion: The Poor and the Social Sciences', in M. Rhodes and Y. Mény (eds.) *The Future of European Welfare: A New Social Contract*. Houndmills: Macmillan.

Proposition (1994/95), *Ändringar i kriminalvårdslagstiftningen (anstaltsindelningen m.m.)*, Proposition 1994/95:124. Stockholm: Regeringskansliet.

——(1995/96), *Tullens befogenheter vid den inre gränsen*, Proposition 1995/96:166. Stockholm: Regeringskansliet.

——(1996/97), *Kriterier för rätt till ersättning i form av sjukpenning och Förtidspension*, Proposition 1996/97:28. Stockholm: Regeringskansliet.

——(1998/99), *Förändrad omvärld – omdanat försvar*, Proposition 1998/99:74. Stockholm: Regeringskansliet.

——(1999/2000a), *Förnyad arbetsmarknadspolitik för delaktighet och tillväxt*, Proposition 1999/2000:98. Stockholm: Regeringskansliet.

——(1999/2000b), *En rättvisare och tydligare arbetslöshetsförsäkring*, Proposition 1999/2000:139. Stockholm: Regeringskansliet.

——(2002/03), *Arbetsmarknadspolitiken förstärks*, Proposition 2002/03:44. Stockholm: Regeringskansliet.

Rawls, J. (1973), *A Theory of Justice*. Oxford: Oxford University Press.

Regeringen (2003a), *Sveriges handlingsplan mot fattigdom och social utestängning 2003–2005*. Stockholm: Regeringskansliet.

——(2003b), *Regleringsbrev för budgetåret 2004 avseende Arbetsmarknadsverket*. Stockholm: Regeringskansliet.

——(2003c), *Regleringsbrev för budgetåret 2004 avseende Tullverket*. Stockholm: Regeringskansliet.

Renn, O. (2008), *Risk Governance: Coping with Uncertainty in a Complex World*. London: Earthscan.

RiR (2004a), *Arbetslöshetsförsäkringens hantering på arbetsförmedlingen*, RiR 2004:3. Stockholm: Riksrevisionen.

——(2004b), *Återfall i brott eller anpassning i samhället*, RiR 2004:5. Stockholm: Riksrevisionen.

——(2005a), *Arbetslöshetsförsäkringen – kontroll och effektivitet*, RiR 2005:3. Stockholm: Riksrevisionen.

——(2005b), *Aktivitetsgarantin. Regeringens och AMS uppföljning och utvärdering*, RiR 2005:17. Stockholm: Riksrevisionen.

Robinson, D. (1995), *The Impact of Cognitive Skills Training on Post-Release Recidivism among Canadian Federal Offenders*, Research Report No R-41. Ottawa: Correctional Service Canada.

Rosanvallon, P. (2000), *The New Social Question*. Princeton: Princeton University Press.

Rose, N. (1998), *Inventing Our Selves: Psychology, Power, and Personhood*. Cambridge: Cambridge University Press.

——(1999), *Powers of Freedom: Reframing Political Thought*. Cambridge: Cambridge University Press.

Rose, N. and Miller, P. (1992), 'Political Power beyond the State: Problematics of Government', *British Journal of Sociology*, 43: 173–205.

Rose, N., O'Malley, P. and Valverde, M. (2006), 'Governmentality', *Annual Review of Law and Social Science*, 2: 83–104.

Rosholm, M., Svarer, M. and Hammer, B. (2004), *A Danish Profiling System*, Working Paper No. 2004–13. University of Aarhus: Department of Economics.

Ross, R. and Fabiano, E. (1981), *Time to Think: Cognition and Crime/link and Remediation*. Ottawa: Department of Criminology.

Roxell, L. (2007), *Fångar i ett nätverk*. Stockholm: Stockholms universitet.

RRV (1996), *Effektiv ledning. Förutsättningar för styrning och uppföljning inom socialförsäkrings- och arbetsmarknadsområdet*, RRV 1996:60. Stockholm: Riksrevisionsverket.

——(1999a), *Effektiviteten i arbetsförmedlingen*, RRV 1999:15. Stockholm: Riksrevisionsverket.

——(1999b), *Effektivare kriminalvård: en hinderanalys. Regeringsuppdrag att granska hinder för ett effektivare resursutnyttjande i kriminalvården*, RRV 1999:27. Stockholm: Riksrevisionsverket.

——(2001a), *Effektivare arbetsförmedling. En samlad bedömning utifrån RRV:s granskningar*, RRV 2001:15. Stockholm: Riksrevisionsverket.

——(2001b), *Tullverkets kontroll av smuggling*, RRV 2001:19. Stockholm: Riksrevisionsverket.

Rudolph, H. (2001), 'Profiling as an Instrument for Early Identifiaction of People at Risk of Long-Term Unemployment', in P. Weinert, M. Baukens and P. Bollerot (eds.) *Employability: From Theory to Practice*. New Brunswick: Transaction Publishers.

Salonen, T. and Ulmestig, R. (2004), *Nedersta trappsteget: en studie om kommunal aktivering*. Växjö: Växjö universitet.

Sennett, R. (2006), *The Culture of the New Capitalism*. New Haven: Yale University Press.

SFS (1974), *Lag (1974:203) om kriminalvård i anstalt*, Svensk författningssamling.

——(1996), *Lag (1996:701) om Tullverkets befogenheter vid Sveriges gräns mot ett annat land inom Europeiska unionen*, Svensk författningssamling.

——(2000a), *Lag (2000:1460) om ändring i lagen (1997:238) om arbetslöshetsförsäkring*, Svensk författningssamling.

——(2000b), *Förordning (2000:634) om arbetsmarknadspolitiska program*, Svensk författningssamling.

——(2001), *Socialtjänstlag (2001:453)*, Svensk författningssamling

Smith, D. (1980), 'Paragons, Pariahs, and Pirates: A Spectrum-Based Theory of Enterprise', *Crime and Delinquency*, 26: 358–86.

SOU (1993) *Verkställighet av fängelsestraff*, SOU 1993:76. Stockholm: Allmänna förlaget.

——(1994), *Skyddet vid den inre gränsen*, SOU 1994:131. Stockholm: Fritzes.

——(1998), *En gräns – en myndighet?* SOU 1998:18. Stockholm: Fritzes.

——(1999), *Ökade socialbidrag – En studie om inkomster och socialbidrag åren 1990 till 1996*, SOU 1999:46. Stockholm: Fritzes.

——(2000a), *Rehabilitering till arbete: en reform med individen i centrum*, SOU 2000:78. Stockholm: Fritzes.

——(2000b), *Vägvalet*, SOU 2000:126. Stockholm: Fritzes.

——(2002), *Psykisk störning, brott och ansvar*, SOU 2002:3. Stockholm: Fritzes.

——(2004), *Var går gränsen?* SOU 2004:86. Stockholm: Fritzes.

——(2005a), *Framtidens kriminalvård*, SOU 2005:54. Stockholm: Fritzes.

——(2005b), *Säkert inlåst?* SOU 2005:6. Stockholm: Fritzes.

Sparks, R., Bottoms, A. and Hay, W. (1996), *Prisons and the Problem of Order*. Oxford: Clarendon.

Statskontoret (2003), *Effektivitetsgranskning av kriminalvården*. Stockholm: Statskontoret.

——(2004a), *Individuella handlingsplaner. En utvärdering*. Stockholm: Statskontoret.

——(2004b), *Det nya Arbetsmarknadsverket*. Stockholm: Statskontoret.

Svensson, L. (2004), 'Lifelong Learning – A Clash between a Production and a Learning Logic', in C. Garsten and K. Jacobsson (eds.) *Learning to be Employable: New Agendas on Work, Responsibility, and Learning in a Globalizing World*. Basingstoke: Palgrave Macmillan.

Sykes, G. (1958), *A Society of Captives: A Study of a Maximum Security Prison*. Princeton: Princeton University Press.

Tham, H. (1995), 'Från behandling till straffvärde. Kriminalpolitik i en förändrad välfärdsstat', in D. Victor (ed.) *Varning för straff. Om vådan av den nyttiga straffrätten*. Stockholm: Fritzes.

——(2003), *Forskare om narkotikapolitiken*. Stockholm: Stockholms universitet.

TU (2001), *Nationell hotbildsanalys för år 2002*. Stockholm: Tullverket Huvudkontoret.

——(2002), *Tullverkets nationella hotbild 2003*. Stockholm: Tullverket Huvudkontoret.

——(2003a), *Omvärldsbevakning: Europeiska unionens utvidgning österut*. Stockholm: Tullverket Huvudkontoret.

——(2003b), *Varför du?* Stockholm: Tullverket Huvudkontoret.

——(2004a), *Tullverkets nationella hotbildsanalys 2005–06*. Stockholm: Tullverket Huvudkontoret.

——(2004b), *En berättelse om året som gått*. Stockholm: Tullverket Huvudkontoret.

——(2004c), *Tullverkets Årsredovisning budgetåret 2003*. Stockholm: Tullverket Huvudkontoret.

——(2004d), *Omvärldsbevakning: Uppföljande statusrapport nr 5 – slutrapport*. Stockholm: Tullverket Huvudkontoret.

Useem, B. and Kimball, P. (1989), *States of Siege: U.S. Prison Riots, 1971–1986*. Oxford: Oxford University Press.

van Berkel, R. and Hornemann Møller, I. (2002a), 'The Concept of Activation', in R. van Berkel and I. Hornemann Møller (eds.) *Active Social Policies in the EU. Inclusion through Participation?* Bristol: Policy Press.

——(2002b), 'Introduction', in R. van Berkel and I. Hornemann Møller (eds.) *Active Social Policies in the EU. Inclusion through Participation?* Bristol: Policy Press.

van den Berg, G. and van der Klaauw, B. (2005), *Job Search Monitoring and Sanctions – A Brief Survey of Some Recent Results*, IFAU Report 2005:8. Uppsala: Institutet för arbetsmarknadspolitisk utvärdering.

Wacquant, L. (2008), 'The Place of the Prison in the New Government of Poverty', in M. L. Frampton, I. Haney-López and J. Simon (eds.) *After the War on Crime: Race, Democracy, and a New Reconstruction*. New York: New York University Press.

Weber, M. (1972 [1922]), *Wirtschaft und Gesellschaft*. Tübingen: J. C. B. Mohr.

Whitehead, S. (2002), *Men and Masculinities: Key Themes and New Directions*. Cambridge: Polity Press.

Wilson, D., Bouffard, L. and MacKenzie, D. (2005), 'A Quantitative Review of Structured, Group-Oriented, Cognitive-Behavioural Programs for Offenders', *Criminal Justice and Behaviour*, 32: 172–204.

Wolf, L. J. (1991), *Prison Disturbances, April 1990*. London: HMSO.

Zizek, S. (1994), 'The Spectre of Ideology', in S. Zizek (ed.) *Mapping Ideology*. London: Verso.

Index